THE THEORY
OF THE
LEISURE CLASS

Thorstein Veblen

The Theory
of the
Leisure Class

Introduction by Alan Wolfe

Notes by James Danly

THE MODERN LIBRARY

NEW YORK

2001 Modern Library Paperback Edition

LIBRARY OF CONGRESS CATALOGING-IN-PUBLICATION DATA
Veblen, Thorstein, 1857–1929.
The theory of the leisure class / by Thorstein Veblen;
introduction by Alan Wolfe;
notes by James Danly.
p.   cm.—(Modern Library classics)
Originally published: New York: Macmillan, 1899.
Includes bibliographical references and index.
ISBN 0-375-75787-2
1. Leisure class. I. Title. II. Series.
HB831 .V4 2001
305.5'234—dc21
2001041759

Modern Library website address: www.modernlibrary.com
Printed in the United States of America

2 4 6 8 9 7 5 3 1

THORSTEIN VEBLEN

Thorstein Veblen, the maverick economist who shook the complacency of America in the early twentieth century with his incisive criticisms of our social and economic systems, was born on July 30, 1857, on a frontier farm near Cato, Wisconsin. His parents were Norwegian immigrants who moved the family to a Scandinavian farming community in Minnesota in 1865. A precocious child, Veblen was often excused from chores so that he might pursue intellectual interests. Like his siblings, he attended local schools, and at the age of seventeen he entered Carleton College, a small liberal-arts institution in nearby Northfield, Minnesota. Upon graduation in 1880 Veblen briefly studied philosophy at Johns Hopkins University but subsequently transferred to Yale, where in 1884 he earned a doctorate in philosophy and political economy. Unable to secure a teaching position because he was not a practicing Christian, Veblen returned to the family homestead and spent the next several years reading extensively and writing occasionally. In 1888 he married Ellen Rolfe, the daughter of a prominent Midwestern family. After completing a fellowship in economics and finance at Cornell in 1892, he was hired by the University of Chicago as an instructor, and in 1896 he began editing the newly founded *Journal of Political Economy.*

The Theory of the Leisure Class, Veblen's first and greatest work, caused an uproar in academia when it was published in 1899. The book challenged two cherished doctrines of classical economics: that the self-interest of the capitalist coincides with the interests of the community and that the competitive system provides the dynamic of economic progress. Veblen's quintessential work, for which he coined the term "conspicuous consumption," proved surprisingly popular in literary circles. William Dean Howells, whose long and highly favorable review launched it as a popular success, interpreted *The Theory of the Leisure Class* as primarily a social satire. Likewise, *Time* magazine later praised Veblen as "the most impressive American satirist of his day." Critic Alfred Kazin would declare that "the satiric element in Veblen's book is almost pyrotechnical in its elaboration.... He was one of the most extraordinary figures in the history of the American imagination."

A century later the book endures as a classic not only of economic theory but of sociology and history as well. "*The Theory of the Leisure Class* brilliantly and truthfully illuminates the effect of wealth on behavior," said Harvard economist John Kenneth Galbraith. "It is a marvelous book; it is also, in its particular way, a masterpiece of English prose [and] the most comprehensive [tract] ever written on snobbery and social pretense. Some of it has application to American society at the end of the [nineteenth] century—at the height of the gilded age of American capitalism—but more is wonderfully relevant to modern affluence.... No one who has read this book ever again sees the consumption of goods by the rich in the same light."

Veblen attracted further notoriety with *The Theory of Business Enterprise* (1904). A head-on, heretical assault on the American business system, it aroused suspicion that Veblen was a Marxist. Yet he soon made a point of disassociating himself from Marx on technical grounds, stating emphatically: "The Marxian system is not only not tenable, it is not even intelligible." Controversy surrounded Veblen's personal life as well. An extramarital affair with the wife of a fellow professor resulted in his dismissal from the University of Chicago in 1906. Likewise, the scandals surrounding his dalliances with various women caused his removal from the teaching staff of Stanford University in 1909.

In 1911 Veblen joined the faculty of the University of Missouri and entered a period of great productivity. *The Instinct of Workmanship and the State of the Industrial Arts* (1914), which Veblen regarded as his best work, expanded on ideas first introduced in *The Theory of the Leisure Class*. As war broke out in Europe, he reflected on the economic policies underlying Germany's dynastic and militant state in *Imperial Germany and the Industrial Revolution* (1915), and later he examined the threat to peace inherent in the capitalist system in *An Inquiry into the Nature of Peace and the Terms of Its Perpetuation* (1917). In *The Higher Learning in America* (1918) Veblen vigorously argued that this country's colleges and universities were totally subservient to business interests. He made another noteworthy contribution to economic and social literature with *The Place of Science in Modern Civilisation* (1919).

During the last decade of his life Veblen lectured at the progressive New School for Social Research in New York City. His works on economic management dating from this time include *The Vested Interests and the State of the Industrial Arts* (1919, later published as *The Vested Interests and the Common Man*), *The Engineers and the Price System* (1921), and *Absentee Ownership and Business Enterprise in Recent Times* (1923). In 1925 Veblen completed a translation of *The Laxdaela Saga* from the original chronicle of Icelandic legends he recalled from childhood. Thorstein Veblen died in relative obscurity near Palo Alto, California, on August 3, 1929, shortly before the Great Depression he had long predicted. His final book, *Essays in Our Changing Order,* was published posthumously in 1934.

"[Veblen was] the foremost analyst, after Marx, of the social contradictions in our economic order," reflected social philosopher Lewis Mumford. "His books, in their combination of erudition and irony, of refined analysis and almost tortured understatement, with their austere surfaces and their molten flow of feeling underneath, feeling that bubbles up through the fissures in the thought—his books truly reflect the personality [of] a stick of dynamite wrapped up to look like a stick of candy. . . . Veblen's thought was like an x-ray which penetrates a hitherto opaque organism and alters one's whole picture of its internal structure. Above all, he was the eccentric pathologist, who traced back to their sources in history the derangements of function that are visible in our present economic order." The New Deal economist Stuart Chase stated: "Veblen was like an astronomer constructing orbits for future generations. At the turn of the [twentieth] century he gathered his facts, synthesized them in one of the boldest interpretations in the history of economics, and foretold the mold into which that history must fall for decades to come." And John Kenneth Galbraith concluded: "No man of his time, or since, looked with such a cool and penetrating eye not so much at pecuniary gain as at the way its pursuit makes men and women behave."

CONTENTS

INTRODUCTION

Alan Wolfe

One could hardly imagine a more subversive dismissal of the very rich than the one found in Thorstein Veblen's 1899 classic, *The Theory of the Leisure Class.* Karl Marx is usually upheld as the great enemy of capitalism, but *The Communist Manifesto* actually praised the bourgeoisie for giving "a cosmopolitan character to production and consumption in every country." Veblen, by contrast, incapable of offering even backhanded compliments to the bourgeoisie, treated the consumption patterns of the rich as a throwback to feudalism.

The Theory of the Leisure Class is best known for its scathing descriptions of upper-class frivolity. If your aim is to prove to others how much money you have, the best way to do so is by pretending that money means nothing to you. Reversing all previous economic logic, the very rich hire servants and expect them to be unproductive, thereby demonstrating how oblivious they are to such mundane considerations as efficiency. The rich choose their clothing not because of its comfort, but because of its value in display; since items of dress are always "in evidence" and therefore afford "an indication of our pecuniary standing to all observers at the first glance," the clothing of the upper classes has little relationship to its original function of protecting the person against the elements. Devoted to conspicuous leisure, waste, and consumption, the man of wealth "becomes a connoisseur in creditable viands of various degrees of merit, in manly beverages and trinkets, in seemly apparel and architecture, in weapons, games, dancers, and the narcotics." It is as if capitalists look to the future and can see only the past. As their factories spin out products that revolutionize the world, their lifestyle comes to ape the grandeur associated with the Renaissance.

Marx and Engels assumed that the workers of the world would unite and overthrow the capitalist class. Veblen, more cynic than revolutionary, seeks to prick the image the rich have of themselves. Since at least the eighteenth century, the rich have believed themselves to be the virtuous class, and the great virtue they have believed they possess—and are certain the poor do not—is frugality. "He who buys need have 100 Eyes," wrote Benjamin Franklin in *Poor Richard's Almanac* in 1745, "but one's enough for him that sells the Stuff." By keeping their wants to a minimum, by sacrificing today's pleasures for tomorrow's profits, by investing rather than consuming, capitalists should not only acquire wealth but acquit themselves in the eyes of God. Using Benjamin Franklin to illustrate the point, the German sociologist Max Weber, a contemporary of Veblen's, demonstrated the ways in which the Protestant search for God's grace through simple piety was essential to the capitalist revolution.

The harshest charge that Veblen levels against the rich is that, whatever their religious beliefs, their patterns of consumption conjure up the Catholicism against which the Protestant Reformation waged war. Veblen is not given to developing precise concepts and specifying historical periods, so he does not mention actual religions. But the words he selects to characterize conspicuous consumption are the very words Protestants so often used to condemn Catholicism. Oriented toward display rather than utility, consumption in modern society, he writes, takes on a "ceremonial" or "sacramental" character. Such consumption can best be characterized as "devout," concentrated as it is on "sacred buildings" whose "expensive splendour" has "an appreciable uplifting and mellowing effect upon the worshipper's frame of mind." In such buildings live people—both owners and their servants—who, in order to demonstrate their superiority, "must appear . . . clothed in garments of a special, ornate character." Since Luther—Veblen, of Norwegian descent, was born into the Lutheran church—Protestants have viewed the Catholic propensity for ritual and symbolic display as a penchant for superstition and miracle unworthy of reasonable people. Through his choice of language, Veblen reiterates the charge; conspicuous consumption can best be understood as a cultic atavism that appeals not to reason, but to the emotions.

From Veblen's time to the present, one of the persistent complaints made by people of privilege against people of poverty is that emotions all too often sway the latter. The rich believe that the poor, seduced by the glitter around them, pursue immediate gratification at the expense of long-term reward; they believe that the poor, addicted to the bottle and unable to control their tempers, fashion lives that are, in the famous words of Thomas Hobbes, nasty, brutish, and short. But in Veblen's world, the rich, in their determination to enjoy life's pleasures, have more in common with the poor than they realize. Against the notion that the rich are civilized while the poor are barbarian, Veblen points out how both are attracted to violence: "It is only the high-bred gentleman and the rowdy that normally resort to blows as the universal solvent of differences of opinion." The distinction between dueling and street fighting escapes Veblen. In both cases, one sees "an arrested development of the man's moral nature," manifested in appeals to the frenzy of the crowd and a determination to uphold one's reputation in the eyes of others.

Sports are for Veblen just as irrational as violence, and, in their own way, just as harmful. Veblen can think of no greater insult to level against the sporting life than to compare it to the religious life, and once again he links the rich and the poor in their common attraction to superstition. Both the delinquent and the well-bred sportsman, he writes, "are on an average more apt to be adherents of some accredited creed, and are also rather more inclined to devout observances, than the general average of the community." Veblen would not have been surprised by the tendency of modern athletes to cross themselves before shooting foul shots or to thank Jesus for ensuring victory. To Veblen, religion and sports are equally premodern in the emphasis their adherents place on luck, as if these adherents believe that a person's capacity to achieve God's grace and the outcomes of football games are both predestined. So long as sports play a major role in society—and Veblen was convinced that so long as a regime of conspicuous consumption persisted, they would—society will give pride of place to "an archaic scheme of life which has outlived much of its usefulness for the economic exigencies of the collective life of to-day."

In Veblen's day, as in our own, sports dominated the culture of the university. While professors may have looked with disdain on the hoopla promoted by the athletic departments of their colleges, higher learning itself had its own predatory temptations. Universities, with their rituals and their particular garb, such as caps and gowns, were dominated by "a specialised priestly class" of scholars who passed on their authority from one generation to the next through "some sort of a scholarly apostolic succession." Veblen has little to criticize about "the lower, technological, or practical grades and branches" of the higher education system, because engineering schools and community colleges are too close to the realities of the harsh world of work to become part of the leisure class. But what we would today call elite colleges and universities are, in his view, "conservative," even "reactionary," institutions serving no particular public function other than making the useless members of the upper class feel useful. Not for nothing were universities originally religious institutions; in Veblen's view, they remain "seminaries of the higher learning," dedicated to such archaic practices as teaching the classics and the humanities and in that way supporting "a conspicuous waste of time and labour on the part of the general body of students in acquiring such knowledge." No doubt Veblen's clinical dissection of the university is related to the university's rejection of him; in his time, economics was not the branch of applied mathematics that it has become in ours, but it was conservative enough in outlook and narrow-gauged enough in method to find little of value in Veblen's more speculative enterprises.

As if to demonstrate that he would have no truck with a life of leisure, Veblen wrote in a style that demanded hard concentration on the part of his readers, filling his text with obscure references— "the pervading belief in the *hamingia* or *gipta* (*gæfa, auðna*) which lends so much of colour to the Icelandic sagas." He treats the United States of his time as if he were a visiting anthropologist puzzled by local customs. He offers explanations for his observations based upon fashionable Darwinian accounts of natural selection. A fascination with obscure racial and phrenological categories—"the dolichocephalic-blond, the brachycephalic-brunette, and the Mediterranean"—runs through his writing. Although Veblen added many terms to the English language, none more common than "conspicuous consumption," his sentences surround a problem as opposed to attacking it. His are not the kind of books one reads in one sitting to idle away a rainy day. His words have to be digested slowly, a chapter at a time.

Still, one of the words that has entered the English language as a result of *The Theory of the Leisure Class* is "Veblenesque." The discipline of economics is even less hospitable to Veblen's kind of writing now than it was a hundred years ago, yet a number of economists known to the general public—if not all that well regarded among their professional colleagues—write in a tradition inspired by Veblen, including John Kenneth Galbraith, Juliet Schor, and Robert Frank. To call someone "Veblenesque" is to suggest that he or she engages in pointing out foibles of contemporary capitalism that are obvious to nearly everyone but the professional economist. Is it rational to want to buy a house near a pristine lake when, if enough other people have the same desire, the lake will no longer be pristine? Should corporate executives be rewarded with stock options for firing employees from their jobs? Can we say that the numbers rackets of the inner cities ought to be illegal when the form of gambling called the NASDAQ is perfectly legal? These are the kinds of questions that require Veblen's ironic sensibility to be addressed fully.

xvi · Introduction

Modern life, like life in Veblen's time, is unfair. A younger version of George W. Bush would be unlikely to get into Yale these days if he had the president's grades, but he would still, as a result of his family's money and connections, have advantages in life outstripping those of a poor person with more brains. The stock-market boom of the 1990s poured wealth into the pockets of many people who were lucky rather than skilled. Trophy homes—indeed, trophy wives, a depressing feature of contemporary society anticipated by Veblen—flourished at the end of the twentieth century in much the same way that they flourished at the end of the nineteenth. Veblen praised engineers and mechanics for their practicality, distrusting as he did the appeals to the emotions he associated with the rich. Yet his attack on the rich of his day, if not motivated by an emotion like envy, was certainly shaped by one like anger. For Veblen, contempt and satire may not have been the best revenge, but they were the only tools at his disposal, and by deploying them so skillfully, he wrote a book that will be read so long as the rich are different from the rest of us—which, if the future is anything like the past, they always will be.

———

ALAN WOLFE is the director of the Boisi Center for Religion and American Public Life at Boston College and the author of *One Nation, After All* and *Moral Freedom*.

THE THEORY
OF THE
LEISURE CLASS

CHAPTER I

INTRODUCTORY

The institution of a leisure class is found in its best development at the higher stages of the barbarian culture; as, for instance, in feudal Europe or feudal Japan. In such communities the distinction between classes is very rigorously observed; and the feature of most striking economic significance in these class differences is the distinction maintained between the employments proper to the several classes. The upper classes are by custom exempt or excluded from industrial occupations, and are reserved for certain employments to which a degree of honour attaches. Chief among the honourable employments in any feudal community is warfare; and priestly service is commonly second to warfare. If the barbarian community is not notably warlike, the priestly office may take the precedence, with that of the warrior second. But the rule holds with but slight exceptions that, whether warriors or priests, the upper classes are exempt from industrial employments, and this exemption is the economic expression of their superior rank. Brahmin India affords a fair illustration of the industrial exemption of both these classes. In the communities belonging to the higher barbarian culture there is a considerable differentiation of sub-classes within what may be comprehensively called the leisure class; and there is a corresponding differentiation of employments between these sub-classes. The leisure class as a whole comprises the noble and the priestly classes, together with much of their retinue. The occupations of the class are correspondingly diversified; but they have the common economic characteristic of being non-industrial. These non-industrial upper-class occupations may be roughly comprised under government, warfare, religious observances, and sports.

At an earlier, but not the earliest, stage of barbarism, the leisure class is found in a less differentiated form. Neither the class distinctions nor the distinctions between leisure-class occupations are so minute and intricate. The Polynesian islanders generally show this stage of the development in good form, with the exception that, owing to the absence of large game, hunting does not hold the usual place of honour in their scheme of life. The Icelandic community in the time of the Sagas also affords a fair instance. In such a community there is a rigorous distinction between classes and between the occupations peculiar to each class. Manual labour, industry, whatever has to do directly with the everyday work of getting a livelihood, is the exclusive occupation of the inferior class. This inferior class includes slaves and other dependents, and ordinarily also all the women. If there are several grades of aristocracy, the women of high rank are commonly exempt from industrial employment, or at least from the more vulgar kinds of manual labour. The men of the upper classes are not only exempt, but by prescriptive custom they are debarred, from all industrial occupations. The range of employments open to them is rigidly defined. As on the higher plane already spoken of, these employments are government, warfare, religious observances, and sports. These four lines of activity govern the scheme of life of the upper classes, and for the highest rank—the kings or chieftains—these are the only kinds of activity that custom or the common sense of the community will allow. Indeed, where the scheme is well developed even sports are accounted doubtfully legitimate for the members of the highest rank. To the lower grades of the leisure class certain other employments are open, but they are employments that are subsidiary to one or another of these typical leisure-class occupations. Such are, for instance, the manufacture and care of arms and accoutrements and of war canoes, the dressing and handling of horses, dogs, and hawks, the preparation of sacred apparatus, etc. The lower classes are excluded from these secondary honourable employments, except from such as are plainly of an industrial character and are only remotely related to the typical leisure-class occupations.

If we go a step back of this exemplary barbarian culture, into the lower stages of barbarism, we no longer find the leisure class in fully developed form. But this lower barbarism shows the usages, motives, and circumstances out of which the institution of a leisure class has arisen, and indicates the steps of its early growth. Nomadic hunting tribes in various parts of the world illustrate these more primitive phases of the differentiation. Any one of the North American hunting tribes may be taken as a convenient illustration. These tribes can scarcely be said to have a defined leisure class. There is a differentiation of function, and there is a distinction between classes on the basis of this difference of function, but the exemption of the superior class from work has not gone far enough to make the designation "leisure class" altogether applicable. The tribes belonging on this economic level have carried the economic differentiation to the point at which a marked distinction is made between the occupations of men and women, and this distinction is of an invidious character. In nearly all these tribes the women are, by prescriptive custom, held to those employments out of which the industrial occupations proper develop at the next advance. The men are exempt from these vulgar employments and are reserved for war, hunting, sports, and devout observances. A very nice discrimination is ordinarily shown in this matter.

This division of labour coincides with the distinction between the working and the leisure class as it appears in the higher barbarian culture. As the diversification and specialisation of employments proceed, the line of demarcation so drawn comes to divide the industrial from the non-industrial employments. The man's occupation as it stands at the earlier barbarian stage is not the original out of which any appreciable portion of later industry has developed. In the later development it survives only in employments that are not classed as industrial,—war, politics, sports, learning, and the priestly office. The only notable exceptions are a portion of the fishery industry and certain slight employments that are doubtfully to be classed as industry; such as the manufacture of arms, toys, and sporting goods. Virtually the whole range of industrial employments is an outgrowth of what is classed as woman's work in the primitive barbarian community.

The work of the men in the lower barbarian culture is no less indispensable to the life of the group than the work done by the women. It may even be that the men's work contributes as much to the food supply and the other necessary consumption of the group. Indeed, so obvious is this "productive" character of the men's work that in the conventional economic writings the hunter's work is taken as the type of primitive industry. But such is not the barbarian's sense of the matter. In his own eyes he is not a labourer, and he is not to be classed with the women in this respect; nor is his effort to be classed with the women's drudgery, as labour or industry, in such a sense as to admit of its being confounded with the latter. There is in all barbarian communities a profound sense of the disparity between man's and woman's work. His work may conduce to the maintenance of the group, but it is felt that it does so through an excellence and an efficacy of a kind that cannot without derogation be compared with the uneventful diligence of the women.

At a farther step backward in the cultural scale—among savage groups—the differentiation of employments is still less elaborate and the invidious distinction between classes and employments is less consistent and less rigorous. Unequivocal instances of a primitive savage culture are hard to find. Few of those groups or communities that are classed as "savage" show no traces of regression from a more advanced cultural stage. But there are groups—some of them apparently not the result of retrogression—which show the traits of primitive savagery with some fidelity. Their culture differs from that of the barbarian communities in the absence of a leisure class and the absence, in great measure, of the animus or spiritual attitude on which the institution of a leisure class rests.

These communities of primitive savages in which there is no hierarchy of economic classes make up but a small and inconspicuous fraction of the human race. As good an instance of this phase of culture as may be had is afforded by the tribes of the Andamans,[1] or by the Todas[2] of the Nilgiri Hills. The scheme of life of these groups at the time of their earliest contact with Europeans seems to have been nearly typical, so far as regards the absence of a leisure class. As a further instance might be cited the Ainu of Yezo, and, more doubtfully, also some Bushman and Eskimo groups. Some Pueblo communities are less confidently to be included in the same class. Most, if not all, of the communities here cited may well be cases of degeneration from a higher barbarism, rather than bearers of a culture that has never risen above its present level. If so, they are for the present purpose to be taken with allowance, but they may serve none the less as evidence to the same effect as if they were really "primitive" populations.

These communities that are without a defined leisure class resemble one another also in certain other features of their social structure and manner of life. They are small groups and of a simple (archaic) structure; they are commonly peaceable and sedentary; they are poor; and individual ownership is not a dominant feature of their economic system. At the same time it does not follow that these are the smallest of existing communities, or that their social structure is in all respects the least differentiated; nor does the class necessarily include all primitive communities which have no defined system of individual ownership. But it is to be noted that the class seems to include the most peaceable—perhaps all the characteristically peaceable—primitive groups of men. Indeed, the most notable trait common to members of such communities is a certain amiable inefficiency when confronted with force or fraud.

The evidence afforded by the usages and cultural traits of communities at a low stage of development indicates that the institution of a leisure class has emerged gradually during the transition from primitive savagery to barbarism; or more precisely, during the transition from a peaceable to a consistently warlike habit of life.

The conditions apparently necessary to its emergence in a consistent form are: (1) the community must be of a predatory habit of life (war or the hunting of large game or both); that is to say, the men, who constitute the inchoate leisure class in these cases, must be habituated to the infliction of injury by force and stratagem; (2) subsistence must be obtainable on sufficiently easy terms to admit of the exemption of a considerable portion of the community from steady application to a routine of labour. The institution of a leisure class is the outgrowth of an early discrimination between employments, according to which some employments are worthy and others unworthy. Under this ancient distinction the worthy employments are those which may be classed as exploit; unworthy are those necessary everyday employments into which no appreciable element of exploit enters.

This distinction has but little obvious significance in a modern industrial community, and it has, therefore, received but slight attention at the hands of economic writers. When viewed in the light of that modern common sense which has guided economic discussion, it seems formal and insubstantial. But it persists with great tenacity as a commonplace preconception even in modern life, as is shown, for instance, by our habitual aversion to menial employments. It is a distinction of a personal kind—of superiority and inferiority. In the earlier stages of culture, when the personal force of the individual counted more immediately and obviously in shaping the course of events, the element of exploit counted for more in the everyday scheme of life. Interest centred about this fact to a greater degree. Consequently a distinction proceeding on this ground seemed more imperative and more definitive then than is the case to-day. As a fact in the sequence of development, therefore, the distinction is a substantial one and rests on sufficiently valid and cogent grounds.

The ground on which a discrimination between facts is habitually made changes as the interest from which the facts are habitually viewed changes. Those features of the facts at hand are salient and substantial upon which the dominant interest of the time throws its light. Any given ground of distinction will seem insubstantial to any one who habitually apprehends the facts in question from a different point of view and values them for a different purpose. The habit of distinguishing and classifying the various purposes and directions of activity prevails of necessity always and everywhere; for it is indispensable in reaching a working theory or scheme of life. The particular point of view, or the particular characteristic that is pitched upon as definitive in the classification of the facts of life depends upon the interest from which a discrimination of the facts is sought. The grounds of discrimination, and the norm of procedure in classifying the facts, therefore, progressively change as the growth of culture proceeds; for the end for which the facts of life are apprehended changes, and the point of view consequently changes also. So that what are recognised as the salient and decisive features of a class of activities or of a social class at one stage of culture will not retain the same relative importance for the purposes of classification at any subsequent stage.

But the change of standards and points of view is gradual only, and it seldom results in the subversion or entire suppression of a standpoint once accepted. A distinction is still habitually made between industrial and non-industrial occupations; and this modern distinction is a transmuted form of the barbarian distinction between exploit and drudgery. Such employments as warfare, politics, public worship, and public merrymaking, are felt, in the popular apprehension, to differ intrinsically from the labour that has to do with elaborating the material means of life. The precise line of demarcation is not the same as it was in the early barbarian scheme, but the broad distinction has not fallen into disuse.

The tacit, common-sense distinction to-day is, in effect, that any effort is to be accounted industrial only so far as its ultimate purpose is the utilisation of non-human things. The coercive utilisation of man by man is not felt to be an industrial function; but all effort directed to enhance human life by taking advantage of the non-human environment is classed together as industrial activity. By the economists who have best retained and adapted the classical tradition, man's "power over nature" is currently postulated as the characteristic fact of industrial productivity. This industrial power over nature is taken to include man's power over the life of the beasts and over all the elemental forces. A line is in this way drawn between mankind and brute creation.

In other times and among men imbued with a different body of preconceptions, this line is not drawn precisely as we draw it today. In the savage or the barbarian scheme of life it is drawn in a different place and in another way. In all communities under the barbarian culture there is an alert and pervading sense of antithesis between two comprehensive groups of phenomena, in one of which barbarian man includes himself, and in the other, his victual. There is a felt antithesis between economic and non-economic phenomena, but it is not conceived in the modern fashion; it lies not between man and brute creation, but between animate and inert things.

It may be an excess of caution at this day to explain that the barbarian notion which it is here intended to convey by the term "animate" is not the same as would be conveyed by the word "living." The term does not cover all living things, and it does cover a great many others. Such a striking natural phenomenon as a storm, a disease, a waterfall, are recognised as "animate"; while fruits and herbs, and even inconspicuous animals, such as house-flies, maggots, lemmings, sheep, are not ordinarily apprehended as "animate" except when taken collectively. As here used the term does not necessarily imply an indwelling soul or spirit. The concept includes such things as in the apprehension of the animistic savage or barbarian are formidable by virtue of a real or imputed habit of initiating action. This category comprises a large number and range of natural objects and phenomena. Such a distinction between the inert and the active is still present in the habits of thought of unreflecting persons, and it still profoundly affects the prevalent theory of human life and of natural processes; but it does not pervade our daily life to the extent or with the far-reaching practical consequences that are apparent at earlier stages of culture and belief.

To the mind of the barbarian, the elaboration and utilisation of what is afforded by inert nature is activity on quite a different plane from his dealings with "animate" things and forces. The line of demarcation may be vague and shifting, but the broad distinction is sufficiently real and cogent to influence the barbarian scheme of life. To the class of things apprehended as animate, the barbarian fancy imputes an unfolding of activity directed to some end. It is this teleological unfolding of activity that constitutes any object or phenomenon an "animate" fact. Wherever the unsophisticated savage or barbarian meets with activity that is at all obtrusive, he construes it in the only terms that are ready to hand—the terms immediately given in his consciousness of his own actions. Activity is, therefore, assimilated to human action, and active objects are in so far assimilated to the human agent. Phenomena of this character—especially those whose behaviour is notably formidable or baffling—have to be met in a different spirit and with proficiency of a different kind from what is required in dealing with inert things. To deal successfully with such phenomena is a work of exploit rather than of industry. It is an assertion of prowess, not of diligence.

Under the guidance of this naïve discrimination between the inert and the animate, the activities of the primitive social group tend to fall into two classes, which would in modern phrase be called exploit and industry. Industry is effort that goes to create a new thing, with a new purpose given it by the fashioning hand of its maker out of passive ("brute") material; while exploit, so far as it results in an outcome useful to the agent, is the conversion to his own ends of energies previously directed to some other end by another agent. We still speak of "brute matter" with something of the barbarian's realisation of a profound significance in the term.

The distinction between exploit and drudgery coincides with a difference between the sexes. The sexes differ, not only in stature and muscular force, but perhaps even more decisively in temperament, and this must early have given rise to a corresponding division of labour. The general range of activities that come under the head of exploit falls to the males as being the stouter, more massive, better capable of a sudden and violent strain, and more readily inclined to self-assertion, active emulation, and aggression. The difference in mass, in physiological character, and in temperament may be slight among the members of the primitive group; it appears, in fact, to be relatively slight and inconsequential in some of the more archaic communities with which we are acquainted—as for instance the tribes of the Andamans. But so soon as a differentiation of function has well begun on the lines marked out by this difference in physique and animus, the original difference between the sexes will itself widen. A cumulative process of selective adaptation to the new distribution of employments will set in, especially if the habitat or the fauna with which the group is in contact is such as to call for a considerable exercise of the sturdier virtues. The habitual pursuit of large game requires more of the manly qualities of massiveness, agility, and ferocity, and it can therefore scarcely fail to hasten and widen the differentiation of functions between the sexes. And so soon as the group comes into hostile contact with other groups, the divergence of function will take on the developed form of a distinction between exploit and industry.

In such a predatory group of hunters it comes to be the able-bodied men's office to fight and hunt. The women do what other work there is to do—other members who are unfit for man's work being for this purpose classed with the women. But the men's hunting and fighting are both of the same general character. Both are of a predatory nature; the warrior and the hunter alike reap where they have not strewn. Their aggressive assertion of force and sagacity differs obviously from the women's assiduous and uneventful shaping of materials; it is not to be accounted productive labour, but rather an acquisition of substance by seizure. Such being the barbarian man's work, in its best development and widest divergence from women's work, any effort that does not involve an assertion of prowess comes to be unworthy of the man. As the tradition gains consistency, the common sense of the community erects it into a canon of conduct; so that no employment and no acquisition is morally possible to the self-respecting man at this cultural stage, except such as proceeds on the basis of prowess—force or fraud. When the predatory habit of life has been settled upon the group by long habituation, it becomes the able-bodied man's accredited office in the social economy to kill, to destroy such competitors in the struggle for existence as attempt to resist or elude him, to overcome and reduce to subservience those alien forces that assert themselves refractorily in the environment. So tenaciously and with such nicety is this theoretical distinction between exploit and drudgery adhered to that in many hunting tribes the man must not bring home the game which he has killed, but must send his woman to perform that baser office.

———

As has already been indicated, the distinction between exploit and drudgery is an invidious distinction between employments. Those employments which are to be classed as exploit are worthy, honourable, noble; other employments, which do not contain this element of exploit, and especially those which imply subservience or submission, are unworthy, debasing, ignoble. The concept of dignity, worth, or honour, as applied either to persons or conduct, is of first-rate consequence in the development of classes and of class distinctions, and it is therefore necessary to say something of its derivation and meaning. Its psychological ground may be indicated in outline as follows.

As a matter of selective necessity, man is an agent. He is, in his own apprehension, a centre of unfolding impulsive activity—"teleological" activity. He is an agent seeking in every act the accomplishment of some concrete, objective, impersonal end. By force of his being such an agent he is possessed of a taste for effective work, and a distaste for futile effort. He has a sense of the merit of serviceability or efficiency and of the demerit of futility, waste, or incapacity. This aptitude or propensity may be called the instinct of workmanship. Wherever the circumstances or traditions of life lead to an habitual comparison of one person with another in point of efficiency, the instinct of workmanship works out in an emulative or invidious comparison of persons. The extent to which this result follows depends in some considerable degree on the temperament of the population. In any community where such an invidious comparison of persons is habitually made, visible success becomes an end sought for its own utility as a basis of esteem. Esteem is gained and dispraise is avoided by putting one's efficiency in evidence. The result is that the instinct of workmanship works out in an emulative demonstration of force.

During that primitive phase of social development, when the community is still habitually peaceable, perhaps sedentary, and without a developed system of individual ownership, the efficiency of the individual can be shown chiefly and most consistently in some employment that goes to further the life of the group. What emulation of an economic kind there is between the members of such a group will be chiefly emulation in industrial serviceability. At the same time the incentive to emulation is not strong, nor is the scope for emulation large.

When the community passes from peaceable savagery to a predatory phase of life, the conditions of emulation change. The opportunity and the incentive to emulation increase greatly in scope and urgency. The activity of the men more and more takes on the character of exploit; and an invidious comparison of one hunter or warrior with another grows continually easier and more habitual. Tangible evidences of prowess—trophies—find a place in men's habits of thought as an essential feature of the paraphernalia of life. Booty, trophies of the chase or of the raid, come to be prized as evidence of preëminent force. Aggression becomes the accredited form of action, and booty serves as *prima facie* evidence of successful aggression. As accepted at this cultural stage, the accredited, worthy form of self-assertion is contest; and useful articles or services obtained by seizure or compulsion, serve as a conventional evidence of successful contest. Therefore, by contrast, the obtaining of goods by other methods than seizure comes to be accounted unworthy of man in his best estate. The performance of productive work, or employment in personal service, falls under the same odium for the same reason. An invidious distinction in this way arises between exploit and acquisition by seizure on the one hand and industrial employment on the other hand. Labour acquires a character of irksomeness by virtue of the indignity imputed to it.

With the primitive barbarian, before the simple content of the notion has been obscured by its own ramifications and by a secondary growth of cognate ideas, "honourable" seems to connote nothing else than assertion of superior force. "Honourable" is "formidable"; "worthy" is "prepotent." A honorific act is in the last analysis little if anything else than a recognised successful act of aggression; and where aggression means conflict with men and beasts, the activity which comes to be especially and primarily honourable is the assertion of the strong hand. The naïve, archaic habit of construing all manifestations of force in terms of personality or "will power" greatly fortifies this conventional exaltation of the strong hand. Honorific epithets, in vogue among barbarian tribes as well as among peoples of a more advanced culture, commonly bear the stamp of this unsophisticated sense of honour. Epithets and titles used in addressing chieftains, and in the propitiation of kings and gods, very commonly impute a propensity for overbearing violence and an irresistible devastating force to the person who is to be propitiated. This holds true to an extent also in the more civilised communities of the present day. The predilection shown in heraldic devices for the more rapacious beasts and birds of prey goes to enforce the same view.

Under this common-sense barbarian appreciation of worth or honour, the taking of life—the killing of formidable competitors, whether brute or human—is honourable in the highest degree. And this high office of slaughter, as an expression of the slayer's prepotence, casts a glamour of worth over every act of slaughter and over all the tools and accessories of the act. Arms are honourable, and the use of them, even in seeking the life of the meanest creatures of the fields, becomes a honorific employment. At the same time, employment in industry becomes correspondingly odious, and, in the common-sense apprehension, the handling of the tools and implements of industry falls beneath the dignity of able-bodied men. Labour becomes irksome.

———

It is here assumed that in the sequence of cultural evolution primitive groups of men have passed from an initial peaceable stage to a subsequent stage at which fighting is the avowed and characteristic employment of the group. But it is not implied that there has been an abrupt transition from unbroken peace and good-will to a later or higher phase of life in which the fact of combat occurs for the first time. Neither is it implied that all peaceful industry disappears on the transition to the predatory phase of culture. Some fighting, it is safe to say, would be met with at any early stage of social development. Fights would occur with more or less frequency through sexual competition. The known habits of primitive groups, as well as the habits of the anthropoid apes, argue to that effect, and the evidence from the well-known promptings of human nature enforces the same view.

It may therefore be objected that there can have been no such initial stage of peaceable life as is here assumed. There is no point in cultural evolution prior to which fighting does not occur. But the point in question is not as to the occurrence of combat, occasional or sporadic, or even more or less frequent and habitual; it is a question as to the occurrence of an habitual bellicose frame of mind— a prevalent habit of judging facts and events from the point of view of the fight. The predatory phase of culture is attained only when the predatory attitude has become the habitual and accredited spiritual attitude for the members of the group; when the fight has become the dominant note in the current theory of life; when the common-sense appreciation of men and things has come to be an appreciation with a view to combat.

The substantial difference between the peaceable and the predatory phase of culture, therefore, is a spiritual difference, not a mechanical one. The change in spiritual attitude is the outgrowth of a change in the material facts of the life of the group, and it comes on gradually as the material circumstances favourable to a predatory attitude supervene. The inferior limit of the predatory culture is an industrial limit. Predation cannot become the habitual, conventional resource of any group or any class until industrial methods have been developed to such a degree of efficiency as to leave a margin worth fighting for, above the subsistence of those engaged in getting a living. The transition from peace to predation therefore depends on the growth of technical knowledge and the use of tools. A predatory culture is similarly impracticable in early times, until weapons have been developed to such a point as to make man a formidable animal. The early development of tools and of weapons is of course the same fact seen from two different points of view.

The life of a given group would be characterised as peaceable so long as habitual recourse to combat has not brought the fight into the foreground in men's everyday thoughts, as a dominant feature of the life of man. A group may evidently attain such a predatory attitude with a greater or less degree of completeness, so that its scheme of life and canons of conduct may be controlled to a greater or less extent by the predatory animus. The predatory phase of culture is therefore conceived to come on gradually, through a cumulative growth of predatory aptitudes, habits, and traditions; this growth being due to a change in the circumstances of the group's life, of such a kind as to develop and conserve those traits of human nature and those traditions and norms of conduct that make for a predatory rather than a peaceable life.

The evidence for the hypothesis that there has been such a peaceable stage of primitive culture is in great part drawn from psychology rather than from ethnology, and cannot be detailed here. It will be recited in part in a later chapter, in discussing the survival of archaic traits of human nature under the modern culture.

CHAPTER II

Pecuniary Emulation

In the sequence of cultural evolution the emergence of a leisure class coincides with the beginning of ownership. This is necessarily the case, for these two institutions result from the same set of economic forces. In the inchoate phase of their development they are but different aspects of the same general facts of social structure.

It is as elements of social structure—conventional facts—that leisure and ownership are matters of interest for the purpose in hand. An habitual neglect of work does not constitute a leisure class; neither does the mechanical fact of use and consumption constitute ownership. The present inquiry, therefore, is not concerned with the beginning of indolence, nor with the beginning of the appropriation of useful articles to individual consumption. The point in question is the origin and nature of a conventional leisure class on the one hand and the beginnings of individual ownership as a conventional right or equitable claim on the other hand.

The early differentiation out of which the distinction between a leisure and a working class arises is a division maintained between men's and women's work in the lower stages of barbarism. Likewise the earliest form of ownership is an ownership of the women by the able-bodied men of the community. The facts may be expressed in more general terms, and truer to the import of the barbarian theory of life, by saying that it is an ownership of the woman by the man.

There was undoubtedly some appropriation of useful articles before the custom of appropriating women arose. The usages of existing archaic communities in which there is no ownership of women is warrant for such a view. In all communities the members, both male and female, habitually appropriate to their individual use a variety of useful things; but these useful things are not thought of as owned by the person who appropriates and consumes them. The habitual appropriation and consumption of certain slight personal effects goes on without raising the question of ownership; that is to say, the question of a conventional, equitable claim to extraneous things.

The ownership of women begins in the lower barbarian stages of culture, apparently with the seizure of female captives. The original reason for the seizure and appropriation of women seems to have been their usefulness as trophies. The practice of seizing women from the enemy as trophies, gave rise to a form of ownership-marriage, resulting in a household with a male head. This was followed by an extension of slavery to other captives and inferiors, besides women, and by an extension of ownership-marriage to other women than those seized from the enemy. The outcome of emulation under the circumstances of a predatory life, therefore, has been on the one hand a form of marriage resting on coercion, and on the other hand the custom of ownership. The two institutions are not distinguishable in the initial phase of their development; both arise from the desire of the successful men to put their prowess in evidence by exhibiting some durable result of their exploits. Both also minister to that propensity for mastery which pervades all predatory communities. From the ownership of women the concept of ownership extends itself to include the products of their industry, and so there arises the ownership of things as well as of persons.

In this way a consistent system of property in goods is gradually installed. And although in the latest stages of the development, the serviceability of goods for consumption has come to be the most obtrusive element of their value, still, wealth has by no means yet lost its utility as a honorific evidence of the owner's prepotence.

———

Wherever the institution of private property is found, even in a slightly developed form, the economic process bears the character of a struggle between men for the possession of goods. It has been customary in economic theory, and especially among those economists who adhere with least faltering to the body of modernised classical doctrines, to construe this struggle for wealth as being substantially a struggle for subsistence. Such is, no doubt, its character in large part during the earlier and less efficient phases of industry. Such is also its character in all cases where the "niggardliness of nature" is so strict as to afford but a scanty livelihood to the community in return for strenuous and unremitting application to the business of getting the means of subsistence. But in all progressing communities an advance is presently made beyond this early stage of technological development. Industrial efficiency is presently carried to such a pitch as to afford something appreciably more than a bare livelihood to those engaged in the industrial process. It has not been unusual for economic theory to speak of the further struggle for wealth on this new industrial basis as a competition for an increase of the comforts of life,—primarily for an increase of the physical comforts which the consumption of goods affords.

The end of acquisition and accumulation is conventionally held to be the consumption of the goods accumulated—whether it is consumption directly by the owner of the goods or by the household attached to him and for this purpose identified with him in theory. This is at least felt to be the economically legitimate end of acquisition, which alone it is incumbent on the theory to take account of. Such consumption may of course be conceived to serve the consumer's physical wants—his physical comfort—or his so-called higher wants—spiritual, æsthetic, intellectual, or what not; the latter class of wants being served indirectly by an expenditure of goods, after the fashion familiar to all economic readers.

But it is only when taken in a sense far removed from its naïve meaning that consumption of goods can be said to afford the incentive from which accumulation invariably proceeds. The motive that lies at the root of ownership is emulation; and the same motive of emulation continues active in the further development of the institution to which it has given rise and in the development of all those features of the social structure which this institution of ownership touches. The possession of wealth confers honour; it is an invidious distinction. Nothing equally cogent can be said for the consumption of goods, nor for any other conceivable incentive to acquisition, and especially not for any incentive to the accumulation of wealth.

It is of course not to be overlooked that in a community where nearly all goods are private property the necessity of earning a livelihood is a powerful and ever-present incentive for the poorer members of the community. The need of subsistence and of an increase of physical comfort may for a time be the dominant motive of acquisition for those classes who are habitually employed at manual labour, whose subsistence is on a precarious footing, who possess little and ordinarily accumulate little; but it will appear in the course of the discussion that even in the case of these impecunious classes the predominance of the motive of physical want is not so decided as has sometimes been assumed. On the other hand, so far as regards those members and classes of the community who are chiefly concerned in the accumulation of wealth, the incentive of subsistence or of physical comfort never plays a considerable part. Ownership began and grew into a human institution on grounds unrelated to the subsistence minimum. The dominant incentive was from the outset the invidious distinction attaching to wealth, and, save temporarily and by exception, no other motive has usurped the primacy at any later stage of the development.

Property set out with being booty held as trophies of the successful raid. So long as the group had departed but little from the primitive communal organisation, and so long as it still stood in close contact with other hostile groups, the utility of things or persons owned lay chiefly in an invidious comparison between their possessor and the enemy from whom they were taken. The habit of distinguishing between the interests of the individual and those of the group to which he belongs is apparently a later growth. Invidious comparison between the possessor of the honorific booty and his less successful neighbours within the group was no doubt present early as an element of the utility of the things possessed, though this was not at the outset the chief element of their value. The man's prowess was still primarily the group's prowess, and the possessor of the booty felt himself to be primarily the keeper of the honour of his group. This appreciation of exploit from the communal point of view is met with also at later stages of social growth, especially as regards the laurels of war.

But so soon as the custom of individual ownership begins to gain consistency, the point of view taken in making the invidious comparison on which private property rests will begin to change. Indeed, the one change is but the reflex of the other. The initial phase of ownership, the phase of acquisition by naïve seizure and conversion, begins to pass into the subsequent stage of an incipient organisation of industry on the basis of private property (in slaves); the horde develops into a more or less self-sufficing industrial community; possessions then come to be valued not so much as evidence of successful foray, but rather as evidence of the prepotence of the possessor of these goods over other individuals within the community. The invidious comparison now becomes primarily a comparison of the owner with the other members of the group. Property is still of the nature of trophy, but, with the cultural advance, it becomes more and more a trophy of successes scored in the game of ownership carried on between the members of the group under the quasi-peaceable methods of nomadic life.

Gradually, as industrial activity further displaces predatory activity in the community's everyday life and in men's habits of thought, accumulated property more and more replaces trophies of predatory exploit as the conventional exponent of prepotence and success. With the growth of settled industry, therefore, the possession of wealth gains in relative importance and effectiveness as a customary basis of repute and esteem. Not that esteem ceases to be awarded on the basis of other, more direct evidence of prowess; not that successful predatory aggression or warlike exploit ceases to call out the approval and admiration of the crowd, or to stir the envy of the less successful competitors; but the opportunities for gaining distinction by means of this direct manifestation of superior force grow less available both in scope and frequency. At the same time opportunities for industrial aggression, and for the accumulation of property by the quasi-peaceable methods of nomadic industry, increase in scope and availability. And it is even more to the point that property now becomes the most easily recognised evidence of a reputable degree of success as distinguished from heroic or signal achievement. It therefore becomes the conventional basis of esteem. Its possession in some amount becomes necessary in order to any reputable standing in the community. It becomes indispensable to accumulate, to acquire property, in order to retain one's good name. When accumulated goods have in this way once become the accepted badge of efficiency, the possession of wealth presently assumes the character of an independent and definitive basis of esteem. The possession of goods, whether acquired aggressively by one's own exertion or passively by transmission through inheritance from others, becomes a conventional basis of reputability. The possession of wealth, which was at the outset valued simply as an evidence of efficiency, becomes, in popular apprehension, itself a meritorious act. Wealth is now itself intrinsically honourable and confers honour on its possessor. By a further refinement, wealth acquired passively by transmission from ancestors or other antecedents presently becomes even more honorific than wealth acquired by the possessor's own effort; but this distinction belongs at a later stage in the evolution of the pecuniary culture and will be spoken of in its place.

Prowess and exploit may still remain the basis of award of the highest popular esteem, although the possession of wealth has become the basis of commonplace reputability and of a blameless social standing. The predatory instinct and the consequent approbation of predatory efficiency are deeply ingrained in the habits of thought of those peoples who have passed under the discipline of a protracted predatory culture. According to popular award, the highest honours within human reach may, even yet, be those gained by an unfolding of extraordinary predatory efficiency in war, or by a quasi-predatory efficiency in statecraft; but for the purposes of a commonplace decent standing in the community these means of repute have been replaced by the acquisition and accumulation of goods. In order to stand well in the eyes of the community, it is necessary to come up to a certain, somewhat indefinite, conventional standard of wealth; just as in the earlier predatory stage it is necessary for the barbarian man to come up to the tribe's standard of physical endurance, cunning, and skill at arms. A certain standard of wealth in the one case, and of prowess in the other, is a necessary condition of reputability, and anything in excess of this normal amount is meritorious.

Those members of the community who fall short of this, somewhat indefinite, normal degree of prowess or of property suffer in the esteem of their fellow-men; and consequently they suffer also in their own esteem, since the usual basis of self-respect is the respect accorded by one's neighbours. Only individuals with an aberrant temperament can in the long run retain their self-esteem in the face of the disesteem of their fellows. Apparent exceptions to the rule are met with, especially among people with strong religious convictions. But these apparent exceptions are scarcely real exceptions, since such persons commonly fall back on the putative approbation of some supernatural witness of their deeds.

So soon as the possession of property becomes the basis of popular esteem, therefore, it becomes also a requisite to that complacency which we call self-respect. In any community where goods are held in severalty it is necessary, in order to his own peace of mind, that an individual should possess as large a portion of goods as others with whom he is accustomed to class himself; and it is extremely gratifying to possess something more than others. But as fast as a person makes new acquisitions, and becomes accustomed to the resulting new standard of wealth, the new standard forthwith ceases to afford appreciably greater satisfaction than the earlier standard did. The tendency in any case is constantly to make the present pecuniary standard the point of departure for a fresh increase of wealth; and this in turn gives rise to a new standard of sufficiency and a new pecuniary classification of one's self as compared with one's neighbours. So far as concerns the present question, the end sought by accumulation is to rank high in comparison with the rest of the community in point of pecuniary strength. So long as the comparison is distinctly unfavourable to himself, the normal, average individual will live in chronic dissatisfaction with his present lot; and when he has reached what may be called the normal pecuniary standard of the community, or of his class in the community, this chronic dissatisfaction will give place to a restless straining to place a wider and ever-widening pecuniary interval between himself and this average standard. The invidious comparison can never become so favourable to the individual making it that he would not gladly rate himself still higher relatively to his competitors in the struggle for pecuniary reputability.

In the nature of the case, the desire for wealth can scarcely be satiated in any individual instance, and evidently a satiation of the average or general desire for wealth is out of the question. However widely, or equally, or "fairly," it may be distributed, no general increase of the community's wealth can make any approach to satiating this need, the ground of which is the desire of every one to excel every one else in the accumulation of goods. If, as is sometimes assumed, the incentive to accumulation were the want of subsistence or of physical comfort, then the aggregate economic wants of a community might conceivably be satisfied at some point in the advance of industrial efficiency; but since the struggle is substantially a race for reputability on the basis of an invidious comparison, no approach to a definitive attainment is possible.

What has just been said must not be taken to mean that there are no other incentives to acquisition and accumulation than this desire to excel in pecuniary standing and so gain the esteem and envy of one's fellow-men. The desire for added comfort and security from want is present as a motive at every stage of the process of accumulation in a modern industrial community; although the standard of sufficiency in these respects is in turn greatly affected by the habit of pecuniary emulation. To a great extent this emulation shapes the methods and selects the objects of expenditure for personal comfort and decent livelihood.

Besides this, the power conferred by wealth also affords a motive to accumulation. That propensity for purposeful activity and that repugnance to all futility of effort which belong to man by virtue of his character as an agent do not desert him when he emerges from the naïve communal culture where the dominant note of life is the unanalysed and undifferentiated solidarity of the individual with the group with which his life is bound up. When he enters upon the predatory stage, where self-seeking in the narrower sense becomes the dominant note, this propensity goes with him still, as the pervasive trait that shapes his scheme of life. The propensity for achievement and the repugnance to futility remain the underlying economic motive. The propensity changes only in the form of its expression and in the proximate objects to which it directs the man's activity. Under the régime of individual ownership the most available means of visibly achieving a purpose is that afforded by the acquisition and accumulation of goods; and as the self-regarding antithesis between man and man reaches fuller consciousness, the propensity for achievement—the instinct of workmanship—tends more and more to shape itself into a straining to excel others in pecuniary achievement. Relative success, tested by an invidious pecuniary comparison with other men, becomes the conventional end of action. The currently accepted legitimate end of effort becomes the achievement of a favourable comparison with other men; and therefore the repugnance to futility to a good extent coalesces with the incentive of emulation. It acts to accentuate the struggle for pecuniary reputability by visiting with a sharper disapproval all shortcoming and all evidence of shortcoming in point of pecuniary success. Purposeful effort comes to mean, primarily, effort directed to or resulting in a more creditable showing of accumulated wealth. Among the motives which lead men to accumulate wealth, the primacy, both in scope and intensity, therefore, continues to belong to this motive of pecuniary emulation.

In making use of the term "invidious," it may perhaps be unnecessary to remark, there is no intention to extol or depreciate, or to commend or deplore any of the phenomena which the word is used to characterise. The term is used in a technical sense as describing a comparison of persons with a view to rating and grading them in respect of relative worth or value—in an æsthetic or moral sense—and so awarding and defining the relative degrees of complacency with which they may legitimately be contemplated by themselves and by others. An invidious comparison is a process of valuation of persons in respect of worth.

CHAPTER III

Conspicuous Leisure

If its working were not disturbed by other economic forces or other features of the emulative process, the immediate effect of such a pecuniary struggle as has just been described in outline would be to make men industrious and frugal. This result actually follows, in some measure, so far as regards the lower classes, whose ordinary means of acquiring goods is productive labour. This is more especially true of the labouring classes in a sedentary community which is at an agricultural stage of industry, in which there is a considerable subdivision of property, and whose laws and customs secure to these classes a more or less definite share of the product of their industry. These lower classes can in any case not avoid labour, and the imputation of labour is therefore not greatly derogatory to them, at least not within their class. Rather, since labour is their recognised and accepted mode of life, they take some emulative pride in a reputation for efficiency in their work, this being often the only line of emulation that is open to them. For those for whom acquisition and emulation is possible only within the field of productive efficiency and thrift, the struggle for pecuniary reputability will in some measure work out in an increase of diligence and parsimony. But certain secondary features of the emulative process, yet to be spoken of, come in to very materially circumscribe and modify emulation in these directions among the pecuniarily inferior classes as well as among the superior class.

But it is otherwise with the superior pecuniary class, with which we are here immediately concerned. For this class also the incentive to diligence and thrift is not absent; but its action is so greatly qualified by the secondary demands of pecuniary emulation, that any inclination in this direction is practically overborne and any incentive to diligence tends to be of no effect. The most imperative of these secondary demands of emulation, as well as the one of widest scope, is the requirement of abstention from productive work. This is true in an especial degree for the barbarian stage of culture. During the predatory culture labour comes to be associated in men's habits of thought with weakness and subjection to a master. It is therefore a mark of inferiority, and therefore comes to be accounted unworthy of man in his best estate. By virtue of this tradition labour is felt to be debasing, and this tradition has never died out. On the contrary, with the advance of social differentiation it has acquired the axiomatic force due to ancient and unquestioned prescription.

In order to gain and to hold the esteem of men it is not sufficient merely to possess wealth or power. The wealth or power must be put in evidence, for esteem is awarded only on evidence. And not only does the evidence of wealth serve to impress one's importance on others and to keep their sense of his importance alive and alert, but it is of scarcely less use in building up and preserving one's self-complacency. In all but the lowest stages of culture the normally constituted man is comforted and upheld in his self-respect by "decent surroundings" and by exemption from "menial offices." Enforced departure from his habitual standard of decency, either in the paraphernalia of life or in the kind and amount of his everyday activity, is felt to be a slight upon his human dignity, even apart from all conscious consideration of the approval or disapproval of his fellows.

The archaic theoretical distinction between the base and the honourable in the manner of a man's life retains very much of its ancient force even to-day. So much so that there are few of the better class who are not possessed of an instinctive repugnance for the vulgar forms of labour. We have a realising sense of ceremonial uncleanness attaching in an especial degree to the occupations which are associated in our habits of thought with menial service. It is felt by all persons of refined taste that a spiritual contamination is inseparable from certain offices that are conventionally required of servants. Vulgar surroundings, mean (that is to say, inexpensive) habitations, and vulgarly productive occupations are unhesitatingly condemned and avoided. They are incompatible with life on a satisfactory spiritual plane—with "high thinking." From the days of the Greek philosophers to the present, a degree of leisure and of exemption from contact with such industrial processes as serve the immediate everyday purposes of human life has ever been recognised by thoughtful men as a prerequisite to a worthy or beautiful, or even a blameless, human life. In itself and in its consequences the life of leisure is beautiful and ennobling in all civilised men's eyes.

This direct, subjective value of leisure and of other evidences of wealth is no doubt in great part secondary and derivative. It is in part a reflex of the utility of leisure as a means of gaining the respect of others, and in part it is the result of a mental substitution. The performance of labour has been accepted as a conventional evidence of inferior force; therefore it comes itself, by a mental short-cut, to be regarded as intrinsically base.

During the predatory stage proper, and especially during the earlier stages of the quasi-peaceable development of industry that follows the predatory stage, a life of leisure is the readiest and most conclusive evidence of pecuniary strength, and therefore of superior force; provided always that the gentleman of leisure can live in manifest ease and comfort. At this stage wealth consists chiefly of slaves, and the benefits accruing from the possession of riches and power take the form chiefly of personal service and the immediate products of personal service. Conspicuous abstention from labour therefore becomes the conventional mark of superior pecuniary achievement and the conventional index of reputability; and conversely, since application to productive labour is a mark of poverty and subjection, it becomes inconsistent with a reputable standing in the community. Habits of industry and thrift, therefore, are not uniformly furthered by a prevailing pecuniary emulation. On the contrary, this kind of emulation indirectly discountenances participation in productive labour. Labour would unavoidably become dishonourable, as being an evidence of poverty, even if it were not already accounted indecorous under the ancient tradition handed down from an earlier cultural stage. The ancient tradition of the predatory culture is that productive effort is to be shunned as being unworthy of able-bodied men, and this tradition is reinforced rather than set aside in the passage from the predatory to the quasi-peaceable manner of life.

Even if the institution of a leisure class had not come in with the first emergence of individual ownership, by force of the dishonour attaching to productive employment, it would in any case have come in as one of the early consequences of ownership. And it is to be remarked that while the leisure class existed in theory from the beginning of predatory culture, the institution takes on a new and fuller meaning with the transition from the predatory to the next succeeding pecuniary stage of culture. It is from this time forth a "leisure class" in fact as well as in theory. From this point dates the institution of the leisure class in its consummate form.

During the predatory stage proper the distinction between the leisure and the labouring class is in some degree a ceremonial distinction only. The able-bodied men jealously stand aloof from whatever is, in their apprehension, menial drudgery; but their activity in fact contributes appreciably to the sustenance of the group. The subsequent stage of quasi-peaceable industry is usually characterised by an established chattel slavery, herds of cattle, and a servile class of herdsmen and shepherds; industry has advanced so far that the community is no longer dependent for its livelihood on the chase or on any other form of activity that can fairly be classed as exploit. From this point on, the characteristic feature of leisure-class life is a conspicuous exemption from all useful employment.

The normal and characteristic occupations of the class in this mature phase of its life history are in form very much the same as in its earlier days. These occupations are government, war, sports, and devout observances. Persons unduly given to difficult theoretical niceties may hold that these occupations are still incidentally and indirectly "productive"; but it is to be noted as decisive of the question in hand that the ordinary and ostensible motive of the leisure class in engaging in these occupations is assuredly not an increase of wealth by productive effort. At this as at any other cultural stage, government and war are, at least in part, carried on for the pecuniary gain of those who engage in them; but it is gain obtained by the honourable method of seizure and conversion. These occupations are of the nature of predatory, not of productive, employment. Something similar may be said of the chase, but with a difference. As the community passes out of the hunting stage proper, hunting gradually becomes differentiated into two distinct employments. On the one hand it is a trade, carried on chiefly for gain; and from this the element of exploit is virtually absent, or it is at any rate not present in a sufficient degree to clear the pursuit of the imputation of gainful industry. On the other hand, the chase is also a sport—an exercise of the predatory impulse simply. As such it does not afford any appreciable pecuniary incentive, but it contains a more or less obvious element of exploit. It is this latter development of the chase—purged of all imputation of handicraft—that alone is meritorious and fairly belongs in the scheme of life of the developed leisure class.

Abstention from labour is not only a honorific or meritorious act, but it presently comes to be a requisite of decency. The insistence on property as the basis of reputability is very naïve and very imperious during the early stages of the accumulation of wealth. Abstention from labour is the conventional evidence of wealth and is therefore the conventional mark of social standing; and this insistence on the meritoriousness of wealth leads to a more strenuous insistence on leisure. *Nota notæ est nota rei ipsius.*[1] According to well-established laws of human nature, prescription presently seizes upon this conventional evidence of wealth and fixes it in men's habits of thought as something that is in itself substantially meritorious and ennobling; while productive labour at the same time and by a like process becomes in a double sense intrinsically unworthy. Prescription ends by making labour not only disreputable in the eyes of the community, but morally impossible to the noble, free-born man, and incompatible with a worthy life.

This tabu on labour has a further consequence in the industrial differentiation of classes. As the population increases in density and the predatory group grows into a settled industrial community, the constituted authorities and the customs governing ownership gain in scope and consistency. It then presently becomes impracticable to accumulate wealth by simple seizure, and, in logical consistency, acquisition by industry is equally impossible for high-minded and impecunious men. The alternative open to them is beggary or privation. Wherever the canon of conspicuous leisure has a chance undisturbed to work out its tendency, there will therefore emerge a secondary, and in a sense spurious, leisure class—abjectly poor and living a precarious life of want and discomfort, but morally unable to stoop to gainful pursuits. The decayed gentleman and the lady who has seen better days are by no means unfamiliar phenomena even now. This pervading sense of the indignity of the slightest manual labour is familiar to all civilised peoples, as well as to peoples of a less advanced pecuniary culture. In persons of delicate sensibility, who have long been habituated to gentle manners, the sense of the shamefulness of manual labour may become so strong that, at a critical juncture, it will even set aside the instinct of self-preservation. So, for instance, we are told of certain Polynesian chiefs, who, under the stress of good form, preferred to starve rather than carry their food to their mouths with their own hands. It is true, this conduct may have been due, at least in part, to an excessive sanctity or tabu attaching to the chief's person. The tabu would have been communicated by the contact of his hands, and so would have made anything touched by him unfit for human food. But the tabu is itself a derivative of the unworthiness or moral incompatibility of labour; so that even when construed in this sense the conduct of the Polynesian chiefs is truer to the canon of honorific leisure than would at first appear. A better illustration, or at least a more unmistakable one, is afforded by a certain king of France, who is said to have lost his life through an excess of moral stamina in the observance of good form. In the absence of the functionary whose office it was to shift his master's seat, the king sat uncomplaining before the fire and suffered his royal person to be toasted beyond recovery. But in so doing he saved his Most Christian Majesty from menial contamination.

> Summum crede nefas animam præferre pudori,
> Et propter vitam vivendi perdere causas.[2]

It has already been remarked that the term "leisure," as here used, does not connote indolence or quiescence. What it connotes is non-productive consumption of time. Time is consumed non-productively (1) from a sense of the unworthiness of productive work, and (2) as an evidence of pecuniary ability to afford a life of idleness. But the whole of the life of the gentleman of leisure is not spent before the eyes of the spectators who are to be impressed with that spectacle of honorific leisure which in the ideal scheme makes up his life. For some part of the time his life is perforce withdrawn from the public eye, and of this portion which is spent in private the gentleman of leisure should, for the sake of his good name, be able to give a convincing account. He should find some means of putting in evidence the leisure that is not spent in the sight of the spectators. This can be done only indirectly, through the exhibition of some tangible, lasting results of the leisure so spent—in a manner analogous to the familiar exhibition of tangible, lasting products of the labour performed for the gentleman of leisure by handicraftsmen and servants in his employ.

The lasting evidence of productive labour is its material product—commonly some article of consumption. In the case of exploit it is similarly possible and usual to procure some tangible result that may serve for exhibition in the way of trophy or booty. At a later phase of the development it is customary to assume some badge or insignia of honour that will serve as a conventionally accepted mark of exploit, and which at the same time indicates the quantity or degree of exploit of which it is the symbol. As the population increases in density, and as human relations grow more complex and numerous, all the details of life undergo a process of elaboration and selection; and in this process of elaboration the use of trophies develops into a system of rank, titles, degrees and insignia, typical examples of which are heraldic devices, medals, and honorary decorations.

As seen from the economic point of view, leisure, considered as an employment, is closely allied in kind with the life of exploit; and the achievements which characterise a life of leisure, and which remain as its decorous criteria, have much in common with the trophies of exploit. But leisure in the narrower sense, as distinct from exploit and from any ostensibly productive employment of effort on objects which are of no intrinsic use, does not commonly leave a material product. The criteria of a past performance of leisure therefore commonly take the form of "immaterial" goods. Such immaterial evidences of past leisure are quasi-scholarly or quasi-artistic accomplishments and a knowledge of processes and incidents which do not conduce directly to the furtherance of human life. So, for instance, in our time there is the knowledge of the dead languages and the occult sciences; of correct spelling; of syntax and prosody; of the various forms of domestic music and other household art; of the latest proprieties of dress, furniture, and equipage; of games, sports, and fancy-bred animals, such as dogs and race-horses. In all these branches of knowledge the initial motive from which their acquisition proceeded at the outset, and through which they first came into vogue, may have been something quite different from the wish to show that one's time had not been spent in industrial employment; but unless these accomplishments had approved themselves as serviceable evidence of an unproductive expenditure of time, they would not have survived and held their place as conventional accomplishments of the leisure class.

These accomplishments may, in some sense, be classed as branches of learning. Beside and beyond these there is a further range of social facts which shade off from the region of learning into that of physical habit and dexterity. Such are what is known as manners and breeding, polite usage, decorum, and formal and ceremonial observances generally. This class of facts are even more immediately and obtrusively presented to the observation, and they are therefore more widely and more imperatively insisted on as required evidences of a reputable degree of leisure. It is worth while to remark that all that class of ceremonial observances which are classed under the general head of manners hold a more important place in the esteem of men during the stage of culture at which conspicuous leisure has the greatest vogue as a mark of reputability, than at later stages of the cultural development. The barbarian of the quasi-peaceable stage of industry is notoriously a more high-bred gentleman, in all that concerns decorum, than any but the very exquisite among the men of a later age. Indeed, it is well known, or at least it is currently believed, that manners have progressively deteriorated as society has receded from the patriarchal stage. Many a gentleman of the old school has been provoked to remark regretfully upon the underbred manners and bearing of even the better classes in the modern industrial communities; and the decay of the ceremonial code—or as it is otherwise called, the vulgarisation of life—among the industrial classes proper has become one of the chief enormities of latter-day civilisation in the eyes of all persons of delicate sensibilities. The decay which the code has suffered at the hands of a busy people testifies—all deprecation apart—to the fact that decorum is a product and an exponent of leisure-class life and thrives in full measure only under a régime of status.

The origin, or better the derivation, of manners is, no doubt, to be sought elsewhere than in a conscious effort on the part of the well-mannered to show that much time has been spent in acquiring them. The proximate end of innovation and elaboration has been the higher effectiveness of the new departure in point of beauty or of expressiveness. In great part the ceremonial code of decorous usages owes its beginning and its growth to the desire to conciliate or to show good-will, as anthropologists and sociologists are in the habit of assuming, and this initial motive is rarely if ever absent from the conduct of well-mannered persons at any stage of the later development. Manners, we are told, are in part an elaboration of gesture, and in part they are symbolical and conventionalised survivals representing former acts of dominance or of personal service or of personal contact. In large part they are an expression of the relation of status,—a symbolic pantomime of mastery on the one hand and of subservience on the other. Wherever at the present time the predatory habit of mind, and the consequent attitude of mastery and of subservience, gives its character to the accredited scheme of life, there the importance of all punctilios of conduct is extreme, and the assiduity with which the ceremonial observance of rank and titles is attended to approaches closely to the ideal set by the barbarian of the quasi-peaceable nomadic culture. Some of the Continental countries afford good illustrations of this spiritual survival. In these communities the archaic ideal is similarly approached as regards the esteem accorded to manners as a fact of intrinsic worth.

Decorum set out with being symbol and pantomime and with having utility only as an exponent of the facts and qualities symbolised; but it presently suffered the transmutation which commonly passes over symbolical facts in human intercourse. Manners presently came, in popular apprehension, to be possessed of a substantial utility in themselves; they acquired a sacramental character, in great measure independent of the facts which they originally prefigured. Deviations from the code of decorum have become intrinsically odious to all men, and good breeding is, in everyday apprehension, not simply an adventitious mark of human excellence, but an integral feature of the worthy human soul. There are few things that so touch us with instinctive revulsion as a breach of decorum; and so far have we progressed in the direction of imputing intrinsic utility to the ceremonial observances of etiquette that few of us, if any, can dissociate an offence against etiquette from a sense of the substantial unworthiness of the offender. A breach of faith may be condoned, but a breach of decorum can not. "Manners maketh man."

None the less, while manners have this intrinsic utility, in the

apprehension of the performer and the beholder alike, this sense of
the intrinsic rightness of decorum is only the proximate ground of
the vogue of manners and breeding. Their ulterior, economic
ground is to be sought in the honorific character of that leisure or
non-productive employment of time and effort without which
good manners are not acquired. The knowledge and habit of good
form come only by long-continued use. Refined tastes, manners,
and habits of life are a useful evidence of gentility, because good
breeding requires time, application, and expense, and can therefore
not be compassed by those whose time and energy are taken up
with work. A knowledge of good form is *prima facie* evidence that
that portion of the well-bred person's life which is not spent under
the observation of the spectator has been worthily spent in acquiring accomplishments that are of no lucrative effect. In the last
analysis the value of manners lies in the fact that they are the
voucher of a life of leisure. Therefore, conversely, since leisure is
the conventional means of pecuniary repute, the acquisition of
some proficiency in decorum is incumbent on all who aspire to a
modicum of pecuniary decency.

So much of the honourable life of leisure as is not spent in the
sight of spectators can serve the purposes of reputability only in so
far as it leaves a tangible, visible result that can be put in evidence
and can be measured and compared with products of the same
class exhibited by competing aspirants for repute. Some such effect, in the way of leisurely manners and carriage, etc., follows from
simple persistent abstention from work, even where the subject
does not take thought of the matter and studiously acquire an air of
leisurely opulence and mastery. Especially does it seem to be true
that a life of leisure in this way persisted in through several generations will leave a persistent, ascertainable effect in the conformation of the person, and still more in his habitual bearing and
demeanour. But all the suggestions of a cumulative life of leisure,
and all the proficiency in decorum that comes by the way of passive
habituation, may be further improved upon by taking thought and
assiduously acquiring the marks of honourable leisure, and then
carrying the exhibition of these adventitious marks of exemption

from employment out in a strenuous and systematic discipline. Plainly, this is a point at which a diligent application of effort and expenditure may materially further the attainment of a decent proficiency in the leisure-class proprieties. Conversely, the greater the degree of proficiency and the more patent the evidence of a high degree of habituation to observances which serve no lucrative or other directly useful purpose, the greater the consumption of time and substance impliedly involved in their acquisition, and the greater the resultant good repute. Hence, under the competitive struggle for proficiency in good manners, it comes about that much pains is taken with the cultivation of habits of decorum; and hence the details of decorum develop into a comprehensive discipline, conformity to which is required of all who would be held blameless in point of repute. And hence, on the other hand, this conspicuous leisure of which decorum is a ramification grows gradually into a laborious drill in deportment and an education in taste and discrimination as to what articles of consumption are decorous and what are the decorous methods of consuming them.

In this connection it is worthy of notice that the possibility of producing pathological and other idiosyncrasies of person and manner by shrewd mimicry and a systematic drill have been turned to account in the deliberate production of a cultured class—often with a very happy effect. In this way, by the process vulgarly known as snobbery, a syncopated evolution of gentle birth and breeding is achieved in the case of a goodly number of families and lines of descent. This syncopated gentle birth gives results which, in point of serviceability as a leisure-class factor in the population, are in no wise substantially inferior to others who may have had a longer but less arduous training in the pecuniary proprieties.

There are, moreover, measureable degrees of conformity to the latest accredited code of the punctilios as regards decorous means and methods of consumption. Differences between one person and another in the degree of conformity to the ideal in these respects can be compared, and persons may be graded and scheduled with some accuracy and effect according to a progressive scale of manners and breeding. The award of reputability in this regard is commonly made in good faith, on the ground of conformity to accepted canons of taste in the matters concerned, and without conscious regard to the pecuniary standing or the degree of leisure practised by any given candidate for reputability; but the canons of taste according to which the award is made are constantly under the surveillance of the law of conspicuous leisure, and are indeed constantly undergoing change and revision to bring them into closer conformity with its requirements. So that while the proximate ground of discrimination may be of another kind, still the pervading principle and abiding test of good breeding is the requirement of a substantial and patent waste of time. There may be some considerable range of variation in detail within the scope of this principle, but they are variations of form and expression, not of substance.

Much of the courtesy of everyday intercourse is of course a direct expression of consideration and kindly good-will, and this element of conduct has for the most part no need of being traced back to any underlying ground of reputability to explain either its presence or the approval with which it is regarded; but the same is not true of the code of proprieties. These latter are expressions of status. It is of course sufficiently plain, to any one who cares to see, that our bearing towards menials and other pecuniarily dependent inferiors is the bearing of the superior member in a relation of status, though its manifestation is often greatly modified and softened from the original expression of crude dominance. Similarly, our bearing towards superiors, and in great measure towards equals, expresses a more or less conventionalised attitude of subservience. Witness the masterful presence of the high-minded gentleman or lady, which testifies to so much of dominance and independence of economic circumstances, and which at the same time appeals with such convincing force to our sense of what is right and gracious. It is among this highest leisure class, who have no superiors and few peers, that decorum finds its fullest and maturest expression; and it is this highest class also that gives decorum that definitive formulation which serves as a canon of conduct for the classes beneath. And here also the code is most obviously a code of status and shows most plainly its incompatibility with all vulgarly productive work. A divine assurance and an imperious complaisance, as of one habituated to require subservience and to take no thought for the morrow, is the birthright and the criterion of the gentleman at his best; and it is in popular apprehension even more than that, for this demeanour is accepted as an intrinsic attribute of superior worth, before which the base-born commoner delights to stoop and yield.

———

As has been indicated in an earlier chapter, there is reason to believe that the institution of ownership has begun with the ownership of persons, primarily women. The incentives to acquiring such property have apparently been: (1) a propensity for dominance and coercion; (2) the utility of these persons as evidence of the prowess of their owner; (3) the utility of their services.

Personal service holds a peculiar place in the economic development. During the stage of quasi-peaceable industry, and especially during the earlier development of industry within the limits of this general stage, the utility of their services seems commonly to be the dominant motive to the acquisition of property in persons. Servants are valued for their services. But the dominance of this motive is not due to a decline in the absolute importance of the other two utilities possessed by servants. It is rather that the altered circumstances of life accentuate the utility of servants for this last-named purpose. Women and other slaves are highly valued, both as an evidence of wealth and as a means of accumulating wealth. Together with cattle, if the tribe is a pastoral one, they are the usual form of investment for a profit. To such an extent may female slavery give its character to the economic life under the quasi-peaceable culture that the woman even comes to serve as a unit of value among peoples occupying this cultural stage—as for instance in Homeric times. Where this is the case there need be little question but that the basis of the industrial system is chattel slavery and that the women are commonly slaves. The great, pervading human relation in such a system is that of master and servant. The accepted evidence of wealth is the possession of many women, and presently also of other slaves engaged in attendance on their master's person and in producing goods for him.

A division of labour presently sets in, whereby personal service and attendance on the master becomes the special office of a portion of the servants, while those who are wholly employed in industrial occupations proper are removed more and more from all immediate relation to the person of their owner. At the same time those servants whose office is personal service, including domestic duties, come gradually to be exempted from productive industry carried on for gain.

This process of progressive exemption from the common run of industrial employment will commonly begin with the exemption of the wife, or the chief wife. After the community has advanced to settled habits of life, wife-capture from hostile tribes becomes impracticable as a customary source of supply. Where this cultural advance has been achieved, the chief wife is ordinarily of gentle blood, and the fact of her being so will hasten her exemption from vulgar employment. The manner in which the concept of gentle blood originates, as well as the place which it occupies in the development of marriage, cannot be discussed in this place. For the purpose in hand it will be sufficient to say that gentle blood is blood which has been ennobled by protracted contact with accumulated wealth or unbroken prerogative. The woman with these antecedents is preferred in marriage, both for the sake of a resulting alliance with her powerful relatives and because a superior worth is felt to inhere in blood which has been associated with many goods and great power. She will still be her husband's chattel, as she was her father's chattel before her purchase, but she is at the same time of her father's gentle blood; and hence there is a moral incongruity in her occupying herself with the debasing employments of her fellow-servants. However completely she may be subject to her master, and however inferior to the male members of the social stratum in which her birth has placed her, the principle that gentility is transmissible will act to place her above the common slave; and so soon as this principle has acquired a prescriptive authority it will act to invest her in some measure with that prerogative of leisure which is the chief mark of gentility. Furthered by this principle of transmissible gentility the wife's exemption gains in scope, if the wealth of her owner permits it, until it includes exemption from debasing menial service as well as from handicraft. As the industrial development goes on and property becomes massed in relatively fewer hands, the conventional standard of wealth of the upper class rises. The same tendency to exemption from handicraft, and in the course of time from menial domestic employments, will then assert itself as regards the other wives, if such there are, and also as regards other servants in immediate attendance upon the person of their master. The exemption comes more tardily the remoter the relation in which the servant stands to the person of the master.

If the pecuniary situation of the master permits it, the development of a special class of personal or body servants is also furthered by the very grave importance which comes to attach to this personal service. The master's person, being the embodiment of worth and honour, is of the most serious consequence. Both for his reputable standing in the community and for his self-respect, it is a matter of moment that he should have at his call efficient specialised servants, whose attendance upon his person is not diverted from this their chief office by any by-occupation. These specialised servants are useful more for show than for service actually performed. In so far as they are not kept for exhibition simply, they afford gratification to their master chiefly in allowing scope to his propensity for dominance. It is true, the care of the continually increasing household apparatus may require added labour; but since the apparatus is commonly increased in order to serve as a means of good repute rather than as a means of comfort, this qualification is not of great weight. All these lines of utility are better served by a larger number of more highly specialised servants. There results, therefore, a constantly increasing differentiation and multiplication of domestic and body servants, along with a concomitant progressive exemption of such servants from productive labour. By virtue of their serving as evidence of ability to pay, the office of such domestics regularly tends to include continually fewer duties, and their service tends in the end to become nominal only. This is especially true of those servants who are in most immediate and obvious attendance upon their master. So that the utility of these comes to consist, in great part, in their conspicuous exemption from productive labour and in the evidence which this exemption affords of their master's wealth and power.

After some considerable advance has been made in the practice of employing a special corps of servants for the performance of a conspicuous leisure in this manner, men begin to be preferred above women for services that bring them obtrusively into view. Men, especially lusty, personable fellows, such as footmen and other menials should be, are obviously more powerful and more expensive than women. They are better fitted for this work, as showing a larger waste of time and of human energy. Hence it comes about that in the economy of the leisure class the busy housewife of the early patriarchal days, with her retinue of hard-working handmaidens, presently gives place to the lady and the lackey.

In all grades and walks of life, and at any stage of the economic development, the leisure of the lady and of the lackey differs from the leisure of the gentleman in his own right in that it is an occupation of an ostensibly laborious kind. It takes the form, in large measure, of a painstaking attention to the service of the master, or to the maintenance and elaboration of the household paraphernalia; so that it is leisure only in the sense that little or no productive work is performed by this class, not in the sense that all appearance of labour is avoided by them. The duties performed by the lady, or by the household or domestic servants, are frequently arduous enough, and they are also frequently directed to ends which are considered extremely necessary to the comfort of the entire household. So far as these services conduce to the physical efficiency or comfort of the master or the rest of the household, they are to be accounted productive work. Only the residue of employment left after deduction of this effective work is to be classed as a performance of leisure.

But much of the services classed as household cares in modern everyday life, and many of the "utilities" required for a comfortable existence by civilised man, are of a ceremonial character. They are, therefore, properly to be classed as a performance of leisure in the sense in which the term is here used. They may be none the less imperatively necessary from the point of view of decent existence; they may be none the less requisite for personal comfort even, although they may be chiefly or wholly of a ceremonial character. But in so far as they partake of this character they are imperative and requisite because we have been taught to require them under pain of ceremonial uncleanness or unworthiness. We feel discomfort in their absence, but not because their absence results directly in physical discomfort; nor would a taste not trained to discriminate between the conventionally good and the conventionally bad take offence at their omission. In so far as this is true the labour spent in these services is to be classed as leisure; and when performed by others than the economically free and self-directing head of the establishment, they are to be classed as vicarious leisure.

The vicarious leisure performed by housewives and menials, under the head of household cares, may frequently develop into drudgery, especially where the competition for reputability is close and strenuous. This is frequently the case in modern life. Where this happens, the domestic service which comprises the duties of this servant class might aptly be designated as wasted effort, rather than as vicarious leisure. But the latter term has the advantage of indicating the line of derivation of these domestic offices, as well as of neatly suggesting the substantial economic ground of their utility; for these occupations are chiefly useful as a method of imputing pecuniary reputability to the master or to the household on the ground that a given amount of time and effort is conspicuously wasted in that behalf.

In this way, then, there arises a subsidiary or derivative leisure class, whose office is the performance of a vicarious leisure for the behoof of the reputability of the primary or legitimate leisure class. This vicarious leisure class is distinguished from the leisure class proper by a characteristic feature of its habitual mode of life.

The leisure of the master class is, at least ostensibly, an indulgence of a proclivity for the avoidance of labour and is presumed to enhance the master's own well-being and fulness of life; but the leisure of the servant class exempt from productive labour is in some sort a performance exacted from them, and is not normally or primarily directed to their own comfort. The leisure of the servant is not his own leisure. So far as he is a servant in the full sense, and not at the same time a member of a lower order of the leisure class proper, his leisure normally passes under the guise of specialised service directed to the furtherance of his master's fulness of life. Evidence of this relation of subservience is obviously present in the servant's carriage and manner of life. The like is often true of the wife throughout the protracted economic stage during which she is still primarily a servant—that is to say, so long as the household with a male head remains in force. In order to satisfy the requirements of the leisure-class scheme of life, the servant should show not only an attitude of subservience, but also the effects of special training and practice in subservience. The servant or wife should not only perform certain offices and show a servile disposition, but it is quite as imperative that they should show an acquired facility in the tactics of subservience—a trained conformity to the canons of effectual and conspicuous subservience. Even to-day it is this aptitude and acquired skill in the formal manifestation of the servile relation that constitutes the chief element of utility in our highly paid servants, as well as one of the chief ornaments of the well-bred housewife.

The first requisite of a good servant is that he should conspicuously know his place. It is not enough that he knows how to effect certain desired mechanical results; he must, above all, know how to effect these results in due form. Domestic service might be said to be a spiritual rather than a mechanical function. Gradually there grows up an elaborate system of good form, specifically regulating the manner in which this vicarious leisure of the servant class is to be performed. Any departure from these canons of form is to be deprecated, not so much because it evinces a shortcoming in mechanical efficiency, or even that it shows an absence of the servile attitude and temperament, but because, in the last analysis, it shows the absence of special training. Special training in personal service costs time and effort, and where it is obviously present in a high degree, it argues that the servant who possesses it, neither is nor has been habitually engaged in any productive occupation. It is *prima facie* evidence of a vicarious leisure extending far back in the past. So that trained service has utility, not only as gratifying the master's instinctive liking for good and skilful workmanship and his propensity for conspicuous dominance over those whose lives are subservient to his own, but it has utility also as putting in evidence a much larger consumption of human service than would be shown by the mere present conspicuous leisure performed by an untrained person. It is a serious grievance if a gentleman's butler or footman performs his duties about his master's table or carriage in such unformed style as to suggest that his habitual occupation may be ploughing or sheepherding. Such bungling work would imply inability on the master's part to procure the service of specially trained servants; that is to say, it would imply inability to pay for the consumption of time, effort, and instruction required to fit a trained servant for special service under an exacting code of forms. If the performance of the servant argues lack of means on the part of his master, it defeats its chief substantial end; for the chief use of servants is the evidence they afford of the master's ability to pay.

What has just been said might be taken to imply that the offence of an under-trained servant lies in a direct suggestion of inexpensiveness or of usefulness. Such, of course, is not the case. The connection is much less immediate. What happens here is what happens generally. Whatever approves itself to us on any ground at the outset, presently comes to appeal to us as a gratifying thing in itself; it comes to rest in our habits of thought as substantially right. But in order that any specific canon of deportment shall maintain itself in favour, it must continue to have the support of, or at least not be incompatible with, the habit or aptitude which constitutes the norm of its development. The need of vicarious leisure, or conspicuous consumption of service, is a dominant incentive to the keeping of servants. So long as this remains true it may be set down without much discussion that any such departure from accepted usage as would suggest an abridged apprenticeship in service would presently be found insufferable. The requirement of an expensive vicarious leisure acts indirectly, selectively, by guiding the formation of our taste,—of our sense of what is right in these matters,—and so weeds out unconformable departures by withholding approval of them.

As the standard of wealth recognized by common consent advances, the possession and exploitation of servants as a means of showing superfluity undergoes a refinement. The possession and maintenance of slaves employed in the production of goods argues wealth and prowess, but the maintenance of servants who produce nothing argues still higher wealth and position. Under this principle there arises a class of servants, the more numerous the better, whose sole office is fatuously to wait upon the person of their owner, and so to put in evidence his ability unproductively to consume a large amount of service. There supervenes a division of labour among the servants or dependents whose life is spent in maintaining the honour of the gentleman of leisure. So that, while one group produces goods for him, another group, usually headed by the wife, or chief wife, consumes for him in conspicuous leisure; thereby putting in evidence his ability to sustain large pecuniary damage without impairing his superior opulence.

This somewhat idealized and diagrammatic outline of the development and nature of domestic service comes nearest being true for that cultural stage which has here been named the "quasi-peaceable" stage of industry. At this stage personal service first rises to the position of an economic institution, and it is at this stage that it occupies the largest place in the community's scheme of life. In the cultural sequence, the quasi-peaceable stage follows the predatory stage proper, the two being successive phases of barbarian life. Its characteristic feature is a formal observance of peace and order, at the same time that life at this stage still has too much of coercion and class antagonism to be called peaceable in the full sense of the word. For many purposes, and from another point of view than the economic one, it might as well be named the stage of status. The method of human relation during this stage, and the spiritual attitude of men at this level of culture, is well summed up under that term. But as a descriptive term to characterise the prevailing methods of industry, as well as to indicate the trend of industrial development at this point in economic evolution, the term "quasi-peaceable" seems preferable. So far as concerns the communities of the Western culture, this phase of economic development probably lies in the past; except for a numerically small though very conspicuous fraction of the community in whom the habits of thought peculiar to the barbarian culture have suffered but a relatively slight disintegration.

Personal service is still an element of great economic importance, especially as regards the distribution and consumption of goods; but its relative importance even in this direction is no doubt less than it once was. The best development of this vicarious leisure lies in the past rather than in the present; and its best expression in the present is to be found in the scheme of life of the upper leisure class. To this class the modern culture owes much in the way of the conservation of traditions, usages, and habits of thought which belong on a more archaic cultural plane, so far as regards their widest acceptance and their most effective development.

In the modern industrial communities the mechanical contrivances available for the comfort and convenience of everyday life are highly developed. So much so that body servants, or, indeed, domestic servants of any kind, would now scarcely be employed by anybody except on the ground of a canon of reputability carried over by tradition from earlier usage. The only exception would be servants employed to attend on the persons of the infirm and the feeble-minded. But such servants properly come under the head of trained nurses rather than under that of domestic servants, and they are, therefore, an apparent rather than a real exception to the rule.

The proximate reason for keeping domestic servants, for instance, in the moderately well-to-do household of to-day, is (ostensibly) that the members of the household are unable without discomfort to compass the work required by such a modern establishment. And the reason for their being unable to accomplish it is (1) that they have too many "social duties," and (2) that the work to be done is too severe and that there is too much of it. These two reasons may be restated as follows: (1) Under a mandatory code of decency, the time and effort of the members of such a household are required to be ostensibly all spent in a performance of conspicuous leisure, in the way of calls, drives, clubs, sewing-circles, sports, charity organisations, and other like social functions. Those persons whose time and energy are employed in these matters privately avow that all these observances, as well as the incidental attention to dress and other conspicuous consumption, are very irksome but altogether unavoidable. (2) Under the requirement of conspicuous consumption of goods, the apparatus of living has grown so elaborate and cumbrous, in the way of dwellings, furniture, bric-a-brac, wardrobe and meals, that the consumers of these things cannot make way with them in the required manner without help. Personal contact with the hired persons whose aid is called in to fulfil the routine of decency is commonly distasteful to the occupants of the house, but their presence is endured and paid for, in order to delegate to them a share in this onerous consumption of household goods. The presence of domestic servants, and of the special class of body servants in an eminent degree, is a concession of physical comfort to the moral need of pecuniary decency.

The largest manifestation of vicarious leisure in modern life is made up of what are called domestic duties. These duties are fast becoming a species of services performed, not so much for the individual behoof of the head of the household as for the reputability of the household taken as a corporate unit—a group of which the housewife is a member on a footing of ostensible equality. As fast as the household for which they are performed departs from its archaic basis of ownership-marriage, these household duties of course tend to fall out of the category of vicarious leisure in the original sense; except so far as they are performed by hired servants. That is to say, since vicarious leisure is possible only on a basis of status or of hired service, the disappearance of the relation of status from human intercourse at any point carries with it the disappearance of vicarious leisure so far as regards that much of life. But it is to be added, in qualification of this qualification, that so long as the household subsists, even with a divided head, this class of non-productive labour performed for the sake of household reputability must still be classed as vicarious leisure, although in a slightly altered sense. It is now leisure performed for the quasi-personal corporate household, instead of, as formerly, for the proprietary head of the household.

CHAPTER IV

CONSPICUOUS CONSUMPTION

In what has been said of the evolution of the vicarious leisure class and its differentiation from the general body of the working classes, reference has been made to a further division of labour,—that between different servant classes. One portion of the servant class, chiefly those persons whose occupation is vicarious leisure, come to undertake a new, subsidiary range of duties—the vicarious consumption of goods. The most obvious form in which this consumption occurs is seen in the wearing of liveries and the occupation of spacious servants' quarters. Another, scarcely less obtrusive or less effective form of vicarious consumption, and a much more widely prevalent one, is the consumption of food, clothing, dwelling, and furniture by the lady and the rest of the domestic establishment.

But already at a point in economic evolution far antedating the emergence of the lady, specialised consumption of goods as an evidence of pecuniary strength had begun to work out in a more or less elaborate system. The beginning of a differentiation in consumption even antedates the appearance of anything that can fairly be called pecuniary strength. It is traceable back to the initial phase of predatory culture, and there is even a suggestion that an incipient differentiation in this respect lies back of the beginnings of the predatory life. This most primitive differentiation in the consumption of goods is like the later differentiation with which we are all so intimately familiar, in that it is largely of a ceremonial character, but unlike the latter it does not rest on a difference in accumulated wealth. The utility of consumption as an evidence of wealth is to be classed as a derivative growth. It is an adaptation to a new end, by a selective process, of a distinction previously existing and well established in men's habits of thought.

In the earlier phases of the predatory culture the only economic differentiation is a broad distinction between an honourable superior class made up of the able-bodied men on the one side, and a base inferior class of labouring women on the other. According to the ideal scheme of life in force at that time it is the office of the men to consume what the women produce. Such consumption as falls to the women is merely incidental to their work; it is a means to their continued labour, and not a consumption directed to their own comfort and fulness of life. Unproductive consumption of goods is honourable, primarily as a mark of prowess and a perquisite of human dignity; secondarily it becomes substantially honourable in itself, especially the consumption of the more desirable things. The consumption of choice articles of food, and frequently also of rare articles of adornment, becomes tabu to the women and children; and if there is a base (servile) class of men, the tabu holds also for them. With a further advance in culture this tabu may change into simple custom of a more or less rigorous character; but whatever be the theoretical basis of the distinction which is maintained, whether it be a tabu or a larger conventionality, the features of the conventional scheme of consumption do not change easily. When the quasi-peaceable stage of industry is reached, with its fundamental institution of chattel slavery, the general principle, more or less rigorously applied, is that the base, industrious class should consume only what may be necessary to their subsistence. In the nature of things, luxuries and the comforts of life belong to the leisure class. Under the tabu, certain victuals, and more particularly certain beverages, are strictly reserved for the use of the superior class.

The ceremonial differentiation of the dietary is best seen in the use of intoxicating beverages and narcotics. If these articles of consumption are costly, they are felt to be noble and honorific. Therefore the base classes, primarily the women, practise an enforced continence with respect to these stimulants, except in countries where they are obtainable at a very low cost. From archaic times down through all the length of the patriarchal régime it has been the office of the women to prepare and administer these luxuries, and it has been the perquisite of the men of gentle birth and breeding to consume them. Drunkenness and the other pathological consequences of the free use of stimulants therefore tend in their turn to become honorific, as being a mark, at the second remove, of the superior status of those who are able to afford the indulgence. Infirmities induced by over-indulgence are among some peoples freely recognised as manly attributes. It has even happened that the name for certain diseased conditions of the body arising from such an origin has passed into everyday speech as a synonym for "noble" or "gentle." It is only at a relatively early stage of culture that the symptoms of expensive vice are conventionally accepted as marks of a superior status, and so tend to become virtues and command the deference of the community; but the reputability that attaches to certain expensive vices long retains so much of its force as to appreciably lessen the disapprobation visited upon the men of the wealthy or noble class for any excessive indulgence. The same invidious distinction adds force to the current disapproval of any indulgence of this kind on the part of women, minors, and inferiors. This invidious traditional distinction has not lost its force even among the more advanced peoples of to-day. Where the example set by the leisure class retains its imperative force in the regulation of the conventionalities, it is observable that the women still in great measure practise the same traditional continence with regard to stimulants.

This characterisation of the greater continence in the use of stimulants practised by the women of the reputable classes may seem an excessive refinement of logic at the expense of common sense. But facts within easy reach of any one who cares to know them go to say that the greater abstinence of women is in some part due to an imperative conventionality; and this conventionality is, in a general way, strongest where the patriarchal tradition—the tradition that the woman is a chattel—has retained its hold in greatest vigour. In a sense which has been greatly qualified in scope and rigour, but which has by no means lost its meaning even yet; this tradition says that the woman, being a chattel, should consume only what is necessary to her sustenance,—except so far as her further consumption contributes to the comfort or the good repute of her master. The consumption of luxuries, in the true sense, is a consumption directed to the comfort of the consumer himself, and is, therefore, a mark of the master. Any such consumption by others can take place only on a basis of sufferance. In communities where the popular habits of thought have been profoundly shaped by the patriarchal tradition we may accordingly look for survivals of the tabu on luxuries at least to the extent of a conventional deprecation of their use by the unfree and dependent class. This is more particularly true as regards certain luxuries, the use of which by the dependent class would detract sensibly from the comfort or pleasure of their masters, or which are held to be of doubtful legitimacy on other grounds. In the apprehension of the great conservative middle class of Western civilisation the use of these various stimulants is obnoxious to at least one, if not both, of these objections; and it is a fact too significant to be passed over that it is precisely among these middle classes of the Germanic culture, with their strong surviving sense of the patriarchal proprieties, that the women are to the greatest extent subject to a qualified tabu on narcotics and alcoholic beverages. With many qualifications—with more qualifications as the patriarchal tradition has gradually weakened—the general rule is felt to be right and binding that women should consume only for the benefit of their masters. The objection of course presents itself that expenditure on women's dress and household paraphernalia is an obvious exception to this rule; but it will appear in the sequel that this exception is much more obvious than substantial.

During the earlier stages of economic development, consumption of goods without stint, especially consumption of the better grades of goods,—ideally all consumption in excess of the subsistence minimum,—pertains normally to the leisure class. This restriction tends to disappear, at least formally, after the later peaceable stage has been reached, with private ownership of goods and an industrial system based on wage labour or on the petty household economy. But during the earlier quasi-peaceable stage, when so many of the traditions through which the institution of a leisure class has affected the economic life of later times were taking form and consistency, this principle has had the force of a conventional law. It has served as the norm to which consumption has tended to conform, and any appreciable departure from it is to be regarded as an aberrant form, sure to be eliminated sooner or later in the further course of development.

The quasi-peaceable gentleman of leisure, then, not only consumes of the staff of life beyond the minimum required for subsistence and physical efficiency, but his consumption also undergoes a specialisation as regards the quality of the goods consumed. He consumes freely and of the best, in food, drink, narcotics, shelter, services, ornaments, apparel, weapons and accoutrements, amusements, amulets, and idols or divinities. In the process of gradual amelioration which takes place in the articles of his consumption, the motive principle and the proximate aim of innovation is no doubt the higher efficiency of the improved and more elaborate products for personal comfort and well-being. But that does not remain the sole purpose of their consumption. The canon of reputability is at hand and seizes upon such innovations as are, according to its standard, fit to survive. Since the consumption of these more excellent goods is an evidence of wealth, it becomes honorific; and conversely, the failure to consume in due quantity and quality becomes a mark of inferiority and demerit.

This growth of punctilious discrimination as to qualitative excellence in eating, drinking, etc., presently affects not only the manner of life, but also the training and intellectual activity of the gentleman of leisure. He is no longer simply the successful, aggressive male,—the man of strength, resource, and intrepidity. In order to avoid stultification he must also cultivate his tastes, for it now becomes incumbent on him to discriminate with some nicety between the noble and the ignoble in consumable goods. He becomes a connoisseur in creditable viands of various degrees of merit, in manly beverages and trinkets, in seemly apparel and architecture, in weapons, games, dancers, and the narcotics. This cultivation of the aesthetic faculty requires time and application, and the demands made upon the gentleman in this direction therefore tend to change his life of leisure into a more or less arduous application to the business of learning how to live a life of ostensible leisure in a becoming way. Closely related to the requirement that the gentleman must consume freely and of the right kind of goods, there is the requirement that he must know how to consume them in a seemly manner. His life of leisure must be conducted in due form. Hence arise good manners in the way pointed out in an earlier chapter. High-bred manners and ways of living are items of conformity to the norm of conspicuous leisure and conspicuous consumption.

Conspicuous consumption of valuable goods is a means of reputability to the gentleman of leisure. As wealth accumulates on his hands, his own unaided effort will not avail to sufficiently put his opulence in evidence by this method. The aid of friends and competitors is therefore brought in by resorting to the giving of valuable presents and expensive feasts and entertainments. Presents and feasts had probably another origin than that of naïve ostentation, but they acquired their utility for this purpose very early, and they have retained that character to the present; so that their utility in this respect has now long been the substantial ground on which these usages rest. Costly entertainments, such as the potlatch[1] or the ball, are peculiarly adapted to serve this end. The competitor with whom the entertainer wishes to institute a comparison is, by this method, made to serve as a means to the end. He consumes vicariously for his host at the same time that he is a witness to the consumption of that excess of good things which his host is unable to dispose of single-handed, and he is also made to witness his host's facility in etiquette.

In the giving of costly entertainments other motives, of a more genial kind, are of course also present. The custom of festive gatherings probably originated in motives of conviviality and religion; these motives are also present in the later development, but they do not continue to be the sole motives. The latter-day leisure-class festivities and entertainments may continue in some slight degree to serve the religious need and in a higher degree the needs of recreation and conviviality, but they also serve an invidious purpose; and they serve it none the less effectually for having a colourable non-invidious ground in these more avowable motives. But the economic effect of these social amenities is not therefore lessened, either in the vicarious consumption of goods or in the exhibition of difficult and costly achievements in etiquette.

As wealth accumulates, the leisure class develops further in function and structure, and there arises a differentiation within the class. There is a more or less elaborate system of rank and grades. This differentiation is furthered by the inheritance of wealth and the consequent inheritance of gentility. With the inheritance of gentility goes the inheritance of obligatory leisure; and gentility of a sufficient potency to entail a life of leisure may be inherited without the complement of wealth required to maintain a dignified leisure. Gentle blood may be transmitted without goods enough to afford a reputably free consumption at one's ease. Hence results a class of impecunious gentlemen of leisure, incidentally referred to already. These half-caste gentlemen of leisure fall into a system of hierarchical gradations. Those who stand near the higher and the highest grades of the wealthy leisure class, in point of birth, or in point of wealth, or both, outrank the remoter-born and the pecuniarily weaker. These lower grades, especially the impecunious, or marginal, gentlemen of leisure, affiliate themselves by a system of dependence or fealty to the great ones; by so doing they gain an increment of repute, or of the means with which to lead a life of leisure, from their patron. They become his courtiers or retainers, servants; and being fed and countenanced by their patron they are indices of his rank and vicarious consumers of his superfluous wealth. Many of these affiliated gentlemen of leisure are at the same time lesser men of substance in their own right; so that some of them are scarcely at all, others only partially, to be rated as vicarious consumers. So many of them, however, as make up the retainers and hangers-on of the patron may be classed as vicarious consumers without qualification. Many of these again, and also many of the other aristocracy of less degree, have in turn attached to their persons a more or less comprehensive group of vicarious consumers in the persons of their wives and children, their servants, retainers, etc.

Throughout this graduated scheme of vicarious leisure and vicarious consumption the rule holds that these offices must be performed in some such manner, or under some such circumstance or insignia, as shall point plainly to the master to whom this leisure or consumption pertains, and to whom therefore the resulting increment of good repute of right inures. The consumption and leisure executed by these persons for their master or patron represents an investment on his part with a view to an increase of good fame. As regards feasts and largesses this is obvious enough, and the imputation of repute to the host or patron here takes place immediately, on the ground of common notoriety. Where leisure and consumption is performed vicariously by henchmen and retainers, imputation of the resulting repute to the patron is effected by their residing near his person so that it may be plain to all men from what source they draw. As the group whose good esteem is to be secured in this way grows larger, more patent means are required to indicate the imputation of merit for the leisure performed, and to this end uniforms, badges, and liveries come into vogue. The wearing of uniforms or liveries implies a considerable degree of dependence, and may even be said to be a mark of servitude, real or ostensible. The wearers of uniforms and liveries may be roughly divided into two classes—the free and the servile, or the noble and the ignoble. The services performed by them are likewise divisible into noble and ignoble. Of course the distinction is not observed with strict consistency in practice; the less debasing of the base services and the less honorific of the noble functions are not infrequently merged in the same person. But the general distinction is not on that account to be overlooked. What may add some perplexity is the fact that this fundamental distinction between noble and ignoble, which rests on the nature of the ostensible service performed, is traversed by a secondary distinction into honorific and humiliating, resting on the rank of the person for whom the service is performed or whose livery is worn. So, those offices which are by right the proper employment of the leisure class are noble; such are government, fighting, hunting, the care of arms and accoutrements, and the like,—in short, those which may be classed as ostensibly predatory employments. On the other hand, those employments which properly fall to the industrious class are ignoble; such as handicraft or other productive labour, menial services, and the like. But a base service performed for a person of very high degree may become a very honorific office; as for instance the office of a Maid of Honour or of a Lady in Waiting to the Queen, or the King's Master of the Horse or his Keeper of the Hounds. The two offices last named suggest a principle of some general bearing. Whenever, as in these cases, the menial service in question has to do directly with the primary leisure employments of fighting and hunting, it easily acquires a reflected honorific character. In this way great honour may come to attach to an employment which in its own nature belongs to the baser sort.

In the later development of peaceable industry, the usage of employing an idle corps of uniformed men-at-arms gradually lapses. Vicarious consumption by dependents bearing the insignia of their patron or master narrows down to a corps of liveried menials. In a heightened degree, therefore, the livery comes to be a badge of servitude, or rather of servility. Something of a honorific character always attached to the livery of the armed retainer, but this honorific character disappears when the livery becomes the exclusive badge of the menial. The livery becomes obnoxious to nearly all who are required to wear it. We are yet so little removed from a state of effective slavery as still to be fully sensitive to the sting of any imputation of servility. This antipathy asserts itself even in the case of the liveries or uniforms which some corporations prescribe as the distinctive dress of their employees. In this country the aversion even goes the length of discrediting—in a mild and uncertain way—those government employments, military and civil, which require the wearing of a livery or uniform.

With the disappearance of servitude, the number of vicarious consumers attached to any one gentleman tends, on the whole, to decrease. The like is of course true, and perhaps in a still higher degree, of the number of dependents who perform vicarious leisure for him. In a general way, though not wholly nor consistently, these two groups coincide. The dependent who was first delegated for these duties was the wife, or the chief wife; and, as would be expected, in the later development of the institution, when the number of persons by whom these duties are customarily performed gradually narrows, the wife remains the last. In the higher grades of society a large volume of both these kinds of service is required; and here the wife is of course still assisted in the work by a more or less numerous corps of menials. But as we descend the social scale, the point is presently reached where the duties of vicarious leisure and consumption devolve upon the wife alone. In the communities of the Western culture, this point is at present found among the lower middle class.

And here occurs a curious inversion. It is a fact of common observation that in this lower middle class there is no pretence of leisure on the part of the head of the household. Through force of circumstances it has fallen into disuse. But the middle-class wife still carries on the business of vicarious leisure, for the good name of the household and its master. In descending the social scale in any modern industrial community, the primary fact—the conspicuous leisure of the master of the household—disappears at a relatively high point. The head of the middle-class household has been reduced by economic circumstances to turn his hand to gaining a livelihood by occupations which often partake largely of the character of industry, as in the case of the ordinary business man of today. But the derivative fact—the vicarious leisure and consumption rendered by the wife, and the auxiliary vicarious performance of leisure by menials—remains in vogue as a conventionality which the demands of reputability will not suffer to be slighted. It is by no means an uncommon spectacle to find a man applying himself to work with the utmost assiduity, in order that his wife may in due form render for him that degree of vicarious leisure which the common sense of the time demands.

The leisure rendered by the wife in such cases is, of course, not a simple manifestation of idleness or indolence. It almost invariably occurs disguised under some form of work or household duties or social amenities, which prove on analysis to serve little or no ulterior end beyond showing that she does not and need not occupy herself with anything that is gainful or that is of substantial use. As has already been noticed under the head of manners, the greater part of the customary round of domestic cares to which the middle-class housewife gives her time and effort is of this character. Not that the results of her attention to household matters, of a decorative and mundificatory character, are not pleasing to the sense of men trained in middle-class proprieties; but the taste to which these effects of household adornment and tidiness appeal is a taste which has been formed under the selective guidance of a canon of propriety that demands just these evidences of wasted effort. The effects are pleasing to us chiefly because we have been taught to find them pleasing. There goes into these domestic duties much solicitude for a proper combination of form and colour, and for other ends that are to be classed as æsthetic in the proper sense of the term; and it is not denied that effects having some substantial æsthetic value are sometimes attained. Pretty much all that is here insisted on is that, as regards these amenities of life, the housewife's efforts are under the guidance of traditions that have been shaped by the law of conspicuously wasteful expenditure of time and substance. If beauty or comfort is achieved,—and it is a more or less fortuitous circumstance if they are,—they must be achieved by means and methods that commend themselves to the great economic law of wasted effort. The more reputable, "presentable" portion of middle-class household paraphernalia are, on the one hand, items of conspicuous consumption, and on the other hand, apparatus for putting in evidence the vicarious leisure rendered by the housewife.

The requirement of vicarious consumption at the hands of the wife continues in force even at a lower point in the pecuniary scale than the requirement of vicarious leisure. At a point below which little if any pretence of wasted effort, in ceremonial cleanness and the like, is observable, and where there is assuredly no conscious attempt at ostensible leisure, decency still requires the wife to consume some goods conspicuously for the reputability of the household and its head. So that, as the latter-day outcome of this evolution of an archaic institution, the wife, who was at the outset the drudge and chattel of the man, both in fact and in theory,—the producer of goods for him to consume,—has become the ceremonial consumer of goods which he produces. But she still quite unmistakably remains his chattel in theory; for the habitual rendering of vicarious leisure and consumption is the abiding mark of the unfree servant.

This vicarious consumption practised by the household of the middle and lower classes can not be counted as a direct expression of the leisure-class scheme of life, since the household of this pecuniary grade does not belong within the leisure class. It is rather that the leisure-class scheme of life here comes to an expression at the second remove. The leisure class stands at the head of the social structure in point of reputability; and its manner of life and its standards of worth therefore afford the norm of reputability for the community. The observance of these standards, in some degree of approximation, becomes incumbent upon all classes lower in the scale. In modern civilised communities the lines of demarcation between social classes have grown vague and transient, and wherever this happens the norm of reputability imposed by the upper class extends its coercive influence with but slight hindrance down through the social structure to the lowest strata. The result is that the members of each stratum accept as their ideal of decency the scheme of life in vogue in the next higher stratum, and bend their energies to live up to that ideal. On pain of forfeiting their good name and their self-respect in case of failure, they must conform to the accepted code, at least in appearance.

The basis on which good repute in any highly organised industrial community ultimately rests is pecuniary strength; and the means of showing pecuniary strength, and so of gaining or retaining a good name, are leisure and a conspicuous consumption of goods. Accordingly, both of these methods are in vogue as far down the scale as it remains possible; and in the lower strata in which the two methods are employed, both offices are in great part delegated to the wife and children of the household. Lower still, where any degree of leisure, even ostensible, has become impracticable for the wife, the conspicuous consumption of goods remains and is carried on by the wife and children. The man of the household also can do something in this direction, and, indeed, he commonly does; but with a still lower descent into the levels of indigence—along the margin of the slums—the man, and presently also the children, virtually cease to consume valuable goods for appearances, and the woman remains virtually the sole exponent of the household's pecuniary decency. No class of society, not even the most abjectly poor, forgoes all customary conspicuous consumption. The last items of this category of consumption are not given up except under stress of the direst necessity. Very much of squalor and discomfort will be endured before the last trinket or the last pretence of pecuniary decency is put away. There is no class and no country that has yielded so abjectly before the pressure of physical want as to deny themselves all gratification of this higher or spiritual need.

—

From the foregoing survey of the growth of conspicuous leisure and consumption, it appears that the utility of both alike for the purposes of reputability lies in the element of waste that is common to both. In the one case it is a waste of time and effort, in the other it is a waste of goods. Both are methods of demonstrating the possession of wealth, and the two are conventionally accepted as equivalents. The choice between them is a question of advertising expediency simply, except so far as it may be affected by other standards of propriety, springing from a different source. On grounds of expediency the preference may be given to the one or the other at different stages of the economic development. The question is, which of the two methods will most effectively reach the persons whose convictions it is desired to affect. Usage has answered this question in different ways under different circumstances.

So long as the community or social group is small enough and compact enough to be effectually reached by common notoriety alone,—that is to say, so long as the human environment to which the individual is required to adapt himself in respect of reputability is comprised within his sphere of personal acquaintance and neighbourhood gossip,—so long the one method is about as effective as the other. Each will therefore serve about equally well during the earlier stages of social growth. But when the differentiation has gone farther and it becomes necessary to reach a wider human environment, consumption begins to hold over leisure as an ordinary means of decency. This is especially true during the later, peaceable economic stage. The means of communication and the mobility of the population now expose the individual to the observation of many persons who have no other means of judging of his reputability than the display of goods (and perhaps of breeding) which he is able to make while he is under their direct observation.

The modern organisation of industry works in the same direction also by another line. The exigencies of the modern industrial system frequently place individuals and households in juxtaposition between whom there is little contact in any other sense than that of juxtaposition. One's neighbours, mechanically speaking, often are socially not one's neighbours, or even acquaintances; and still their transient good opinion has a high degree of utility. The only practicable means of impressing one's pecuniary ability on these unsympathetic observers of one's everyday life is an unremitting demonstration of ability to pay. In the modern community there is also a more frequent attendance at large gatherings of people to whom one's everyday life is unknown; in such places as churches, theatres, ballrooms, hotels, parks, shops, and the like. In order to impress these transient observers, and to retain one's self-complacency under their observation, the signature of one's pecuniary strength should be written in characters which he who runs may read. It is evident, therefore, that the present trend of the development is in the direction of heightening the utility of conspicuous consumption as compared with leisure.

It is also noticeable that the serviceability of consumption as a means of repute, as well as the insistence on it as an element of decency, is at its best in those portions of the community where the human contact of the individual is widest and the mobility of the population is greatest. Conspicuous consumption claims a relatively larger portion of the income of the urban than of the rural population, and the claim is also more imperative. The result is that, in order to keep up a decent appearance, the former habitually live hand-to-mouth to a greater extent than the latter. So it comes, for instance, that the American farmer and his wife and daughters are notoriously less modish in their dress, as well as less urbane in their manners, than the city artisan's family with an equal income. It is not that the city population is by nature much more eager for the peculiar complacency that comes of a conspicuous consumption, nor has the rural population less regard for pecuniary decency. But the provocation to this line of evidence, as well as its transient effectiveness, are more decided in the city. This method is therefore more readily resorted to, and in the struggle to outdo one another the city population push their normal standard of conspicuous consumption to a higher point, with the result that a relatively greater expenditure in this direction is required to indicate a given degree of pecuniary decency in the city. The requirement of conformity to this higher conventional standard becomes mandatory. The standard of decency is higher, class for class, and this requirement of decent appearance must be lived up to on pain of losing caste.

Consumption becomes a larger element in the standard of living in the city than in the country. Among the country population its place is to some extent taken by savings and home comforts known through the medium of neighbourhood gossip sufficiently to serve the like general purpose of pecuniary repute. These home comforts and the leisure indulged in—where the indulgence is found—are of course also in great part to be classed as items of conspicuous consumption; and much the same is to be said of the savings. The smaller amount of the savings laid by by the artisan class is no doubt due, in some measure, to the fact that in the case of the artisan the savings are a less effective means of advertisement, relative to the environment in which he is placed, than are the savings of the people living on farms and in the small villages. Among the latter, everybody's affairs, especially everybody's pecuniary status, are known to everybody else. Considered by itself simply—taken in the first degree—this added provocation to which the artisan and the urban labouring classes are exposed may not very seriously decrease the amount of savings; but in its cumulative action, through raising the standard of decent expenditure, its deterrent effect on the tendency to save cannot but be very great.

A felicitous illustration of the manner in which this canon of reputability works out its results is seen in the practice of dram-drinking, "treating," and smoking in public places, which is customary among the labourers and handicraftsmen of the towns, and among the lower middle class of the urban population generally. Journeymen printers may be named as a class among whom this form of conspicuous consumption has a great vogue, and among whom it carries with it certain well-marked consequences that are often deprecated. The peculiar habits of the class in this respect are commonly set down to some kind of an ill-defined moral deficiency with which this class is credited, or to a morally deleterious influence which their occupation is supposed to exert, in some unascertainable way, upon the men employed in it. The state of the case for the men who work in the composition and press rooms of the common run of printing-houses may be summed up as follows. Skill acquired in any printing-house or any city is easily turned to account in almost any other house or city; that is to say, the inertia due to special training is slight. Also, this occupation requires more than the average of intelligence and general information, and the men employed in it are therefore ordinarily more ready than many others to take advantage of any slight variation in the demand for their labour from one place to another. The inertia due to the home feeling is consequently also slight. At the same time the wages in the trade are high enough to make movement from place to place relatively easy. The result is a great mobility of the labour employed in printing; perhaps greater than in any other equally well-defined and considerable body of workmen. These men are constantly thrown in contact with new groups of acquaintances, with whom the relations established are transient or ephemeral, but whose good opinion is valued none the less for the time being. The human proclivity to ostentation, reënforced by sentiments of good-fellowship, leads them to spend freely in those directions which will best serve these needs. Here as elsewhere prescription seizes upon the custom as soon as it gains a vogue, and incorporates it in the accredited standard of decency. The next step is to make this standard of decency the point of departure for a new move in advance in the same direction,—for there is no merit in simple spiritless conformity to a standard of dissipation that is lived up to as a matter of course by every one in the trade.

The greater prevalence of dissipation among printers than among the average of workmen is accordingly attributable, at least in some measure, to the greater ease of movement and the more transient character of acquaintance and human contact in this trade. But the substantial ground of this high requirement in dissipation is in the last analysis no other than that same propensity for a manifestation of dominance and pecuniary decency which makes the French peasant-proprietor parsimonious and frugal, and induces the American millionaire to found colleges, hospitals and museums. If the canon of conspicuous consumption were not offset to a considerable extent by other features of human nature, alien to it, any saving should logically be impossible for a population situated as the artisan and labouring classes of the cities are at present, however high their wages or their income might be.

But there are other standards of repute and other, more or less imperative, canons of conduct, besides wealth and its manifestation, and some of these come in to accentuate or to qualify the broad, fundamental canon of conspicuous waste. Under the simple test of effectiveness for advertising, we should expect to find leisure and the conspicuous consumption of goods dividing the field of pecuniary emulation pretty evenly between them at the outset. Leisure might then be expected gradually to yield ground and tend to obsolescence as the economic development goes forward, and the community increases in size; while the conspicuous consumption of goods should gradually gain in importance, both absolutely and relatively, until it had absorbed all the available product, leaving nothing over beyond a bare livelihood. But the actual course of development has been somewhat different from this ideal scheme. Leisure held the first place at the start, and came to hold a rank very much above wasteful consumption of goods, both as a direct exponent of wealth and as an element in the standard of decency, during the quasi-peaceable culture. From that point onward, consumption has gained ground, until, at present, it unquestionably holds the primacy, though it is still far from absorbing the entire margin of production above the subsistence minimum.

The early ascendency of leisure as a means of reputability is traceable to the archaic distinction between noble and ignoble employments. Leisure is honourable and becomes imperative partly because it shows exemption from ignoble labour. The archaic differentiation into noble and ignoble classes is based on an invidious distinction between employments as honorific or debasing; and this traditional distinction grows into an imperative canon of decency during the early quasi-peaceable stage. Its ascendency is furthered by the fact that leisure is still fully as effective an evidence of wealth as consumption. Indeed, so effective is it in the relatively small and stable human environment to which the individual is exposed at that cultural stage, that, with the aid of the archaic tradition which deprecates all productive labour, it gives rise to a large impecunious leisure class, and it even tends to limit the production of the community's industry to the subsistence minimum. This extreme inhibition of industry is avoided because slave labour, working under a compulsion more rigorous than that of reputability, is forced to turn out a product in excess of the subsistence minimum of the working class. The subsequent relative decline in the use of conspicuous leisure as a basis of repute is due partly to an increasing relative effectiveness of consumption as an evidence of wealth; but in part it is traceable to another force, alien, and in some degree antagonistic, to the usage of conspicuous waste.

This alien factor is the instinct of workmanship. Other circumstances permitting, that instinct disposes men to look with favour upon productive efficiency and on whatever is of human use. It disposes them to deprecate waste of substance or effort. The instinct of workmanship is present in all men, and asserts itself even under very adverse circumstances. So that however wasteful a given expenditure may be in reality, it must at least have some colourable excuse in the way of an ostensible purpose. The manner in which, under special circumstances, the instinct eventuates in a taste for exploit and an invidious discrimination between noble and ignoble classes has been indicated in an earlier chapter. In so far as it comes into conflict with the law of conspicuous waste, the instinct of workmanship expresses itself not so much in insistence on substantial usefulness as in an abiding sense of the odiousness and æsthetic impossibility of what is obviously futile. Being of the nature of an instinctive affection, its guidance touches chiefly and immediately the obvious and apparent violations of its requirements. It is only less promptly and with less constraining force that it reaches such substantial violations of its requirements as are appreciated only upon reflection.

So long as all labour continues to be performed exclusively or usually by slaves, the baseness of all productive effort is too constantly and deterrently present in the mind of men to allow the instinct of workmanship seriously to take effect in the direction of industrial usefulness; but when the quasi-peaceable stage (with slavery and status) passes into the peaceable stage of industry (with wage labour and cash payment), the instinct comes more effectively into play. It then begins aggressively to shape men's views of what is meritorious, and asserts itself at least as an auxiliary canon of self-complacency. All extraneous considerations apart, those persons (adults) are but a vanishing minority to-day who harbour no inclination to the accomplishment of some end, or who are not impelled of their own motion to shape some object or fact or relation for human use. The propensity may in large measure be overborne by the more immediately constraining incentive to a reputable leisure and an avoidance of indecorous usefulness, and it may therefore work itself out in make-believe only; as for instance in "social duties," and in quasi-artistic or quasi-scholarly accomplishments, in the care and decoration of the house, in sewing-circle activity or dress reform, in proficiency at dress, cards, yachting, golf, and various sports. But the fact that it may under stress of circumstances eventuate in inanities no more disproves the presence of the instinct than the reality of the brooding instinct is disproved by inducing a hen to sit on a nestful of china eggs.

This latter-day uneasy reaching-out for some form of purposeful activity that shall at the same time not be indecorously productive of either individual or collective gain marks a difference of attitude between the modern leisure class and that of the quasi-peaceable stage. At the earlier stage, as was said above, the all-dominating institution of slavery and status acted resistlessly to discountenance exertion directed to other than naïvely predatory ends. It was still possible to find some habitual employment for the inclination to action in the way of forcible aggression or repression directed against hostile groups or against the subject classes within the group; and this served to relieve the pressure and draw off the energy of the leisure class without a resort to actually useful, or even ostensibly useful employments. The practice of hunting also served the same purpose in some degree. When the community developed into a peaceful industrial organisation, and when fuller occupation of the land had reduced the opportunities for the hunt to an inconsiderable residue, the pressure of energy seeking purposeful employment was left to find an outlet in some other direction. The ignominy which attaches to useful effort also entered upon a less acute phase with the disappearance of compulsory labour; and the instinct of workmanship then came to assert itself with more persistence and consistency.

The line of least resistance has changed in some measure, and the energy which formerly found a vent in predatory activity, now in part takes the direction of some ostensibly useful end. Ostensibly purposeless leisure has come to be deprecated, especially among that large portion of the leisure class whose plebeian origin acts to set them at variance with the tradition of the *otium cum dignitate.*[2] But that canon of reputability which discountenances all employment that is of the nature of productive effort is still at hand, and will permit nothing beyond the most transient vogue to any employment that is substantially useful or productive. The consequence is that a change has been wrought in the conspicuous leisure practised by the leisure class; not so much in substance as in form. A reconciliation between the two conflicting requirements is effected by a resort to make-believe. Many and intricate polite observances and social duties of a ceremonial nature are developed; many organisations are founded, with some specious object of amelioration embodied in their official style and title; there is much coming and going, and a deal of talk, to the end that the talkers may not have occasion to reflect on what is the effectual economic value of their traffic. And along with the make-believe of purposeful employment, and woven inextricably into its texture, there is commonly, if not invariably, a more or less appreciable element of purposeful effort directed to some serious end.

In the narrower sphere of vicarious leisure a similar change has gone forward. Instead of simply passing her time in visible idleness, as in the best days of the patriarchal régime, the housewife of the advanced peaceable stage applies herself assiduously to household cares. The salient features of this development of domestic service have already been indicated.

Throughout the entire evolution of conspicuous expenditure, whether of goods or of services or human life, runs the obvious implication that in order to effectually mend the consumer's good fame it must be an expenditure of superfluities. In order to be reputable it must be wasteful. No merit would accrue from the consumption of the bare necessaries of life, except by comparison with the abjectly poor who fall short even of the subsistence minimum; and no standard of expenditure could result from such a comparison, except the most prosaic and unattractive level of decency. A standard of life would still be possible which should admit of invidious comparison in other respects than that of opulence; as, for instance, a comparison in various directions in the manifestation of moral, physical, intellectual, or æsthetic force. Comparison in all these directions is in vogue to-day; and the comparison made in these respects is commonly so inextricably bound up with the pecuniary comparison as to be scarcely distinguishable from the latter. This is especially true as regards the current rating of expressions of intellectual and æsthetic force or proficiency; so that we frequently interpret as æsthetic or intellectual a difference which in substance is pecuniary only.

———

The use of the term "waste" is in one respect an unfortunate one. As used in the speech of everyday life the word carries an undertone of deprecation. It is here used for want of a better term that will adequately describe the same range of motives and of phenomena, and it is not to be taken in an odious sense, as implying an illegitimate expenditure of human products or of human life. In the view of economic theory the expenditure in question is no more and no less legitimate than any other expenditure. It is here called "waste" because this expenditure does not serve human life or human well-being on the whole, not because it is waste or misdirection of effort or expenditure as viewed from the standpoint of the individual consumer who chooses it. If he chooses it, that disposes of the question of its relative utility to him, as compared with other forms of consumption that would not be deprecated on account of their wastefulness. Whatever form of expenditure the consumer chooses, or whatever end he seeks in making his choice, has utility to him by virtue of his preference. As seen from the point of view of the individual consumer, the question of wastefulness does not arise within the scope of economic theory proper. The use of the word "waste" as a technical term, therefore, implies no deprecation of the motives or of the ends sought by the consumer under this canon of conspicuous waste.

But it is, on other grounds, worth noting that the term "waste" in the language of everyday life implies deprecation of what is characterised as wasteful. This common-sense implication is itself an

outcropping of the instinct of workmanship. The popular reprobation of waste goes to say that in order to be at peace with himself
the common man must be able to see in any and all human effort
and human enjoyment an enhancement of life and well-being on
the whole. In order to meet with unqualified approval, any economic fact must approve itself under the test of impersonal usefulness—usefulness as seen from the point of view of the generically
human. Relative or competitive advantage of one individual in
comparison with another does not satisfy the economic conscience,
and therefore competitive expenditure has not the approval of this
conscience.

In strict accuracy nothing should be included under the head of
conspicuous waste but such expenditure as is incurred on the
ground of an invidious pecuniary comparison. But in order to bring
any given item or element in under this head it is not necessary that
it should be recognised as waste in this sense by the person incur-
ring the expenditure. It frequently happens that an element of the
standard of living which set out with being primarily wasteful, ends
with becoming, in the apprehension of the consumer, a necessary
of life; and it may in this way become as indispensable as any other
item of the consumer's habitual expenditure. As items which sometimes fall under this head, and are therefore available as illustrations of the manner in which this principle applies, may be cited
carpets and tapestries, silver table service, waiter's services, silk
hats, starched linen, many articles of jewellery and of dress. The
indispensability of these things after the habit and the convention
have been formed, however, has little to say in the classification of
expenditures as waste or not waste in the technical meaning of the
word. The test to which all expenditure must be brought in an attempt to decide that point is the question whether it serves directly
to enhance human life on the whole—whether it furthers the life
process taken impersonally. For this is the basis of award of the instinct of workmanship, and that instinct is the court of final appeal
in any question of economic truth or adequacy. It is a question as to
the award rendered by a dispassionate common sense. The question is, therefore, not whether, under the existing circumstances of

individual habit and social custom, a given expenditure conduces to the particular consumer's gratification or peace of mind; but whether, aside from acquired tastes and from the canons of usage and conventional decency, its result is a net gain in comfort or in the fulness of life. Customary expenditure must be classed under the head of waste in so far as the custom on which it rests is traceable to the habit of making an invidious pecuniary comparison—in so far as it is conceived that it could not have become customary and prescriptive without the backing of this principle of pecuniary reputability or relative economic success.

It is obviously not necessary that a given object of expenditure should be exclusively wasteful in order to come in under the category of conspicuous waste. An article may be useful and wasteful both, and its utility to the consumer may be made up of use and waste in the most varying proportions. Consumable goods, and even productive goods, generally show the two elements in combination, as constituents of their utility; although, in a general way, the element of waste tends to predominate in articles of consumption, while the contrary is true of articles designed for productive use. Even in articles which appear at first glance to serve for pure ostentation only, it is always possible to detect the presence of some, at least ostensible, useful purpose; and on the other hand, even in special machinery and tools contrived for some particular industrial process, as well as in the rudest appliances of human industry, the traces of conspicuous waste, or at least of the habit of ostentation, usually become evident on a close scrutiny. It would be hazardous to assert that a useful purpose is ever absent from the utility of any article or of any service, however obviously its prime purpose and chief element is conspicuous waste; and it would be only less hazardous to assert of any primarily useful product that the element of waste is in no way concerned in its value, immediately or remotely.

CHAPTER V

THE PECUNIARY STANDARD
OF LIVING

For the great body of the people in any modern community, the proximate ground of expenditure in excess of what is required for physical comfort is not a conscious effort to excel in the expensiveness of their visible consumption, so much as it is a desire to live up to the conventional standard of decency in the amount and grade of goods consumed. This desire is not guided by a rigidly invariable standard, which must be lived up to, and beyond which there is no incentive to go. The standard is flexible; and especially it is indefinitely extensible, if only time is allowed for habituation to any increase in pecuniary ability and for acquiring facility in the new and larger scale of expenditure that follows such an increase. It is much more difficult to recede from a scale of expenditure once adopted than it is to extend the accustomed scale in response to an accession of wealth. Many items of customary expenditure prove on analysis to be almost purely wasteful, and they are therefore honorific only, but after they have once been incorporated into the scale of decent consumption, and so have become an integral part of one's scheme of life, it is quite as hard to give up these as it is to give up many items that conduce directly to one's physical comfort, or even that may be necessary to life and health. That is to say, the conspicuously wasteful honorific expenditure that confers spiritual well-being may become more indispensable than much of that expenditure which ministers to the "lower" wants of physical well-being or sustenance only. It is notoriously just as difficult to recede from a "high" standard of living as it is to lower a standard which is already relatively low; although in the former case the difficulty is a moral one, while in the latter it may involve a material deduction from the physical comforts of life.

But while retrogression is difficult, a fresh advance in conspicuous expenditure is relatively easy; indeed, it takes place almost as a matter of course. In the rare cases where it occurs, a failure to increase one's visible consumption when the means for an increase are at hand is felt in popular apprehension to call for explanation, and unworthy motives of miserliness are imputed to those who fall short in this respect. A prompt response to the stimulus, on the other hand, is accepted as the normal effect. This suggests that the standard of expenditure which commonly guides our efforts is not the average, ordinary expenditure already achieved; it is an ideal of consumption that lies just beyond our reach, or to reach which requires some strain. The motive is emulation—the stimulus of an invidious comparison which prompts us to outdo those with whom we are in the habit of classing ourselves. Substantially the same proposition is expressed in the commonplace remark that each class envies and emulates the class next above it in the social scale, while it rarely compares itself with those below or with those who are considerably in advance. That is to say, in other words, our standard of decency in expenditure, as in other ends of emulation, is set by the usage of those next above us in reputability; until, in this way, especially in any community where class distinctions are somewhat vague, all canons of reputability and decency, and all standards of consumption, are traced back by insensible gradations to the usages and habits of thought of the highest social and pecuniary class—the wealthy leisure class.

It is for this class to determine, in general outline, what scheme of life the community shall accept as decent or honorific; and it is their office by precept and example to set forth this scheme of social salvation in its highest, ideal form. But the higher leisure class can exercise this quasi-sacerdotal office only under certain material limitations. The class cannot at discretion effect a sudden revolution or reversal of the popular habits of thought with respect to any of these ceremonial requirements. It takes time for any change to permeate the mass and change the habitual attitude of the people; and especially it takes time to change the habits of those classes that are socially more remote from the radiant body. The process is slower where the mobility of the population is less or where the intervals between the several classes are wider and more abrupt. But if time be allowed, the scope of the discretion of the leisure class as regards questions of form and detail in the community's scheme of life is large; while as regards the substantial principles of reputability, the changes which it can effect lie within a narrow margin of tolerance. Its example and precept carries the force of prescription for all classes below it; but in working out the precepts which are handed down as governing the form and method of reputability—in shaping the usages and the spiritual attitude of the lower classes—this authoritative prescription constantly works under the selective guidance of the canon of conspicuous waste, tempered in varying degree by the instinct of workmanship. To these norms is to be added another broad principle of human nature—the predatory animus—which in point of generality and of psychological content lies between the two just named. The effect of the latter in shaping the accepted scheme of life is yet to be discussed.

The canon of reputability, then, must adapt itself to the economic circumstances, the traditions, and the degree of spiritual maturity of the particular class whose scheme of life it is to regulate. It is especially to be noted that however high its authority and however true to the fundamental requirements of reputability it may have been at its inception, a specific formal observance can under no circumstances maintain itself in force if with the lapse of time or on its transmission to a lower pecuniary class it is found to run counter to the ultimate ground of decency among civilised peoples, namely, serviceability for the purpose of an invidious comparison in pecuniary success.

It is evident that these canons of expenditure have much to say in determining the standard of living for any community and for any class. It is no less evident that the standard of living which prevails at any time or at any given social altitude will in its turn have much to say as to the forms which honorific expenditure will take, and as to the degree to which this "higher" need will dominate a people's consumption. In this respect the control exerted by the accepted standard of living is chiefly of a negative character; it acts almost solely to prevent recession from a scale of conspicuous expenditure that has once become habitual.

A standard of living is of the nature of habit. It is an habitual scale and method of responding to given stimuli. The difficulty in the way of receding from an accustomed standard is the difficulty of breaking a habit that has once been formed. The relative facility with which an advance in the standard is made means that the life process is a process of unfolding activity and that it will readily unfold in a new direction whenever and wherever the resistance to self-expression decreases. But when the habit of expression along such a given line of low resistance has once been formed, the discharge will seek the accustomed outlet even after a change has taken place in the environment whereby the external resistance has appreciably risen. That heightened facility of expression in a given direction which is called habit may offset a considerable increase in the resistance offered by external circumstances to the unfolding of life in the given direction. As between the various habits, or habitual modes and directions of expression, which go to make up an individual's standard of living, there is an appreciable difference in point of persistence under counteracting circumstances and in point of the degree of imperativeness with which the discharge seeks a given direction.

That is to say, in the language of current economic theory, while men are reluctant to retrench their expenditures in any direction, they are more reluctant to retrench in some directions than in others; so that while any accustomed consumption is reluctantly given up, there are certain lines of consumption which are given up with relatively extreme reluctance. The articles or forms of consumption to which the consumer clings with the greatest tenacity are commonly the so-called necessaries of life, or the subsistence minimum. The subsistence minimum is of course not a rigidly determined allowance of goods, definite and invariable in kind and quantity; but for the purpose in hand it may be taken to comprise a certain, more or less definite, aggregate of consumption required for the maintenance of life. This minimum, it may be assumed, is ordinarily given up last in case of a progressive retrenchment of expenditure. That is to say, in a general way, the most ancient and ingrained of the habits which govern the individual's life—those habits that touch his existence as an organism—are the most persistent and imperative. Beyond these come the higher wants—later-formed habits of the individual or the race—in a somewhat irregular and by no means invariable gradation. Some of these higher wants, as for instance the habitual use of certain stimulants, or the need of salvation (in the eschatological sense), or of good repute, may in some cases take precedence of the lower or more elementary wants. In general, the longer the habituation, the more unbroken the habit, and the more nearly it coincides with previous habitual forms of the life process, the more persistently will the given habit assert itself. The habit will be stronger if the particular traits of human nature which its action involves, or the particular aptitudes that find exercise in it, are traits or aptitudes that are already largely and profoundly concerned in the life process or that are intimately bound up with the life history of the particular racial stock.

The varying degrees of ease with which different habits are formed by different persons, as well as the varying degrees of reluctance with which different habits are given up, goes to say that the formation of specific habits is not a matter of length of habituation simply. Inherited aptitudes and traits of temperament count for quite as much as length of habituation in deciding what range of habits will come to dominate any individual's scheme of life. And the prevalent type of transmitted aptitudes, or in other words the type of temperament belonging to the dominant ethnic element in any community, will go far to decide what will be the scope and form of expression of the community's habitual life process. How greatly the transmitted idiosyncrasies of aptitude may count in the way of a rapid and definitive formation of habit in individuals is illustrated by the extreme facility with which an all-dominating habit of alcoholism is sometimes formed; or in the similar facility and the similarly inevitable formation of a habit of devout observances in the case of persons gifted with a special aptitude in that direction. Much the same meaning attaches to that peculiar facility of habituation to a specific human environment that is called romantic love.

Men differ in respect of transmitted aptitudes, or in respect of the relative facility with which they unfold their life activity in particular directions; and the habits which coincide with or proceed upon a relatively strong specific aptitude or a relatively great specific facility of expression become of great consequence to the man's well-being. The part played by this element of aptitude in determining the relative tenacity of the several habits which constitute the standard of living goes to explain the extreme reluctance with which men give up any habitual expenditure in the way of conspicuous consumption. The aptitudes or propensities to which a habit of this kind is to be referred as its ground are those aptitudes whose exercise is comprised in emulation; and the propensity for emulation—for invidious comparison—is of ancient growth and is a pervading trait of human nature. It is easily called into vigorous activity in any new form, and it asserts itself with great insistence under any form under which it has once found habitual expression. When the individual has once formed the habit of seeking expression in a given line of honorific expenditure,—when a given set of stimuli have come to be habitually responded to in activity of a given kind and direction under the guidance of these alert and deep-reaching propensities of emulation,—it is with extreme reluctance that such an habitual expenditure is given up. And on the other hand, whenever an accession of pecuniary strength puts the individual in a position to unfold his life process in larger scope and with additional reach, the ancient propensities of the race will assert themselves in determining the direction which the new unfolding of life is to take. And those propensities which are already actively in the field under some related form of expression, which are aided by the pointed suggestions afforded by a current accredited scheme of life, and for the exercise of which the material means and opportunities are readily available,—these will especially have much to say in shaping the form and direction in which the new accession to the individual's aggregate force will assert itself. That is to say, in concrete terms, in any community where conspicuous consumption is an element of the scheme of life, an increase in an individual's ability to pay is likely to take the form of an expenditure for some accredited line of conspicuous consumption.

With the exception of the instinct of self-preservation, the propensity for emulation is probably the strongest and most alert and persistent of the economic motives proper. In an industrial community this propensity for emulation expresses itself in pecuniary emulation; and this, so far as regards the Western civilised communities of the present, is virtually equivalent to saying that it expresses itself in some form of conspicuous waste. The need of conspicuous waste, therefore, stands ready to absorb any increase in the community's industrial efficiency or output of goods, after the most elementary physical wants have been provided for. Where this result does not follow, under modern conditions, the reason for the discrepancy is commonly to be sought in a rate of increase in the individual's wealth too rapid for the habit of expenditure to keep abreast of it; or it may be that the individual in question defers the conspicuous consumption of the increment to a later date—ordinarily with a view to heightening the spectacular effect of the aggregate expenditure contemplated. As increased industrial efficiency makes it possible to procure the means of livelihood with less labour, the energies of the industrious members of the community are bent to the compassing of a higher result in conspicuous expenditure, rather than slackened to a more comfortable pace. The strain is not lightened as industrial efficiency increases and makes a lighter strain possible, but the increment of output is turned to use to meet this want, which is indefinitely expansible, after the manner commonly imputed in economic theory to higher or spiritual wants. It is owing chiefly to the presence of this element in the standard of living that J. S. Mill was able to say that "hitherto it is questionable if all the mechanical inventions yet made have lightened the day's toil of any human being."[1]

The accepted standard of expenditure in the community or in the class to which a person belongs largely determines what his standard of living will be. It does this directly by commending itself to his common sense as right and good, through his habitually contemplating it and assimilating the scheme of life in which it belongs; but it does so also indirectly through popular insistence on conformity to the accepted scale of expenditure as a matter of propriety, under pain of disesteem and ostracism. To accept and practise the standard of living which is in vogue is both agreeable and expedient, commonly to the point of being indispensable to personal comfort and to success in life. The standard of living of any class, so far as concerns the element of conspicuous waste, is commonly as high as the earning capacity of the class will permit—with a constant tendency to go higher. The effect upon the serious activities of men is therefore to direct them with great singleness of purpose to the largest possible acquisition of wealth, and to discountenance work that brings no pecuniary gain. At the same time the effect on consumption is to concentrate it upon the lines which are most patent to the observers whose good opinion is sought; while the inclinations and aptitudes whose exercise does not involve a honorific expenditure of time or substance tend to fall into abeyance through disuse.

Through this discrimination in favour of visible consumption it has come about that the domestic life of most classes is relatively shabby, as compared with the éclat of that overt portion of their life that is carried on before the eyes of observers. As a secondary consequence of the same discrimination, people habitually screen their private life from observation. So far as concerns that portion of their consumption that may without blame be carried on in secret, they withdraw from all contact with their neighbours. Hence the exclusiveness of people, as regards their domestic life, in most of the industrially developed communities; and hence, by remoter derivation, the habit of privacy and reserve that is so large a feature in the code of proprieties of the better classes in all communities. The low birthrate of the classes upon whom the requirements of reputable expenditure fall with great urgency is likewise traceable to the exigencies of a standard of living based on conspicuous waste. The conspicuous consumption, and the consequent increased expense, required in the reputable maintenance of a child is very considerable and acts as a powerful deterrent. It is probably the most effectual of the Malthusian[2] prudential checks.

The effect of this factor of the standard of living, both in the way of retrenchment in the obscurer elements of consumption that go to physical comfort and maintenance, and also in the paucity or absence of children, is perhaps seen at its best among the classes given to scholarly pursuits. Because of a presumed superiority and scarcity of the gifts and attainments that characterise their life, these classes are by convention subsumed under a higher social grade than their pecuniary grade should warrant. The scale of decent expenditure in their case is pitched correspondingly high, and it consequently leaves an exceptionally narrow margin disposable for the other ends of life. By force of circumstances, their own habitual sense of what is good and right in these matters, as well as the expectations of the community in the way of pecuniary decency among the learned, are excessively high—as measured by the prevalent degree of opulence and earning capacity of the class, relatively to the non-scholarly classes whose social equals they nominally are. In any modern community where there is no priestly monopoly of these occupations, the people of scholarly pursuits are unavoidably thrown into contact with classes that are pecuniarily their superiors. The high standard of pecuniary decency in force among these superior classes is transfused among the scholarly classes with but little mitigation of its rigour; and as a consequence there is no class of the community that spends a larger proportion of its substance in conspicuous waste than these.

CHAPTER VI

PECUNIARY CANONS OF TASTE

The caution has already been repeated more than once, that while the regulating norm of consumption is in large part the requirement of conspicuous waste, it must not be understood that the motive on which the consumer acts in any given case is this principle in its bald, unsophisticated form. Ordinarily his motive is a wish to conform to established usage, to avoid unfavourable notice and comment, to live up to the accepted canons of decency in the kind, amount, and grade of goods consumed, as well as in the decorous employment of his time and effort. In the common run of cases this sense of prescriptive usage is present in the motives of the consumer and exerts a direct constraining force, especially as regards consumption carried on under the eyes of observers. But a considerable element of prescriptive expensiveness is observable also in consumption that does not in any appreciable degree become known to outsiders—as, for instance, articles of underclothing, some articles of food, kitchen utensils, and other household apparatus designed for service rather than for evidence. In all such useful articles a close scrutiny will discover certain features which add to the cost and enhance the commercial value of the goods in question, but do not proportionately increase the serviceability of these articles for the material purposes which alone they ostensibly are designed to serve.

Under the selective surveillance of the law of conspicuous waste there grows up a code of accredited canons of consumption, the effect of which is to hold the consumer up to a standard of expensiveness and wastefulness in his consumption of goods and in his employment of time and effort. This growth of prescriptive usage has an immediate effect upon economic life, but it has also an indirect and remoter effect upon conduct in other respects as well. Habits of thought with respect to the expression of life in any given direction unavoidably affect the habitual view of what is good and right in life in other directions also. In the organic complex of habits of thought which make up the substance of an individual's conscious life the economic interest does not lie isolated and distinct from all other interests. Something, for instance, has already been said of its relation to the canons of reputability.

The principle of conspicuous waste guides the formation of habits of thought as to what is honest and reputable in life and in commodities. In so doing, this principle will traverse other norms of conduct which do not primarily have to do with the code of pecuniary honour, but which have, directly or incidentally, an economic significance of some magnitude. So the canon of honorific waste may, immediately or remotely, influence the sense of duty, the sense of beauty, the sense of utility, the sense of devotional or ritualistic fitness, and the scientific sense of truth.

It is scarcely necessary to go into a discussion here of the particular points at which, or the particular manner in which, the canon of honorific expenditure habitually traverses the canons of moral conduct. The matter is one which has received large attention and illustration at the hands of those whose office it is to watch and admonish with respect to any departures from the accepted code of morals. In modern communities, where the dominant economic and legal feature of the community's life is the institution of private property, one of the salient features of the code of morals is the sacredness of property. There needs no insistence or illustration to gain assent to the proposition that the habit of holding private property inviolate is traversed by the other habit of seeking wealth for the sake of the good repute to be gained through its conspicuous consumption. Most offences against property, especially offences of an appreciable magnitude, come under this head. It is also a matter of common notoriety and by-word that in offences which result in a large accession of property to the offender he does not ordinarily incur the extreme penalty or the extreme obloquy with which his offence would be visited on the ground of the naïve moral code alone. The thief or swindler who has gained great wealth by his delinquency has a better chance than the small thief of escaping the rigorous penalty of the law; and some good repute accrues to him from his increased wealth and from his spending the irregularly acquired possessions in a seemly manner. A well-bred expenditure of his booty especially appeals with great effect to persons of a cultivated sense of the proprieties, and goes far to mitigate the sense of moral turpitude with which his dereliction is viewed by them. It may be noted also—and it is more immediately to the point—that we are all inclined to condone an offence against property in the case of a man whose motive is the worthy one of providing the means of a "decent" manner of life for his wife and children. If it is added that the wife has been "nurtured in the lap of luxury," that is accepted as an additional extenuating circumstance. That is to say, we are prone to condone such an offence where its aim is the honorific one of enabling the offender's wife to perform for him such an amount of vicarious consumption of time and substance as is demanded by the standard of pecuniary decency. In such a case the habit of approving the accustomed degree of conspicuous waste traverses the habit of deprecating violations of ownership, to the extent even of sometimes leaving the award of praise or blame uncertain. This is peculiarly true where the dereliction involves an appreciable predatory or piratical element.

This topic need scarcely be pursued farther here; but the remark may not be out of place that all that considerable body of morals that clusters about the concept of an inviolable ownership is itself a psychological precipitate of the traditional meritoriousness of wealth. And it should be added that this wealth which is held sacred is valued primarily for the sake of the good repute to be got through its conspicuous consumption.

The bearing of pecuniary decency upon the scientific spirit or the quest of knowledge will be taken up in some detail in a separate chapter. Also as regards the sense of devout or ritual merit and adequacy in this connection, little need be said in this place. That topic will also come up incidentally in a later chapter. Still, this usage of honorific expenditure has much to say in shaping popular tastes as to what is right and meritorious in sacred matters, and the bearing of the principle of conspicuous waste upon some of the commonplace devout observances and conceits may therefore be pointed out.

Obviously, the canon of conspicuous waste is accountable for a great portion of what may be called devout consumption; as, *e.g.*, the consumption of sacred edifices, vestments, and other goods of the same class. Even in those modern cults to whose divinities is imputed a predilection for temples not built with hands, the sacred buildings and the other properties of the cult are constructed and decorated with some view to a reputable degree of wasteful expenditure. And it needs but little either of observation or introspection—and either will serve the turn—to assure us that the expensive splendour of the house of worship has an appreciable uplifting and mellowing effect upon the worshipper's frame of mind. It will serve to enforce the same fact if we reflect upon the sense of abject shamefulness with which any evidence of indigence or squalor about the sacred place affects all beholders. The accessories of any devout observance should be pecuniarily above reproach. This requirement is imperative, whatever latitude may be allowed with regard to these accessories in point of æsthetic or other serviceability.

It may also be in place to notice that in all communities, especially in neighbourhoods where the standard of pecuniary decency for dwellings is not high, the local sanctuary is more ornate, more conspicuously wasteful in its architecture and decoration, than the dwelling-houses of the congregation. This is true of nearly all denominations and cults, whether Christian or Pagan, but it is true in a peculiar degree of the older and maturer cults. At the same time the sanctuary commonly contributes little if anything to the physical comfort of the members. Indeed, the sacred structure not only serves the physical well-being of the members to but a slight extent, as compared with their humbler dwelling-houses; but it is felt by all men that a right and enlightened sense of the true, the beautiful, and the good demands that in all expenditure on the sanctuary anything that might serve the comfort of the worshipper should be conspicuously absent. If any element of comfort is admitted in the fittings of the sanctuary, it should at least be scrupulously screened and masked under an ostensible austerity. In the most reputable latter-day houses of worship, where no expense is spared, the principle of austerity is carried to the length of making the fittings of the place a means of mortifying the flesh, especially in appearance. There are few persons of delicate tastes in the matter of devout consumption to whom this austerely wasteful discomfort does not appeal as intrinsically right and good. Devout consumption is of the nature of vicarious consumption. This canon of devout austerity is based on the pecuniary reputability of conspicuously wasteful consumption, backed by the principle that vicarious consumption should conspicuously not conduce to the comfort of the vicarious consumer.

The sanctuary and its fittings have something of this austerity in all the cults in which the saint or divinity to whom the sanctuary pertains is not conceived to be present and make personal use of the property for the gratification of luxurious tastes imputed to him. The character of the sacred paraphernalia is somewhat different in this respect in those cults where the habits of life imputed to the divinity more nearly approach those of an earthly patriarchal potentate—where he is conceived to make use of these consumable goods in person. In the latter case the sanctuary and its fittings take on more of the fashion given to goods destined for the conspicuous consumption of a temporal master or owner. On the other hand, where the sacred apparatus is simply employed in the divinity's service, that is to say, where it is consumed vicariously on his account by his servants, there the sacred properties take the character suited to goods that are destined for vicarious consumption only.

In the latter case the sanctuary and the sacred apparatus are so contrived as not to enhance the comfort or fulness of life of the vicarious consumer, or at any rate not to convey the impression that the end of their consumption is the consumer's comfort. For the end of vicarious consumption is to enhance, not the fulness of life of the consumer, but the pecuniary repute of the master for whose behoof the consumption takes place. Therefore priestly vestments are notoriously expensive, ornate, and inconvenient; and in the cults where the priestly servitor of the divinity is not conceived to serve him in the capacity of consort, they are of an austere, comfortless fashion. And such it is felt that they should be.

It is not only in establishing a devout standard of decent expensiveness that the principle of waste invades the domain of the canons of ritual serviceability. It touches the ways as well as the means, and draws on vicarious leisure as well as on vicarious consumption. Priestly demeanour at its best is aloof, leisurely, perfunctory, and uncontaminated with suggestions of sensuous pleasure. This holds true, in different degrees of course, for the different cults and denominations; but in the priestly life of all anthropomorphic cults the marks of a vicarious consumption of time are visible.

The same pervading canon of vicarious leisure is also visibly present in the exterior details of devout observances and need only be pointed out in order to become obvious to all beholders. All ritual has a notable tendency to reduce itself to a rehearsal of formulas. This development of formula is most noticeable in the maturer cults, which have at the same time a more austere, ornate, and severe priestly life and garb; but it is perceptible also in the forms and methods of worship of the newer and fresher sects, whose tastes in respect of priests, vestments, and sanctuaries are less exacting. The rehearsal of the service (the term "service" carries a suggestion significant for the point in question) grows more perfunctory as the cult gains in age and consistency, and this perfunctoriness of the rehearsal is very pleasing to the correct devout taste. And with a good reason, for the fact of its being perfunctory goes to say pointedly that the master for whom it is performed is exalted above the vulgar need of actually proficuous service on the part of his servants. They are unprofitable servants, and there is a honorific implication for their master in their remaining unprofitable. It is needless to point out the close analogy at this point between the priestly office and the office of the footman. It is pleasing to our sense of what is fitting in these matters, in either case, to recognise in the obvious perfunctoriness of the service that it is a *pro forma* execution only. There should be no show of agility or of dexterous manipulation in the execution of the priestly office, such as might suggest a capacity for turning off the work.

In all this there is of course an obvious implication as to the temperament, tastes, propensities, and habits of life imputed to the divinity by worshippers who live under the tradition of these pecuniary canons of reputability. Through its pervading men's habits of thought, the principle of conspicuous waste has coloured the worshippers' notions of the divinity and of the relation in which the human subject stands to him. It is of course in the more naïve cults that this suffusion of pecuniary beauty is most patent, but it is visible throughout. All peoples, at whatever stage of culture or degree of enlightenment, are fain to eke out a sensibly scant degree of authentic information regarding the personality and habitual surroundings of their divinities. In so calling in the aid of fancy to enrich and fill in their picture of the divinity's presence and manner of life they habitually impute to him such traits as go to make up their ideal of a worthy man. And in seeking communion with the divinity the ways and means of approach are assimilated as nearly as may be to the divine ideal that is in men's minds at the time. It is felt that the divine presence is entered with the best grace, and with the best effect, according to certain accepted methods and with the accompaniment of certain material circumstances which in popular apprehension are peculiarly consonant with the divine nature. This popularly accepted ideal of the bearing and paraphernalia adequate to such occasions of communion is, of course, to a good extent shaped by the popular apprehension of what is intrinsically worthy and beautiful in human carriage and surroundings on all occasions of dignified intercourse. It would on this account be misleading to attempt an analysis of devout demeanour by referring all evidences of the presence of a pecuniary standard of reputability back directly and baldly to the underlying norm of pecuniary emulation. So it would also be misleading to ascribe to the divinity, as popularly conceived, a jealous regard for his pecuniary standing and a habit of avoiding and condemning squalid situations and surroundings simply because they are under grade in the pecuniary respect.

And still, after all allowance has been made, it appears that the canons of pecuniary reputability do directly or indirectly, materially affect our notions of the attributes of divinity, as well as our notions of what are the fit and adequate manner and circumstances of divine communion. It is felt that the divinity must be of a peculiarly serene and leisurely habit of life. And whenever his local habitation is pictured in poetic imagery, for edification or in appeal to the devout fancy, the devout word-painter, as a matter of course, brings out before his auditors' imagination a throne with a profusion of the insignia of opulence and power, and surrounded by a great number of servitors. In the common run of such presentations of the celestial abodes, the office of this corps of servants is a vicarious leisure, their time and efforts being in great measure taken up with an industrially unproductive rehearsal of the meritorious characteristics and exploits of the divinity; while the background of the presentation is filled with the shimmer of the precious metals and of the more expensive varieties of precious stones. It is only in the crasser expressions of devout fancy that this intrusion of pecuniary canons into the devout ideals reaches such an extreme. An extreme case occurs in the devout imagery of the negro population of the South. Their word-painters are unable to descend to anything cheaper than gold; so that in this case the insistence on pecuniary beauty gives a startling effect in yellow,— such as would be unbearable to a soberer taste. Still, there is probably no cult in which ideals of pecuniary merit have not been called in to supplement the ideals of ceremonial adequacy that guide men's conception of what is right in the matter of sacred apparatus.

Similarly it is felt—and the sentiment is acted upon—that the priestly servitors of the divinity should not engage in industrially productive work; that work of any kind—any employment which is of tangible human use—must not be carried on in the divine presence, or within the precincts of the sanctuary; that whoever comes into the presence should come cleansed of all profane industrial features in his apparel or person, and should come clad in garments of more than everyday expensiveness; that on holidays set apart in honour of or for communion with the divinity no work that is of human use should be performed by any one. Even the remoter, lay dependants should render a vicarious leisure to the extent of one day in seven.

In all these deliverances of men's uninstructed sense of what is fit and proper in devout observance and in the relations of the divinity, the effectual presence of the canons of pecuniary reputability is obvious enough, whether these canons have had their effect on the devout judgment in this respect immediately or at the second remove.

These canons of reputability have had a similar, but more far-reaching and more specifically determinable, effect upon the popular sense of beauty or serviceability in consumable goods. The requirements of pecuniary decency have, to a very appreciable extent, influenced the sense of beauty and of utility in articles of use or beauty. Articles are to an extent preferred for use on account of their being conspicuously wasteful; they are felt to be serviceable somewhat in proportion as they are wasteful and ill adapted to their ostensible use.

The utility of articles valued for their beauty depends closely upon the expensiveness of the articles. A homely illustration will bring out this dependence. A hand-wrought silver spoon, of a commercial value of some ten to twenty dollars, is not ordinarily more serviceable—in the first sense of the word—than a machine-made spoon of the same material. It may not even be more serviceable than a machine-made spoon of some "base" metal, such as aluminum, the value of which may be no more than some ten to twenty cents. The former of the two utensils is, in fact, commonly a less effective contrivance for its ostensible purpose than the latter. The objection is of course ready to hand that, in taking this view of the matter, one of the chief uses, if not the chief use, of the costlier spoon is ignored; the hand-wrought spoon gratifies our taste, our sense of the beautiful, while that made by machinery out of the base metal has no useful office beyond a brute efficiency. The facts are no doubt as the objection states them, but it will be evident on reflection that the objection is after all more plausible than conclusive. It appears (1) that while the different materials of which the two spoons are made each possesses beauty and serviceability for the purpose for which it is used, the material of the hand-wrought spoon is some one hundred times more valuable than the baser metal, without very greatly excelling the latter in intrinsic beauty of grain or colour, and without being in any appreciable degree superior in point of mechanical serviceability; (2) if a close inspection should show that the supposed hand-wrought spoon were in reality only a very clever imitation of hand-wrought goods, but an imitation so cleverly wrought as to give the same impression of line and surface to any but a minute examination by a trained eye, the utility of the article, including the gratification which the user derives from its contemplation as an object of beauty, would immediately decline by some eighty or ninety per cent, or even more; (3) if the two spoons are, to a fairly close observer, so nearly identical in appearance that the lighter weight of the spurious article alone betrays it, this identity of form and colour will scarcely add to the value of the machine-made spoon, nor appreciably enhance the gratification of the user's "sense of beauty" in contemplating it, so long as the cheaper spoon is not a novelty, and so long as it can be procured at a nominal cost.

The case of the spoons is typical. The superior gratification derived from the use and contemplation of costly and supposedly beautiful products is, commonly, in great measure a gratification of our sense of costliness masquerading under the name of beauty. Our higher appreciation of the superior article is an appreciation of its superior honorific character, much more frequently than it is an unsophisticated appreciation of its beauty. The requirement of conspicuous wastefulness is not commonly present, consciously, in our canons of taste, but it is none the less present as a constraining norm selectively shaping and sustaining our sense of what is beautiful, and guiding our discrimination with respect to what may legitimately be approved as beautiful and what may not.

It is at this point, where the beautiful and the honorific meet and blend, that a discrimination between serviceability and wastefulness is most difficult in any concrete case. It frequently happens that an article which serves the honorific purpose of conspicuous waste is at the same time a beautiful object; and the same application of labour to which it owes its utility for the former purpose may, and often does, go to give beauty of form and colour to the article. The question is further complicated by the fact that many objects, as, for instance, the precious stones and metals and some other materials used for adornment and decoration, owe their utility as items of conspicuous waste to an antecedent utility as objects of beauty. Gold, for instance, has a high degree of sensuous beauty; very many if not most of the highly prized works of art are intrinsically beautiful, though often with material qualification; the like is true of some stuffs used for clothing, of some landscapes, and of many other things in less degree. Except for this intrinsic beauty which they possess, these objects would scarcely have been coveted as they are, or have become monopolised objects of pride to their possessors and users. But the utility of these things to the possessor is commonly due less to their intrinsic beauty than to the honour which their possession and consumption confers, or to the obloquy which it wards off.

Apart from their serviceability in other respects, these objects are beautiful and have a utility as such; they are valuable on this account if they can be appropriated or monopolised; they are, therefore, coveted as valuable possessions, and their exclusive enjoyment gratifies the possessor's sense of pecuniary superiority at the same time that their contemplation gratifies his sense of beauty. But their beauty, in the naïve sense of the word, is the occasion rather than the ground of their monopolisation or of their commercial value. "Great as is the sensuous beauty of gems, their rarity and price adds an expression of distinction to them, which they would never have if they were cheap." There is, indeed, in the common run of cases under this head, relatively little incentive to the exclusive possession and use of these beautiful things, except on the ground of their honorific character as items of conspicuous waste. Most objects of this general class, with the partial exception of articles of personal adornment, would serve all other purposes than the honorific one equally well, whether owned by the person viewing them or not; and even as regards personal ornaments it is to be added that their chief purpose is to lend éclat to the person of their wearer (or owner) by comparison with other persons who are compelled to do without. The æsthetic serviceability of objects of beauty is not greatly nor universally heightened by possession.

The generalisation for which the discussion so far affords ground is that any valuable object in order to appeal to our sense of beauty must conform to the requirements of beauty and of expensiveness both. But this is not all. Beyond this the canon of expensiveness also affects our tastes in such a way as to inextricably blend the marks of expensiveness, in our appreciation, with the beautiful features of the object, and to subsume the resultant effect under the head of an appreciation of beauty simply. The marks of expensiveness come to be accepted as beautiful features of the expensive articles. They are pleasing as being marks of honorific costliness, and the pleasure which they afford on this score blends with that afforded by the beautiful form and colour of the object; so that we often declare that an article of apparel, for instance, is "perfectly lovely," when pretty much all that an analysis of the æsthetic value of the article would leave ground for is the declaration that it is pecuniarily honorific.

This blending and confusion of the elements of expensiveness and of beauty is, perhaps, best exemplified in articles of dress and of household furniture. The code of reputability in matters of dress decides what shapes, colours, materials, and general effects in human apparel are for the time to be accepted as suitable; and departures from the code are offensive to our taste, supposedly as being departures from æsthetic truth. The approval with which we look upon fashionable attire is by no means to be accounted pure make-believe. We readily, and for the most part with utter sincerity, find those things pleasing that are in vogue. Shaggy dress-stuffs and pronounced colour effects, for instance, offend us at times when the vogue is goods of a high, glossy finish and neutral colours. A fancy bonnet of this year's model unquestionably appeals to our sensibilities to-day much more forcibly than an equally fancy bonnet of the model of last year; although when viewed in the perspective of a quarter of a century, it would, I apprehend, be a matter of the utmost difficulty to award the palm for intrinsic beauty to the one rather than to the other of these structures. So, again, it may be remarked that, considered simply in their physical juxtaposition with the human form, the high gloss of a gentleman's hat or of a patent-leather shoe has no more of intrinsic beauty than a similarly high gloss on a threadbare sleeve; and yet there is no question but that all well-bred people (in the Occidental civilised communities) instinctively and unaffectedly cleave to the one as a phenomenon of great beauty, and eschew the other as offensive to every sense to which it can appeal. It is extremely doubtful if any one could be induced to wear such a contrivance as the high hat of civilised society, except for some urgent reason based on other than æsthetic grounds.

By further habituation to an appreciative perception of the marks of expensiveness in goods, and by habitually identifying beauty with reputability, it comes about that a beautiful article which is not expensive is accounted not beautiful. In this way it has happened, for instance, that some beautiful flowers pass conventionally for offensive weeds; others that can be cultivated with relative ease are accepted and admired by the lower middle class, who can afford no more expensive luxuries of this kind; but these varieties are rejected as vulgar by those people who are better able to pay for expensive flowers and who are educated to a higher schedule of pecuniary beauty in the florist's products; while still other flowers, of no greater intrinsic beauty than these, are cultivated at great cost and call out much admiration from flower-lovers whose tastes have been matured under the critical guidance of a polite environment.

The same variation in matters of taste, from one class of society to another, is visible also as regards many other kinds of consumable goods, as, for example, is the case with furniture, houses, parks, and gardens. This diversity of views as to what is beautiful in these various classes of goods is not a diversity of the norm according to which the unsophisticated sense of the beautiful works. It is not a constitutional difference of endowments in the æsthetic respect, but rather a difference in the code of reputability which specifies what objects properly lie within the scope of honorific consumption for the class to which the critic belongs. It is a difference in the traditions of propriety with respect to the kinds of things which may, without derogation to the consumer, be consumed under the head of objects of taste and art. With a certain allowance for variations to be accounted for on other grounds, these traditions are determined, more or less rigidly, by the pecuniary plane of life of the class.

Everyday life affords many curious illustrations of the way in which the code of pecuniary beauty in articles of use varies from class to class, as well as of the way in which the conventional sense of beauty departs in its deliverances from the sense untutored by the requirements of pecuniary repute. Such a fact is the lawn, or the close-cropped yard or park, which appeals so unaffectedly to the taste of the Western peoples. It appears especially to appeal to the tastes of the well-to-do classes in those communities in which the dolicho[1]-blond element predominates in an appreciable degree. The lawn unquestionably has an element of sensuous beauty, simply as an object of apperception, and as such no doubt it appeals pretty directly to the eye of nearly all races and all classes; but it is, perhaps, more unquestionably beautiful to the eye of the dolicho-blond than to most other varieties of men. This higher appreciation of a stretch of greensward in this ethnic element than in the other elements of the population, goes along with certain other features of the dolicho-blond temperament that indicate that this racial element has once been for a long time a pastoral people inhabiting a region with a humid climate. The close-cropped lawn is beautiful in the eyes of a people whose inherited bent it is to readily find pleasure in contemplating a well-preserved pasture or grazing land.

For the æsthetic purpose the lawn is a cow pasture; and in some cases to-day—where the expensiveness of the attendant circumstances bars out any imputation of thrift—the idyl of the dolicho-blond is rehabilitated in the introduction of a cow into a lawn or private ground. In such cases the cow made use of is commonly of an expensive breed. The vulgar suggestion of thrift, which is nearly inseparable from the cow, is a standing objection to the decorative use of this animal. So that in all cases, except where luxurious surroundings negative this suggestion, the use of the cow as an object of taste must be avoided. Where the predilection for some grazing animal to fill out the suggestion of the pasture is too strong to be suppressed, the cow's place is often given to some more or less inadequate substitute, such as deer, antelopes, or some such exotic beast. These substitutes, although less beautiful to the pastoral eye of Western man than the cow, are in such cases preferred because of their superior expensiveness or futility, and their consequent repute. They are not vulgarly lucrative either in fact or in suggestion.

Public parks of course fall in the same category with the lawn; they too, at their best, are imitations of the pasture. Such a park is of course best kept by grazing, and the cattle on the grass are themselves no mean addition to the beauty of the thing, as need scarcely be insisted on with any one who has once seen a well-kept pasture. But it is worth noting, as an expression of the pecuniary element in popular taste, that such a method of keeping public grounds is seldom resorted to. The best that is done by skilled workmen under the supervision of a trained keeper is a more or less close imitation of a pasture, but the result invariably falls somewhat short of the artistic effect of grazing. But to the average popular apprehension a herd of cattle so pointedly suggests thrift and usefulness that their presence in the public pleasure ground would be intolerably cheap. This method of keeping grounds is comparatively inexpensive, therefore it is indecorous.

Of the same general bearing is another feature of public grounds. There is a studious exhibition of expensiveness coupled with a make-believe of simplicity and crude serviceability. Private grounds also show the same physiognomy wherever they are in the management or ownership of persons whose tastes have been formed under middle-class habits of life or under the upper-class traditions of no later a date than the childhood of the generation that is now passing. Grounds which conform to the instructed tastes of the latter-day upper class do not show these features in so marked a degree. The reason for this difference in tastes between the past and the incoming generation of the well-bred lies in the changing economic situation. A similar difference is perceptible in other respects, as well as in the accepted ideals of pleasure grounds. In this country as in most others, until the last half century but a very small proportion of the population were possessed of such wealth as would exempt them from thrift. Owing to imperfect means of communication, this small fraction were scattered and out of effective touch with one another. There was therefore no basis for a growth of taste in disregard of expensiveness. The revolt of the well-bred taste against vulgar thrift was unchecked. Wherever the unsophisticated sense of beauty might show itself sporadically in an approval of inexpensive or thrifty surroundings, it would lack the "social confirmation" which nothing but a considerable body of like-minded people can give. There was, therefore, no effective upper-class opinion that would overlook evidences of possible inexpensiveness in the management of grounds; and there was consequently no appreciable divergence between the leisure-class and the lower middle-class ideal in the physiognomy of pleasure grounds. Both classes equally constructed their ideals with the fear of pecuniary disrepute before their eyes.

To-day a divergence in ideals is beginning to be apparent. The portion of the leisure class that has been consistently exempt from work and from pecuniary cares for a generation or more is now large enough to form and sustain an opinion in matters of taste. Increased mobility of the members has also added to the facility with which a "social confirmation" can be attained within the class. Within this select class the exemption from thrift is a matter so commonplace as to have lost much of its utility as a basis of pecuniary decency. Therefore the latter-day upper-class canons of taste do not so consistently insist on an unremitting demonstration of expensiveness and a strict exclusion of the appearance of thrift. So, a predilection for the rustic and the "natural" in parks and grounds makes its appearance on these higher social and intellectual levels. This predilection is in large part an outcropping of the instinct of workmanship; and it works out its results with varying degrees of consistency. It is seldom altogether unaffected, and at times it shades off into something not widely different from that make-believe of rusticity which has been referred to above.

A weakness for crudely serviceable contrivances that pointedly suggest immediate and wasteless use is present even in the middle-class tastes; but it is there kept well in hand under the unbroken dominance of the canon of reputable futility. Consequently it works out in a variety of ways and means for shamming service-ability,—in such contrivances as rustic fences, bridges, bowers, pavilions, and the like decorative features. An expression of this affectation of serviceability, at what is perhaps its widest divergence from the first promptings of the sense of economic beauty, is afforded by the cast-iron rustic fence and trellis or by a circuitous drive laid across level ground.

The select leisure class has outgrown the use of these pseudo-serviceable variants of pecuniary beauty, at least at some points. But the taste of the more recent accessions to the leisure class proper and of the middle and lower classes still requires a pecuniary beauty to supplement the æsthetic beauty, even in those objects which are primarily admired for the beauty that belongs to them as natural growths.

The popular taste in these matters is to be seen in the prevalent high appreciation of topiary work and of the conventional flower-beds of public grounds. Perhaps as happy an illustration as may be had of this dominance of pecuniary beauty over æsthetic beauty in middle-class tastes is seen in the reconstruction of the grounds lately occupied by the Columbian Exposition.[2] The evidence goes to show that the requirement of reputable expensiveness is still present in good vigour even where all ostensibly lavish display is avoided. The artistic effects actually wrought in this work of reconstruction diverge somewhat widely from the effect to which the same ground would have lent itself in hands not guided by pecuniary canons of taste. And even the better class of the city's population view the progress of the work with an unreserved approval which suggests that there is in this case little if any discrepancy between the tastes of the upper and the lower or middle classes of the city. The sense of beauty in the population of this representative city of the advanced pecuniary culture is very chary of any departure from its great cultural principle of conspicuous waste.

The love of nature, perhaps itself borrowed from a higher-class code of taste, sometimes expresses itself in unexpected ways under the guidance of this canon of pecuniary beauty, and leads to results that may seem incongruous to an unreflecting beholder. The well-accepted practice of planting trees in the treeless areas of this country, for instance, has been carried over as an item of honorific expenditure into the heavily wooded areas; so that it is by no means unusual for a village or a farmer in the wooded country to clear the land of its native trees and immediately replant saplings of certain introduced varieties about the farmyard or along the streets. In this way a forest growth of oak, elm, beech, butternut, hemlock, basswood, and birch is cleared off to give room for saplings of soft maple, cottonwood, and brittle willow. It is felt that the inexpensiveness of leaving the forest trees standing would derogate from the dignity that should invest an article which is intended to serve a decorative and honorific end.

The like pervading guidance of taste by pecuniary repute is traceable in the prevalent standards of beauty in animals. The part played by this canon of taste in assigning her place in the popular æsthetic scale to the cow has already been spoken of. Something to the same effect is true of the other domestic animals, so far as they are in an appreciable degree industrially useful to the community—as, for instance, barnyard fowl, hogs, cattle, sheep, goats, draught-horses. They are of the nature of productive goods, and serve a useful, often a lucrative end; therefore beauty is not readily imputed to them. The case is different with those domestic animals which ordinarily serve no industrial end; such as pigeons, parrots and other cage-birds, cats, dogs, and fast horses. These commonly are items of conspicuous consumption, and are therefore honorific in their nature and may legitimately be accounted beautiful. This class of animals are conventionally admired by the body of the upper classes, while the pecuniarily lower classes—and that select minority of the leisure class among whom the rigorous canon that abjures thrift is in a measure obsolescent—find beauty in one class of animals as in another, without drawing a hard and fast line of pecuniary demarcation between the beautiful and the ugly.

In the case of those domestic animals which are honorific and are reputed beautiful, there is a subsidiary basis of merit that should be spoken of. Apart from the birds which belong in the honorific class of domestic animals, and which owe their place in this class to their non-lucrative character alone, the animals which merit particular attention are cats, dogs, and fast horses. The cat is less reputable than the other two just named, because she is less wasteful; she may even serve a useful end. At the same time the cat's temperament does not fit her for the honorific purpose. She lives with man on terms of equality, knows nothing of that relation of status which is the ancient basis of all distinctions of worth, honour, and repute, and she does not lend herself with facility to an invidious comparison between her owner and his neighbours. The exception to this last rule occurs in the case of such scarce and fanciful products as the Angora cat, which have some slight honorific value on the ground of expensiveness, and have, therefore, some special claim to beauty on pecuniary grounds.

The dog has advantages in the way of uselessness as well as in special gifts of temperament. He is often spoken of, in an eminent sense, as the friend of man, and his intelligence and fidelity are praised. The meaning of this is that the dog is man's servant and that he has the gift of an unquestioning subservience and a slave's quickness in guessing his master's mood. Coupled with these traits, which fit him well for the relation of status—and which must for the present purpose be set down as serviceable traits—the dog has some characteristics which are of a more equivocal æsthetic value. He is the filthiest of the domestic animals in his person and the nastiest in his habits. For this he makes up in a servile, fawning attitude towards his master, and a readiness to inflict damage and discomfort on all else. The dog, then, commends himself to our favour by affording play to our propensity for mastery, and as he is also an item of expense, and commonly serves no industrial purpose, he holds a well-assured place in men's regard as a thing of good repute. The dog is at the same time associated in our imagination with the chase—a meritorious employment and an expression of the honourable predatory impulse.

Standing on this vantage ground, whatever beauty of form and motion and whatever commendable mental traits he may possess are conventionally acknowledged and magnified. And even those varieties of the dog which have been bred into grotesque deformity by the dog-fancier are in good faith accounted beautiful by many. These varieties of dogs—and the like is true of other fancy-bred animals—are rated and graded in æsthetic value somewhat in proportion to the degree of grotesqueness and instability of the particular fashion which the deformity takes in the given case. For the purpose in hand, this differential utility on the ground of grotesqueness and instability of structure is reducible to terms of a greater scarcity and consequent expense. The commercial value of canine monstrosities, such as the prevailing styles of pet dogs both for men's and women's use, rests on their high cost of production, and their value to their owners lies chiefly in their utility as items of conspicuous consumption. Indirectly, through reflection upon their honorific expensiveness, a social worth is imputed to them; and so, by an easy substitution of words and ideas, they come to be admired and reputed beautiful. Since any attention bestowed upon these animals is in no sense gainful or useful, it is also reputable; and since the habit of giving them attention is consequently not deprecated, it may grow into an habitual attachment of great tenacity and of a most benevolent character. So that in the affection bestowed on pet animals the canon of expensiveness is present more or less remotely as a norm which guides and shapes the sentiment and the selection of its object. The like is true, as will be noticed presently, with respect to affection for persons also; although the manner in which the norm acts in that case is somewhat different.

The case of the fast horse is much like that of the dog. He is on the whole expensive, or wasteful and useless—for the industrial purpose. What productive use he may possess, in the way of enhancing the well-being of the community or making the way of life easier for men, takes the form of exhibitions of force and facility of motion that gratify the popular æsthetic sense. This is of course a substantial serviceability. The horse is not endowed with the spiritual aptitude for servile dependence in the same measure as the dog; but he ministers effectually to his master's impulse to convert the "animate" forces of the environment to his own use and discretion and so express his own dominating individuality through them. The fast horse is at least potentially a race-horse, of high or low degree; and it is as such that he is peculiarly serviceable to his owner. The utility of the fast horse lies largely in his efficiency as a means of emulation; it gratifies the owner's sense of aggression and dominance to have his own horse outstrip his neighbour's. This use being not lucrative, but on the whole pretty consistently wasteful, and quite conspicuously so, it is honorific, and therefore gives the fast horse a strong presumptive position of reputability. Beyond this, the race-horse proper has also a similarly non-industrial but honorific use as a gambling instrument.

The fast horse, then, is æsthetically fortunate, in that the canon of pecuniary good repute legitimates a free appreciation of whatever beauty or serviceability he may possess. His pretensions have the countenance of the principle of conspicuous waste and the backing of the predatory aptitude for dominance and emulation. The horse is, moreover, a beautiful animal, although the race-horse is so in no peculiar degree to the uninstructed taste of those persons who belong neither in the class of race-horse fanciers nor in the class whose sense of beauty is held in abeyance by the moral constraint of the horse fancier's award. To this untutored taste the most beautiful horse seems to be a form which has suffered less radical alteration than the race-horse under the breeder's selective development of the animal. Still, when a writer or speaker—especially of those whose eloquence is most consistently commonplace—wants an illustration of animal grace and serviceability, for rhetorical use, he habitually turns to the horse; and he commonly makes it plain before he is done that what he has in mind is the race-horse.

It should be noted that in the graduated appreciation of varieties of horses and of dogs, such as one meets with among people of even moderately cultivated tastes in these matters, there is also discernible another and more direct line of influence of the leisure-class canons of reputability. In this country, for instance, leisure-class tastes are to some extent shaped on usages and habits which prevail, or which are apprehended to prevail, among the leisure class of Great Britain. In dogs this is true to a less extent than in horses. In horses, more particularly in saddle horses,—which at their best serve the purpose of wasteful display simply,—it will hold true in a general way that a horse is more beautiful in proportion as he is more English; the English leisure class being, for purposes of reputable usage, the upper leisure class of this country, and so the exemplar for the lower grades. This mimicry in the methods of the apperception of beauty and in the forming of judgments of taste need not result in a spurious, or at any rate not a hypocritical or affected, predilection. The predilection is as serious and as substantial an award of taste when it rests on this basis as when it rests on any other; the difference is that this taste is a taste for the reputably correct, not for the æsthetically true.

The mimicry, it should be said, extends further than to the sense of beauty in horseflesh simply. It includes trappings and horsemanship as well, so that the correct or reputably beautiful seat or posture is also decided by English usage, as well as the equestrian gait. To show how fortuitous may sometimes be the circumstances which decide what shall be becoming and what not under the pecuniary canon of beauty, it may be noted that this English seat, and the peculiarly distressing gait which has made an awkward seat necessary, are a survival from the time when the English roads were so bad with mire and mud as to be virtually impassable for a horse travelling at a more comfortable gait; so that a person of decorous tastes in horsemanship to-day rides a punch with docked tail, in an uncomfortable posture and at a distressing gait, because the English roads during a great part of the last century were impassable for a horse travelling at a more horse-like gait, or for an animal built for moving with ease over the firm and open country to which the horse is indigenous.

It is not only with respect to consumable goods—including domestic animals—that the canons of taste have been coloured by the canons of pecuniary reputability. Something to the like effect is to be said for beauty in persons. In order to avoid whatever may be matter of controversy, no weight will be given in this connection to such popular predilection as there may be for the dignified (leisurely) bearing and portly presence that are by vulgar tradition associated with opulence in mature men. These traits are in some measure accepted as elements of personal beauty. But there are certain elements of feminine beauty, on the other hand, which come in under this head, and which are of so concrete and specific a character as to admit of itemised appreciation. It is more or less a rule that in communities which are at the stage of economic development at which women are valued by the upper class for their service, the ideal of female beauty is a robust, large-limbed woman. The ground of appreciation is the physique, while the conformation of the face is of secondary weight only. A well-known instance of this ideal of the early predatory culture is that of the maidens of the Homeric poems.

This ideal suffers a change in the succeeding development, when, in the conventional scheme, the office of the high-class wife comes to be a vicarious leisure simply. The ideal then includes the characteristics which are supposed to result from or to go with a life of leisure consistently enforced. The ideal accepted under these circumstances may be gathered from descriptions of beautiful women by poets and writers of the chivalric times. In the conventional scheme of those days ladies of high degree were conceived to be in perpetual tutelage, and to be scrupulously exempt from all useful work. The resulting chivalric or romantic ideal of beauty takes cognizance chiefly of the face, and dwells on its delicacy, and on the delicacy of the hands and feet, the slender figure, and especially the slender waist. In the pictured representations of the women of that time, and in modern romantic imitators of the chivalric thought and feeling, the waist is attenuated to a degree that implies extreme debility. The same ideal is still extant among a considerable portion of the population of modern industrial communities; but it is to be said that it has retained its hold most tenaciously in those modern communities which are least advanced in point of economic and civil development, and which show the most considerable survivals of status and of predatory institutions. That is to say, the chivalric ideal is best preserved in those existing communities which are substantially least modern. Survivals of this lackadaisical or romantic ideal occur freely in the tastes of the well-to-do classes of Continental countries.

In modern communities which have reached the higher levels of industrial development, the upper leisure class has accumulated so great a mass of wealth as to place its women above all imputation of vulgarly productive labour. Here the status of women as vicarious consumers is beginning to lose its place in the affections of the body of the people; and as a consequence the ideal of feminine beauty is beginning to change back again from the infirmly delicate, translucent, and hazardously slender, to a woman of the archaic type that does not disown her hands and feet, nor, indeed, the other gross material facts of her person. In the course of economic development the ideal of beauty among the peoples of the Western culture has shifted from the woman of physical presence to the lady, and it is beginning to shift back again to the woman; and all in obedience to the changing conditions of pecuniary emulation. The exigencies of emulation at one time required lusty slaves; at another time they required a conspicuous performance of vicarious leisure and consequently an obvious disability; but the situation is now beginning to outgrow this last requirement, since, under the higher efficiency of modern industry, leisure in women is possible so far down the scale of reputability that it will no longer serve as a definitive mark of the highest pecuniary grade.

Apart from this general control exercised by the norm of conspicuous waste over the ideal of feminine beauty, there are one or two details which merit specific mention as showing how it may exercise an extreme constraint in detail over men's sense of beauty in women. It has already been noticed that at the stages of economic evolution at which conspicuous leisure is much regarded as a means of good repute, the ideal requires delicate and diminutive hands and feet and a slender waist. These features, together with the other, related faults of structure that commonly go with them, go to show that the person so affected is incapable of useful effort and must therefore be supported in idleness by her owner. She is useless and expensive, and she is consequently valuable as evidence of pecuniary strength. It results that at this cultural stage women take thought to alter their persons, so as to conform more nearly to the requirements of the instructed taste of the time; and under the guidance of the canon of pecuniary decency, the men find the resulting artificially induced pathological features attractive. So, for instance, the constricted waist which has had so wide and persistent a vogue in the communities of the Western culture, and so also the deformed foot of the Chinese. Both of these are mutilations of unquestioned repulsiveness to the untrained sense. It requires habituation to become reconciled to them. Yet there is no room to question their attractiveness to men into whose scheme of life they fit as honorific items sanctioned by the requirements of pecuniary reputability. They are items of pecuniary and cultural beauty which have come to do duty as elements of the ideal of womanliness.

The connection here indicated between the æsthetic value and the invidious pecuniary value of things is of course not present in the consciousness of the valuer. So far as a person, in forming a judgment of taste, takes thought and reflects that the object of beauty under consideration is wasteful and reputable, and therefore may legitimately be accounted beautiful; so far the judgment is not a *bona fide* judgment of taste and does not come up for consideration in this connection. The connection which is here insisted on between the reputability and the apprehended beauty of objects lies through the effect which the fact of reputability has upon the valuer's habits of thought. He is in the habit of forming judgments of value of various kinds—economic, moral, æsthetic, or reputable—concerning the objects with which he has to do, and his attitude of commendation towards a given object on any other ground will affect the degree of his appreciation of the object when he comes to value it for the æsthetic purpose. This is more particularly true as regards valuation on grounds so closely related to the æsthetic ground as that of reputability. The valuation for the æsthetic purpose and for the purpose of repute are not held apart as distinctly as might be. Confusion is especially apt to arise between these two kinds of valuation, because the value of objects for repute is not habitually distinguished in speech by the use of a special descriptive term. The result is that the terms in familiar use to designate categories or elements of beauty are applied to cover this unnamed element of pecuniary merit, and the corresponding confusion of ideas follows by easy consequence. The demands of reputability in this way coalesce in the popular apprehension with the demands of the sense of beauty, and beauty which is not accompanied by the accredited marks of good repute is not accepted. But the requirements of pecuniary reputability and those of beauty in the naïve sense do not in any appreciable degree coincide. The elimination from our surroundings of the pecuniarily unfit, therefore, results in a more or less thorough elimination of that considerable range of elements of beauty which do not happen to conform to the pecuniary requirement.

The underlying norms of taste are of very ancient growth, probably far antedating the advent of the pecuniary institutions that are here under discussion. Consequently, by force of the past selective adaptation of men's habits of thought, it happens that the requirements of beauty, simply, are for the most part best satisfied by inexpensive contrivances and structures which in a straightforward manner suggest both the office which they are to perform and the method of serving their end.

It may be in place to recall the modern psychological position. Beauty of form seems to be a question of facility of apperception. The proposition could perhaps safely be made broader than this. If abstraction is made from association, suggestion, and "expression," classed as elements of beauty, then beauty in any perceived object means that the mind readily unfolds its apperceptive activity in the directions which the object in question affords. But the directions in which activity readily unfolds or expresses itself are the directions to which long and close habituation has made the mind prone. So far as concerns the essential elements of beauty, this habituation is an habituation so close and long as to have induced not only a proclivity to the apperceptive form in question, but an adaptation of physiological structure and function as well. So far as the economic interest enters into the constitution of beauty, it enters as a suggestion or expression of adequacy to a purpose, a manifest and readily inferable subservience to the life process. This expression of economic facility or economic serviceability in any object— what may be called the economic beauty of the object—is best served by neat and unambiguous suggestion of its office and its efficiency for the material ends of life.

On this ground, among objects of use the simple and unadorned article is æsthetically the best. But since the pecuniary canon of reputability rejects the inexpensive in articles appropriated to individual consumption, the satisfaction of our craving for beautiful things must be sought by way of compromise. The canons of beauty must be circumvented by some contrivance which will give evidence of a reputably wasteful expenditure, at the same time that it meets the demands of our critical sense of the useful and the beautiful, or at least meets the demand of some habit which has come to do duty in place of that sense. Such an auxiliary sense of taste is the sense of novelty; and this latter is helped out in its surrogateship by the curiosity with which men view ingenious and puzzling contrivances. Hence it comes that most objects alleged to be beautiful, and doing duty as such, show considerable ingenuity of design and are calculated to puzzle the beholder—to bewilder him with irrelevant suggestions and hints of the improbable—at the same time that they give evidence of an expenditure of labour in excess of what would give them their fullest efficiency for their ostensible economic end.

This may be shown by an illustration taken from outside the range of our everyday habits and everyday contact, and so outside the range of our bias. Such are the remarkable feather mantles of Hawaii, or the well-known carved handles of the ceremonial adzes of several Polynesian islands. These are undeniably beautiful, both in the sense that they offer a pleasing composition of form, lines, and colour, and in the sense that they evince great skill and ingenuity in design and construction. At the same time the articles are manifestly ill fitted to serve any other economic purpose. But it is not always that the evolution of ingenious and puzzling contrivances under the guidance of the canon of wasted effort works out so happy a result. The result is quite as often a virtually complete suppression of all elements that would bear scrutiny as expressions of beauty, or of serviceability, and the substitution of evidences of misspent ingenuity and labour, backed by a conspicuous ineptitude; until many of the objects with which we surround ourselves in everyday life, and even many articles of everyday dress and ornament, are such as would not be tolerated except under the stress of prescriptive tradition. Illustrations of this substitution of ingenuity and expense in place of beauty and serviceability are to be seen, for instance, in domestic architecture, in domestic art or fancy work, in various articles of apparel, especially of feminine and priestly apparel.

The canon of beauty requires expression of the generic. The "novelty" due to the demands of conspicuous waste traverses this canon of beauty, in that it results in making the physiognomy of our objects of taste a congeries of idiosyncracies; and the idiosyncracies are, moreover, under the selective surveillance of the canon of expensiveness.

This process of selective adaptation of designs to the end of conspicuous waste, and the substitution of pecuniary beauty for æsthetic beauty, has been especially effective in the development of architecture. It would be extremely difficult to find a modern civilised residence or public building which can claim anything better than relative inoffensiveness in the eyes of any one who will dissociate the elements of beauty from those of honorific waste. The endless variety of fronts presented by the better class of tenements and apartment houses in our cities is an endless variety of architectural distress and of suggestions of expensive discomfort. Considered as objects of beauty, the dead walls of the sides and back of these structures, left untouched by the hands of the artist, are commonly the best feature of the building.

What has been said of the influence of the law of conspicuous waste upon the canons of taste will hold true, with but a slight change of terms, of its influence upon our notions of the serviceability of goods for other ends than the æsthetic one. Goods are produced and consumed as a means to the fuller unfolding of human life; and their utility consists, in the first instance, in their efficiency as means to this end. The end is, in the first instance, the fulness of life of the individual, taken in absolute terms. But the human proclivity to emulation has seized upon the consumption of goods as a means to an invidious comparison, and has thereby invested consumable goods with a secondary utility as evidence of relative ability to pay. This indirect or secondary use of consumable goods lends a honorific character to consumption, and presently also to the goods which best serve this emulative end of consumption. The consumption of expensive goods is meritorious, and the goods which contain an appreciable element of cost in excess of what goes to give them serviceability for their ostensible mechanical purpose are honorific. The marks of superfluous costliness in the goods are therefore marks of worth—of high efficiency for the indirect, invidious end to be served by their consumption; and conversely, goods are humilific, and therefore unattractive, if they show too thrifty an adaptation to the mechanical end sought and do not include a margin of expensiveness on which to rest a complacent invidious comparison. This indirect utility gives much of their value to the "better" grades of goods. In order to appeal to the cultivated sense of utility, an article must contain a modicum of this indirect utility.

While men may have set out with disapproving an inexpensive manner of living because it indicated inability to spend much, and so indicated a lack of pecuniary success, they end by falling into the habit of disapproving cheap things as being intrinsically dishonourable or unworthy because they are cheap. As time has gone on, each succeeding generation has received this tradition of meritorious expenditure from the generation before it, and has in its turn further elaborated and fortified the traditional canon of pecuniary reputability in goods consumed; until we have finally reached such a degree of conviction as to the unworthiness of all inexpensive things, that we have no longer any misgivings in formulating the maxim, "Cheap and nasty." So thoroughly has this habit of approving the expensive and disapproving the inexpensive been ingrained into our thinking that we instinctively insist upon at least some measure of wasteful expensiveness in all our consumption, even in the case of goods which are consumed in strict privacy and without the slightest thought of display. We all feel, sincerely and without misgiving, that we are the more lifted up in spirit for having, even in the privacy of our own household, eaten our daily meal by the help of hand-wrought silver utensils, from hand-painted china (often of dubious artistic value) laid on high-priced table linen. Any retrogression from the standard of living which we are accustomed to regard as worthy in this respect is felt to be a grievous violation of our human dignity. So, also, for the last dozen years candles have been a more pleasing source of light at dinner than any other. Candle-light is now softer, less distressing to well-bred eyes, than oil, gas, or electric light. The same could not have been said thirty years ago, when candles were, or recently had been, the cheapest available light for domestic use. Nor are candles even now found to give an acceptable or effective light for any other than a ceremonial illumination.

A political sage still living has summed up the conclusion of this whole matter in the dictum: "A cheap coat makes a cheap man," and there is probably no one who does not feel the convincing force of the maxim.

The habit of looking for the marks of superfluous expensiveness in goods, and of requiring that all goods should afford some utility of the indirect or invidious sort, leads to a change in the standards by which the utility of goods is gauged. The honorific element and the element of brute efficiency are not held apart in the consumer's appreciation of commodities, and the two together go to make up the unanalysed aggregate serviceability of the goods. Under the resulting standard of serviceability, no article will pass muster on the strength of material sufficiency alone. In order to completeness and full acceptability to the consumer it must also show the honorific element. It results that the producers of articles of consumption direct their efforts to the production of goods that shall meet this demand for the honorific element. They will do this with all the more alacrity and effect, since they are themselves under the dominance of the same standard of worth in goods, and would be sincerely grieved at the sight of goods which lack the proper honorific finish. Hence it has come about that there are to-day no goods supplied in any trade which do not contain the honorific element in greater or less degree. Any consumer who might, Diogenes[3]-like, insist on the elimination of all honorific or wasteful elements from his consumption, would be unable to supply his most trivial wants in the modern market. Indeed, even if he resorted to supplying his wants directly by his own efforts, he would find it difficult if not impossible to divest himself of the current habits of thought on this head; so that he could scarcely compass a supply of the necessaries of life for a day's consumption without instinctively and by oversight incorporating in his home-made product something of this honorific, quasi-decorative element of wasted labour.

It is notorious that in their selection of serviceable goods in the retail market, purchasers are guided more by the finish and workmanship of the goods than by any marks of substantial serviceability. Goods, in order to sell, must have some appreciable amount of labour spent in giving them the marks of decent expensiveness, in addition to what goes to give them efficiency for the material use which they are to serve. This habit of making obvious costliness a canon of serviceability of course acts to enhance the aggregate cost of articles of consumption. It puts us on our guard against cheapness by identifying merit in some degree with cost. There is ordinarily a consistent effort on the part of the consumer to obtain goods of the required serviceability at as advantageous a bargain as may be; but the conventional requirement of obvious costliness, as a voucher and a constituent of the serviceability of the goods, leads him to reject as under grade such goods as do not contain a large element of conspicuous waste.

It is to be added that a large share of those features of consumable goods which figure in popular apprehension as marks of serviceability, and to which reference is here had as elements of conspicuous waste, commend themselves to the consumer also on other grounds than that of expensiveness alone. They usually give evidence of skill and effective workmanship, even if they do not contribute to the substantial serviceability of the goods; and it is no doubt largely on some such ground that any particular mark of honorific serviceability first comes into vogue and afterward maintains its footing as a normal constituent element of the worth of an article. A display of efficient workmanship is pleasing simply as such, even where its remoter, for the time unconsidered outcome is futile. There is a gratification of the artistic sense in the contemplation of skilful work. But it is also to be added that no such evidence of skilful workmanship, or of ingenious and effective adaptation of means to end, will, in the long run, enjoy the approbation of the modern civilised consumer unless it has the sanction of the canon of conspicuous waste.

The position here taken is enforced in a felicitous manner by the place assigned in the economy of consumption to machine products. The point of material difference between machine-made goods and the hand-wrought goods which serve the same purposes is, ordinarily, that the former serve their primary purpose more adequately. They are a more perfect product—show a more perfect adaptation of means to end. This does not save them from disesteem and depreciation, for they fall short under the test of honorific waste. Hand labour is a more wasteful method of production; hence the goods turned out by this method are more serviceable for the purpose of pecuniary reputability; hence the marks of hand labour come to be honorific, and the goods which exhibit these marks take rank as of higher grade than the corresponding machine product. Commonly, if not invariably, the honorific marks of hand labour are certain imperfections and irregularities in the lines of the hand-wrought article, showing where the workman has fallen short in the execution of the design. The ground of the superiority of hand-wrought goods, therefore, is a certain margin of crudeness. This margin must never be so wide as to show bungling workmanship, since that would be evidence of low cost, nor so narrow as to suggest the ideal precision attained only by the machine, for that would be evidence of low cost.

The appreciation of those evidences of honorific crudeness to which hand-wrought goods owe their superior worth and charm in the eyes of well-bred people is a matter of nice discrimination. It requires training and the formation of right habits of thought with respect to what may be called the physiognomy of goods. Machine-made goods of daily use are often admired and preferred precisely on account of their excessive perfection by the vulgar and the underbred who have not given due thought to the punctilios of elegant consumption. The ceremonial inferiority of machine products goes to show that the perfection of skill and workmanship embodied in any costly innovations in the finish of goods is not sufficient of itself to secure them acceptance and permanent favour. The innovation must have the support of the canon of conspicuous waste. Any feature in the physiognomy of goods, however pleasing in itself, and however well it may approve itself to the taste for effective work, will not be tolerated if it proves obnoxious to this norm of pecuniary reputability.

The ceremonial inferiority or uncleanness in consumable goods due to "commonness," or in other words to their slight cost of production, has been taken very seriously by many persons. The objection to machine products is often formulated as an objection to the commonness of such goods. What is common is within the (pecuniary) reach of many people. Its consumption is therefore not honorific, since it does not serve the purpose of a favourable invidious comparison with other consumers. Hence the consumption, or even the sight of such goods, is inseparable from an odious suggestion of the lower levels of human life, and one comes away from their contemplation with a pervading sense of meanness that is extremely distasteful and depressing to a person of sensibility. In persons whose tastes assert themselves imperiously, and who have not the gift, habit, or incentive to discriminate between the grounds of their various judgments of taste, the deliverances of the sense of the honorific coalesce with those of the sense of beauty and of the sense of serviceability—in the manner already spoken of; the resulting composite valuation serves as a judgment of the object's beauty or its serviceability, according as the valuer's bias or interest inclines him to apprehend the object in the one or the other of these aspects. It follows not infrequently that the marks of cheapness or commonness are accepted as definitive marks of artistic unfitness, and a code or schedule of æsthetic proprieties on the one hand, and of æsthetic abominations on the other, is constructed on this basis for guidance in questions of taste.

As has already been pointed out, the cheap, and therefore indecorous, articles of daily consumption in modern industrial communities are commonly machine products; and the generic feature of the physiognomy of machine-made goods as compared with the hand-wrought article is their greater perfection in workmanship and greater accuracy in the detail execution of the design. Hence it comes about that the visible imperfections of the hand-wrought goods, being honorific, are accounted marks of superiority in point of beauty, or serviceability, or both. Hence has arisen that exaltation of the defective, of which John Ruskin[4] and William Morris[5] were such eager spokesmen in their time; and on this ground their propaganda of crudity and wasted effort has been taken up and carried forward since their time. And hence also the propaganda for a return to handicraft and household industry. So much of the work and speculations of this group of men as fairly comes under the characterisation here given would have been impossible at a time when the visibly more perfect goods were not the cheaper.

It is of course only as to the economic value of this school of æsthetic teaching that anything is intended to be said or can be said here. What is said is not to be taken in the sense of depreciation, but chiefly as a characterisation of the tendency of this teaching in its effect on consumption and on the production of consumable goods.

The manner in which the bias of this growth of taste has worked itself out in production is perhaps most cogently exemplified in the book manufacture with which Morris busied himself during the later years of his life; but what holds true of the work of the Kelmscott Press in an eminent degree, holds true with but slightly abated force when applied to latter-day artistic book-making generally,—as to type, paper, illustration, binding materials, and binder's work. The claims to excellence put forward by the later products of the book-maker's industry rest in some measure on the degree of its approximation to the crudities of the time when the work of book-making was a doubtful struggle with refractory materials carried on by means of insufficient appliances. These products, since they require hand labour, are more expensive; they are also less convenient for use than the books turned out with a view to serviceability alone; they therefore argue ability on the part of the purchaser to consume freely, as well as ability to waste time and effort. It is on this basis that the printers of to-day are returning to "old-style," and other more or less obsolete styles of type which are less legible and give a cruder appearance to the page than the "modern." Even a scientific periodical, with ostensibly no purpose but the most effective presentation of matter with which its science is concerned, will concede so much to the demands of this pecuniary beauty as to publish its scientific discussions in old-style type, on laid paper, and with uncut edges. But books which are not ostensibly concerned with the effective presentation of their contents alone, of course go farther in this direction. Here we have a somewhat cruder type, printed on hand-laid, deckel-edged paper, with excessive margins and uncut leaves, with bindings of a painstaking crudeness and elaborate ineptitude. The Kelmscott Press reduced the matter to an absurdity—as seen from the point of view of brute serviceability alone—by issuing books for modern use, edited with the obsolete spelling, printed in black-letter, and bound in limp vellum fitted with thongs. As a further characteristic feature which fixes the economic place of artistic book-making, there is the fact that these more elegant books are, at their best, printed in limited editions. A limited edition is in effect a guarantee—somewhat crude, it is true—that this book is scarce and that it therefore is costly and lends pecuniary distinction to its consumer.

The special attractiveness of these book-products to the book-buyer of cultivated taste lies, of course, not in a conscious, naïve recognition of their costliness and superior clumsiness. Here, as in the parallel case of the superiority of hand-wrought articles over machine products, the conscious ground of preference is an intrinsic excellence imputed to the costlier and more awkward article. The superior excellence imputed to the book which imitates the products of antique and obsolete processes is conceived to be chiefly a superior utility in the æsthetic respect; but it is not unusual to find a well-bred book-lover insisting that the clumsier product is also more serviceable as a vehicle of printed speech. So far as regards the superior æsthetic value of the decadent book, the chances are that the book-lover's contention has some ground. The book is designed with an eye single to its beauty, and the result is commonly some measure of success on the part of the designer. What is insisted on here, however, is that the canon of taste under which the designer works is a canon formed under the surveillance of the law of conspicuous waste, and that this law acts selectively to eliminate any canon of taste that does not conform to its demands. That is to say, while the decadent book may be beautiful, the limits within which the designer may work are fixed by requirements of a non-æsthetic kind. The product, if it is beautiful, must also at the same time be costly and ill adapted to its ostensible use. This mandatory canon of taste in the case of the book-designer, however, is not shaped entirely by the law of waste in its first form; the canon is to some extent shaped in conformity to that secondary expression of the predatory temperament, veneration for the archaic or obsolete, which in one of its special developments is called classicism.

In æsthetic theory it might be extremely difficult, if not quite impracticable, to draw a line between the canon of classicism, or regard for the archaic, and the canon of beauty. For the æsthetic purpose such a distinction need scarcely be drawn, and indeed it need not exist. For a theory of taste the expression of an accepted ideal of archaism, on whatever basis it may have been accepted, is perhaps best rated as an element of beauty; there need be no question of its legitimation. But for the present purpose—for the purpose of determining what economic grounds are present in the accepted canons of taste and what is their significance for the distribution and consumption of goods—the distinction is not similarly beside the point.

The position of machine products in the civilised scheme of consumption serves to point out the nature of the relation which subsists between the canon of conspicuous waste and the code of proprieties in consumption. Neither in matters of art and taste proper, nor as regards the current sense of the serviceability of goods, does this canon act as a principle of innovation or initiative. It does not go into the future as a creative principle which makes innovations and adds new items of consumption and new elements of cost. The principle in question is, in a certain sense, a negative rather than a positive law. It is a regulative rather than a creative principle. It very rarely initiates or originates any usage or custom directly. Its action is selective only. Conspicuous wastefulness does not directly afford ground for variation and growth, but conformity to its requirements is a condition to the survival of such innovations as may be made on other grounds. In whatever way usages and customs and methods of expenditure arise, they are all subject to the selective action of this norm of reputability; and the degree in which they conform to its requirements is a test of their fitness to survive in the competition with other similar usages and customs. Other things being equal, the more obviously wasteful usage or method stands the better chance of survival under this law. The law of conspicuous waste does not account for the origin of variations, but only for the persistence of such forms as are fit to survive under its dominance. It acts to conserve the fit, not to originate the acceptable. Its office is to prove all things and to hold fast that which is good for its purpose.

CHAPTER VII

DRESS AS AN EXPRESSION OF THE PECUNIARY CULTURE

It will be in place, by way of illustration, to show in some detail how the economic principles so far set forth apply to everyday facts in some one direction of the life process. For this purpose no line of consumption affords a more apt illustration than expenditure on dress. It is especially the rule of the conspicuous waste of goods that finds expression in dress, although the other, related principles of pecuniary repute are also exemplified in the same contrivances. Other methods of putting one's pecuniary standing in evidence serve their end effectually, and other methods are in vogue always and everywhere; but expenditure on dress has this advantage over most other methods, that our apparel is always in evidence and affords an indication of our pecuniary standing to all observers at the first glance. It is also true that admitted expenditure for display is more obviously present, and is, perhaps, more universally practised in the matter of dress than in any other line of consumption. No one finds difficulty in assenting to the commonplace that the greater part of the expenditure incurred by all classes for apparel is incurred for the sake of a respectable appearance rather than for the protection of the person. And probably at no other point is the sense of shabbiness so keenly felt as it is if we fall short of the standard set by social usage in this matter of dress. It is true of dress in even a higher degree than of most other items of consumption, that people will undergo a very considerable degree of privation in the comforts or the necessaries of life in order to afford what is considered a decent amount of wasteful consumption, so that it is by no means an uncommon occurrence, in an inclement climate, for people to go ill clad in order to appear well dressed. And the commercial value of the goods used for clothing in any modern community is made up to a much larger extent of the fashionableness, the reputability of the goods than of the mechanical service which they render in clothing the person of the wearer. The need of dress is eminently a "higher" or spiritual need.

This spiritual need of dress is not wholly, nor even chiefly, a naïve propensity for display of expenditure. The law of conspicuous waste guides consumption in apparel, as in other things, chiefly at the second remove, by shaping the canons of taste and decency. In the common run of cases the conscious motive of the wearer or purchaser of conspicuously wasteful apparel is the need of conforming to established usage, and of living up to the accredited standard of taste and reputability. It is not only that one must be guided by the code of proprieties in dress in order to avoid the mortification that comes of unfavourable notice and comment, though that motive in itself counts for a great deal; but besides that, the requirement of expensiveness is so ingrained into our habits of thought in matters of dress that any other than expensive apparel is instinctively odious to us. Without reflection or analysis, we feel that what is inexpensive is unworthy. "A cheap coat makes a cheap man." "Cheap and nasty" is recognised to hold true in dress with even less mitigation than in other lines of consumption. On the ground both of taste and of serviceability, an inexpensive article of apparel is held to be inferior, under the maxim "cheap and nasty." We find things beautiful, as well as serviceable, somewhat in proportion as they are costly. With few and inconsequential exceptions, we all find a costly hand-wrought article of apparel much preferable, in point of beauty and of serviceability, to a less expensive imitation of it, however cleverly the spurious article may imitate the costly original; and what offends our sensibilities in the spurious article is not that it falls short in form or colour, or, indeed, in visual effect in any way. The offensive object may be so close an imitation as to defy any but the closest scrutiny; and yet so soon as the counterfeit is detected, its æsthetic value, and its commercial value as well, declines precipitately. Not only that, but it may be asserted with but small risk of contradiction that the æsthetic value of a detected counterfeit in dress declines somewhat in the same proportion as the counterfeit is cheaper than its original. It loses caste æsthetically because it falls to a lower pecuniary grade.

But the function of dress as an evidence of ability to pay does not end with simply showing that the wearer consumes valuable goods in excess of what is required for physical comfort. Simple conspicuous waste of goods is effective and gratifying as far as it goes; it is good *prima facie* evidence of pecuniary success, and consequently *prima facie* evidence of social worth. But dress has subtler and more far-reaching possibilities than this crude, first-hand evidence of wasteful consumption only. If, in addition to showing that the wearer can afford to consume freely and uneconomically, it can also be shown in the same stroke that he or she is not under the necessity of earning a livelihood, the evidence of social worth is enhanced in a very considerable degree. Our dress, therefore, in order to serve its purpose effectually, should not only be expensive, but it should also make plain to all observers that the wearer is not engaged in any kind of productive labour. In the evolutionary process by which our system of dress has been elaborated into its present admirably perfect adaptation to its purpose, this subsidiary line of evidence has received due attention. A detailed examination of what passes in popular apprehension for elegant apparel will show that it is contrived at every point to convey the impression that the wearer does not habitually put forth any useful effort. It goes without saying that no apparel can be considered elegant, or even decent, if it shows the effect of manual labour on the part of the wearer, in the way of soil or wear. The pleasing effect of neat and spotless garments is chiefly, if not altogether, due to their carrying the suggestion of leisure—exemption from personal contact with industrial processes of any kind. Much of the charm that invests the patent-leather shoe, the stainless linen, the lustrous cylindrical hat, and the walking-stick, which so greatly enhance the native dignity of a gentleman, comes of their pointedly suggesting that the wearer cannot when so attired bear a hand in any employment that is directly and immediately of any human use. Elegant dress serves its purpose of elegance not only in that it is expensive, but also because it is the insignia of leisure. It not only shows that the wearer is able to consume a relatively large value, but it argues at the same time that he consumes without producing.

The dress of women goes even farther than that of men in the way of demonstrating the wearer's abstinence from productive employment. It needs no argument to enforce the generalisation that the more elegant styles of feminine bonnets go even farther towards making work impossible than does the man's high hat. The woman's shoe adds the so-called French heel to the evidence of enforced leisure afforded by its polish; because this high heel obviously makes any, even the simplest and most necessary manual work extremely difficult. The like is true even in a higher degree of the skirt and the rest of the drapery which characterises woman's dress. The substantial reason for our tenacious attachment to the skirt is just this: it is expensive and it hampers the wearer at every turn and incapacitates her for all useful exertion. The like is true of the feminine custom of wearing the hair excessively long.

But the woman's apparel not only goes beyond that of the modern man in the degree in which it argues exemption from labour; it also adds a peculiar and highly characteristic feature which differs in kind from anything habitually practised by the men. This feature is the class of contrivances of which the corset is the typical example. The corset is, in economic theory, substantially a mutilation, undergone for the purpose of lowering the subject's vitality and rendering her permanently and obviously unfit for work. It is true, the corset impairs the personal attractions of the wearer, but the loss suffered on that score is offset by the gain in reputability which comes of her visibly increased expensiveness and infirmity. It may broadly be set down that the womanliness of woman's apparel resolves itself, in point of substantial fact, into the more effective hindrance to useful exertion offered by the garments peculiar to women. This difference between masculine and feminine apparel is here simply pointed out as a characteristic feature. The ground of its occurrence will be discussed presently.

So far, then, we have, as the great and dominant norm of dress, the broad principle of conspicuous waste. Subsidiary to this principle, and as a corollary under it, we get as a second norm the principle of conspicuous leisure. In dress construction this norm works out in the shape of divers contrivances going to show that the wearer does not and, as far as it may conveniently be shown, can not engage in productive labour. Beyond these two principles there is a third of scarcely less constraining force, which will occur to any one who reflects at all on the subject. Dress must not only be conspicuously expensive and inconvenient; it must at the same time be up to date. No explanation at all satisfactory has hitherto been offered of the phenomenon of changing fashions. The imperative requirement of dressing in the latest accredited manner, as well as the fact that this accredited fashion constantly changes from season to season, is sufficiently familiar to every one, but the theory of this flux and change has not been worked out. We may of course say, with perfect consistency and truthfulness, that this principle of novelty is another corollary under the law of conspicuous waste. Obviously, if each garment is permitted to serve for but a brief term, and if none of last season's apparel is carried over and made further use of during the present season, the wasteful expenditure on dress is greatly increased. This is good as far as it goes, but it is negative only. Pretty much all that this consideration warrants us in saying is that the norm of conspicuous waste exercises a controlling surveillance in all matters of dress, so that any change in the fashions must conform to the requirement of wastefulness; it leaves unanswered the question as to the motive for making and accepting a change in the prevailing styles, and it also fails to explain why conformity to a given style at a given time is so imperatively necessary as we know it to be.

For a creative principle, capable of serving as motive to invention and innovation in fashions, we shall have to go back to the primitive, non-economic motive with which apparel originated,— the motive of adornment. Without going into an extended discussion of how and why this motive asserts itself under the guidance of the law of expensiveness, it may be stated broadly that each successive innovation in the fashions is an effort to reach some form of display which shall be more acceptable to our sense of form and colour or of effectiveness, than that which it displaces. The changing styles are the expression of a restless search for something which shall commend itself to our æsthetic sense; but as each innovation is subject to the selective action of the norm of conspicuous waste, the range within which innovation can take place is somewhat restricted. The innovation must not only be more beautiful, or perhaps oftener less offensive, than that which it displaces, but it must also come up to the accepted standard of expensiveness.

It would seem at first sight that the result of such an unremitting struggle to attain the beautiful in dress should be a gradual approach to artistic perfection. We might naturally expect that the fashions should show a well-marked trend in the direction of some one or more types of apparel eminently becoming to the human form; and we might even feel that we have substantial ground for the hope that to-day, after all the ingenuity and effort which have been spent on dress these many years, the fashions should have achieved a relative perfection and a relative stability, closely approximating to a permanently tenable artistic ideal. But such is not the case. It would be very hazardous indeed to assert that the styles of to-day are intrinsically more becoming than those of ten years ago, or than those of twenty, or fifty, or one hundred years ago. On the other hand, the assertion freely goes uncontradicted that styles in vogue two thousand years ago are more becoming than the most elaborate and painstaking constructions of to-day.

The explanation of the fashions just offered, then, does not fully explain, and we shall have to look farther. It is well known that certain relatively stable styles and types of costume have been worked out in various parts of the world; as, for instance, among the Japanese, Chinese, and other Oriental nations; likewise among the Greeks,

Romans, and other Eastern peoples of antiquity; so also, in later times, among the peasants of nearly every country of Europe. These national or popular costumes are in most cases adjudged by competent critics to be more becoming, more artistic, than the fluctuating styles of modern civilised apparel. At the same time they are also, at least usually, less obviously wasteful; that is to say, other elements than that of a display of expense are more readily detected in their structure.

These relatively stable costumes are, commonly, pretty strictly and narrowly localised, and they vary by slight and systematic gradations from place to place. They have in every case been worked out by peoples or classes which are poorer than we, and especially they belong in countries and localities and times where the population, or at least the class to which the costume in question belongs, is relatively homogeneous, stable, and immobile. That is to say, stable costumes which will bear the test of time and perspective are worked out under circumstances where the norm of conspicuous waste asserts itself less imperatively than it does in the large modern civilised cities, whose relatively mobile, wealthy population today sets the pace in matters of fashion. The countries and classes which have in this way worked out stable and artistic costumes have been so placed that the pecuniary emulation among them has taken the direction of a competition in conspicuous leisure rather than in conspicuous consumption of goods. So that it will hold true in a general way that fashions are least stable and least becoming in those communities where the principle of a conspicuous waste of goods asserts itself most imperatively, as among ourselves. All this points to an antagonism between expensiveness and artistic apparel. In point of practical fact, the norm of conspicuous waste is incompatible with the requirement that dress should be beautiful or becoming. And this antagonism offers an explanation of that restless change in fashion which neither the canon of expensiveness nor that of beauty alone can account for.

The standard of reputability requires that dress should show wasteful expenditure; but all wastefulness is offensive to native taste. The psychological law has already been pointed out that all men—and women perhaps even in a higher degree—abhor futility, whether of effort or of expenditure,—much as Nature was once said to abhor a vacuum. But the principle of conspicuous waste requires an obviously futile expenditure; and the resulting conspicuous expensiveness of dress is therefore intrinsically ugly. Hence we find that in all innovations in dress, each added or altered detail strives to avoid instant condemnation by showing some ostensible purpose, at the same time that the requirement of conspicuous waste prevents the purposefulness of these innovations from becoming anything more than a somewhat transparent pretence. Even in its freest flights, fashion rarely if ever gets away from a simulation of some ostensible use. The ostensible usefulness of the fashionable details of dress, however, is always so transparent a make-believe, and their substantial futility presently forces itself so baldly upon our attention as to become unbearable, and then we take refuge in a new style. But the new style must conform to the requirement of reputable wastefulness and futility. Its futility presently becomes as odious as that of its predecessor; and the only remedy which the law of waste allows us is to seek relief in some new construction, equally futile and equally untenable. Hence the essential ugliness and the unceasing change of fashionable attire.

Having so explained the phenomenon of shifting fashions, the next thing is to make the explanation tally with everyday facts. Among these everyday facts is the well-known liking which all men have for the styles that are in vogue at any given time. A new style comes into vogue and remains in favour for a season, and, at least so long as it is a novelty, people very generally find the new style attractive. The prevailing fashion is felt to be beautiful. This is due partly to the relief it affords in being different from what went before it, partly to its being reputable. As indicated in the last chapter, the canon of reputability to some extent shapes our tastes, so that under its guidance anything will be accepted as becoming until its novelty wears off, or until the warrant of reputability is transferred to a new and novel structure serving the same general purpose. That the alleged beauty, or "loveliness," of the styles in vogue at any given time is transient and spurious only is attested by the fact that none of the many shifting fashions will bear the test of time. When seen in the perspective of half-a-dozen years or more, the best of our fashions strike us as grotesque, if not unsightly. Our transient attachment to whatever happens to be the latest rests on other than æsthetic grounds, and lasts only until our abiding æsthetic sense has had time to assert itself and reject this latest indigestible contrivance.

The process of developing an æsthetic nausea takes more or less time; the length of time required in any given case being inversely as the degree of intrinsic odiousness of the style in question. This time relation between odiousness and instability in fashions affords ground for the inference that the more rapidly the styles succeed and displace one another, the more offensive they are to sound taste. The presumption, therefore, is that the farther the community, especially the wealthy classes of the community, develop in wealth and mobility and in the range of their human contact, the more imperatively will the law of conspicuous waste assert itself in matters of dress, the more will the sense of beauty tend to fall into abeyance or be overborne by the canon of pecuniary reputability, the more rapidly will fashions shift and change, and the more grotesque and intolerable will be the varying styles that successively come into vogue.

There remains at least one point in this theory of dress yet to be discussed. Most of what has been said applies to men's attire as well as to that of women; although in modern times it applies at nearly all points with greater force to that of women. But at one point the dress of women differs substantially from that of men. In woman's dress there is an obviously greater insistence on such features as testify to the wearer's exemption from or incapacity for all vulgarly productive employment. This characteristic of woman's apparel is of interest, not only as completing the theory of dress, but also as confirming what has already been said of the economic status of women, both in the past and in the present.

As has been seen in the discussion of woman's status under the heads of Vicarious Leisure and Vicarious Consumption, it has in the course of economic development become the office of the woman to consume vicariously for the head of the household; and her apparel is contrived with this object in view. It has come about that obviously productive labour is in a peculiar degree derogatory to respectable women, and therefore special pains should be taken in the construction of women's dress, to impress upon the beholder the fact (often indeed a fiction) that the wearer does not and can not habitually engage in useful work. Propriety requires respectable women to abstain more consistently from useful effort and to make more of a show of leisure than the men of the same social classes. It grates painfully on our nerves to contemplate the necessity of any well-bred woman's earning a livelihood by useful work. It is not "woman's sphere." Her sphere is within the household, which she should "beautify," and of which she should be the "chief orna-ment." The male head of the household is not currently spoken of as its ornament. This feature taken in conjunction with the other fact that propriety requires more unremitting attention to expen-sive display in the dress and other paraphernalia of women, goes to enforce the view already implied in what has gone before. By virtue of its descent from a patriarchal past, our social system makes it the woman's function in an especial degree to put in evidence her household's ability to pay. According to the modern civilised scheme of life, the good name of the household to which she be-longs should be the special care of the woman; and the system of honorific expenditure and conspicuous leisure by which this good name is chiefly sustained is therefore the woman's sphere. In the ideal scheme, as it tends to realise itself in the life of the higher pe-cuniary classes, this attention to conspicuous waste of substance and effort should normally be the sole economic function of the woman.

At the stage of economic development at which the women were still in the full sense the property of the men, the perfor-mance of conspicuous leisure and consumption came to be part of the services required of them. The women being not their own masters, obvious expenditure and leisure on their part would re-dound to the credit of their master rather than to their own credit; and therefore the more expensive and the more obviously unproductive the women of the household are, the more creditable and more effective for the purpose of the reputability of the household or its head will their life be. So much so that the women have been required not only to afford evidence of a life of leisure, but even to disable themselves for useful activity.

It is at this point that the dress of men falls short of that of women, and for a sufficient reason. Conspicuous waste and conspicuous leisure are reputable because they are evidence of pecuniary strength; pecuniary strength is reputable or honorific because, in the last analysis, it argues success and superior force; therefore the evidence of waste and leisure put forth by any individual in his own behalf cannot consistently take such a form or be carried to such a pitch as to argue incapacity or marked discomfort on his part; as the exhibition would in that case show not superior force, but inferiority, and so defeat its own purpose. So, then, wherever wasteful expenditure and the show of abstention from effort is normally, or on an average, carried to the extent of showing obvious discomfort or voluntarily induced physical disability, there the immediate inference is that the individual in question does not perform this wasteful expenditure and undergo this disability for her own personal gain in pecuniary repute, but in behalf of some one else to whom she stands in a relation of economic dependence; a relation which in the last analysis must, in economic theory, reduce itself to a relation of servitude.

To apply this generalisation to women's dress, and put the matter in concrete terms: the high heel, the skirt, the impracticable bonnet, the corset, and the general disregard of the wearer's comfort which is an obvious feature of all civilised women's apparel, are so many items of evidence to the effect that in the modern civilised scheme of life the woman is still, in theory, the economic dependent of the man,—that, perhaps in a highly idealised sense, she still is the man's chattel. The homely reason for all this conspicuous leisure and attire on the part of women lies in the fact that they are servants to whom, in the differentiation of economic functions, has been delegated the office of putting in evidence their master's ability to pay.

There is a marked similarity in these respects between the apparel of women and that of domestic servants, especially liveried servants. In both there is a very elaborate show of unnecessary expensiveness, and in both cases there is also a notable disregard of the physical comfort of the wearer. But the attire of the lady goes farther in its elaborate insistence on the idleness, if not on the physical infirmity of the wearer, than does that of the domestic. And this is as it should be; for in theory, according to the ideal scheme of the pecuniary culture, the lady of the house is the chief menial of the household.

Besides servants, currently recognised as such, there is at least one other class of persons whose garb assimilates them to the class of servants and shows many of the features that go to make up the womanliness of woman's dress. This is the priestly class. Priestly vestments show, in accentuated form, all the features that have been shown to be evidence of a servile status and a vicarious life. Even more strikingly than the everyday habit of the priest, the vestments, properly so called, are ornate, grotesque, inconvenient, and, at least ostensibly, comfortless to the point of distress. The priest is at the same time expected to refrain from useful effort and, when before the public eye, to present an impassively disconsolate countenance, very much after the manner of a well-trained domestic servant. The shaven face of the priest is a further item to the same effect. This assimilation of the priestly class to the class of body servants, in demeanour and apparel, is due to the similarity of the two classes as regards economic function. In economic theory, the priest is a body servant, constructively in attendance upon the person of the divinity whose livery he wears. His livery is of a very expensive character, as it should be in order to set forth in a beseeming manner the dignity of his exalted master; but it is contrived to show that the wearing of it contributes little or nothing to the physical comfort of the wearer, for it is an item of vicarious consumption, and the repute which accrues from its consumption is to be imputed to the absent master, not to the servant.

The line of demarcation between the dress of women, priests, and servants, on the one hand, and of men, on the other hand, is not always consistently observed in practice, but it will scarcely be disputed that it is always present in a more or less definite way in the popular habits of thought. There are of course also free men, and not a few of them, who, in their blind zeal for faultlessly reputable attire, transgress the theoretical line between man's and woman's dress, to the extent of arraying themselves in apparel that is obviously designed to vex the mortal frame; but every one recognises without hesitation that such apparel for men is a departure from the normal. We are in the habit of saying that such dress is "effeminate"; and one sometimes hears the remark that such or such an exquisitely attired gentleman is as well dressed as a footman.

Certain apparent discrepancies under this theory of dress merit a more detailed examination, especially as they mark a more or less evident trend in the later and maturer development of dress. The vogue of the corset offers an apparent exception from the rule of which it has here been cited as an illustration. A closer examination, however, will show that this apparent exception is really a verification of the rule that the vogue of any given element or feature in dress rests on its utility as an evidence of pecuniary standing. It is well known that in the industrially more advanced communities the corset is employed only within certain fairly well defined social strata. The women of the poorer classes, especially of the rural population, do not habitually use it, except as a holiday luxury. Among these classes the women have to work hard, and it avails them little in the way of a pretence of leisure to so crucify the flesh in everyday life. The holiday use of the contrivance is due to imitation of a higher-class canon of decency. Upwards from this low level of indigence and manual labour, the corset was until within a generation or two nearly indispensable to a socially blameless standing for all women, including the wealthiest and most reputable. This rule held so long as there still was no large class of people wealthy enough to be above the imputation of any necessity for manual labour and at the same time large enough to form a self-sufficient, isolated social body whose mass would afford a foundation for special rules of conduct within the class, enforced by the current opinion of the class alone. But now there has grown up a

large enough leisure class possessed of such wealth that any asper-
sion on the score of enforced manual employment would be idle
and harmless calumny; and the corset has therefore in large measure fallen into disuse within this class.

The exceptions under this rule of exemption from the corset are
more apparent than real. They are the wealthy classes of countries
with a lower industrial structure—nearer the archaic, quasi-
industrial type—together with the later accessions of the wealthy
classes in the more advanced industrial communities. The latter
have not yet had time to divest themselves of the plebeian canons
of taste and of reputability carried over from their former, lower
pecuniary grade. Such survival of the corset is not infrequent
among the higher social classes of those American cities, for instance, which have recently and rapidly risen into opulence. If the
word be used as a technical term, without any odious implication,
it may be said that the corset persists in great measure through the
period of snobbery—the interval of uncertainty and of transition
from a lower to the upper levels of pecuniary culture. That is to say,
in all countries which have inherited the corset it continues in use
wherever and so long as it serves its purpose as an evidence of honorific leisure by arguing physical disability in the wearer. The same
rule of course applies to other mutilations and contrivances for decreasing the visible efficiency of the individual.

Something similar should hold true with respect to divers items
of conspicuous consumption, and indeed something of the kind
does seem to hold to a slight degree of sundry features of dress, especially if such features involve a marked discomfort or appearance of discomfort to the wearer. During the past one hundred
years there is a tendency perceptible, in the development of men's
dress especially, to discontinue methods of expenditure and the use
of symbols of leisure which must have been irksome, which may
have served a good purpose in their time, but the continuation of
which among the upper classes to-day would be a work of super-
erogation; as, for instance, the use of powdered wigs and of gold
lace, and the practice of constantly shaving the face. There has of
late years been some slight recrudescence of the shaven face in po-

lite society, but this is probably a transient and unadvised mimicry of the fashion imposed upon body servants, and it may fairly be expected to go the way of the powdered wig of our grandfathers.

These indices, and others which resemble them in point of the boldness with which they point out to all observers the habitual uselessness of those persons who employ them, have been replaced by other, more delicate methods of expressing the same fact; methods which are no less evident to the trained eyes of that smaller, select circle whose good opinion is chiefly sought. The earlier and cruder method of advertisement held its ground so long as the public to which the exhibitor had to appeal comprised large portions of the community who were not trained to detect delicate variations in the evidences of wealth and leisure. The method of advertisement undergoes a refinement when a sufficiently large wealthy class has developed, who have the leisure for acquiring skill in interpreting the subtler signs of expenditure. "Loud" dress becomes offensive to people of taste, as evincing an undue desire to reach and impress the untrained sensibilities of the vulgar. To the individual of high breeding it is only the more honorific esteem accorded by the cultivated sense of the members of his own high class that is of material consequence. Since the wealthy leisure class has grown so large, or the contact of the leisure-class individual with members of his own class has grown so wide, as to constitute a human environment sufficient for the honorific purpose, there arises a tendency to exclude the baser elements of the population from the scheme even as spectators whose applause or mortification should be sought. The result of all this is a refinement of methods, a resort to subtler contrivances, and a spiritualisation of the scheme of symbolism in dress. And as this upper leisure class sets the pace in all matters of decency, the result for the rest of society also is a gradual amelioration of the scheme of dress. As the community advances in wealth and culture, the ability to pay is put in evidence by means which require a progressively nicer discrimination in the beholder. This nicer discrimination between advertising media is in fact a very large element of the higher pecuniary culture.

CHAPTER VIII

INDUSTRIAL EXEMPTION AND CONSERVATISM

The life of man in society, just like the life of other species, is a struggle for existence, and therefore it is a process of selective adaptation. The evolution of social structure has been a process of natural selection of institutions. The progress which has been and is being made in human institutions and in human character may be set down, broadly, to a natural selection of the fittest habits of thought and to a process of enforced adaptation of individuals to an environment which has progressively changed with the growth of the community and with the changing institutions under which men have lived. Institutions are not only themselves the result of a selective and adaptive process which shapes the prevailing or dominant types of spiritual attitude and aptitudes; they are at the same time special methods of life and of human relations, and are therefore in their turn efficient factors of selection. So that the changing institutions in their turn make for a further selection of individuals endowed with the fittest temperament, and a further adaptation of individual temperament and habits to the changing environment through the formation of new institutions.

The forces which have shaped the development of human life and of social structure are no doubt ultimately reducible to terms of living tissue and material environment; but proximately, for the purpose in hand, these forces may best be stated in terms of an environment, partly human, partly non-human, and a human subject with a more or less definite physical and intellectual constitution. Taken in the aggregate or average, this human subject is more or less variable; chiefly, no doubt, under a rule of selective conservation of favourable variations. The selection of favourable variations is perhaps in great measure a selective conservation of ethnic types. In the life history of any community whose population is made up of a mixture of divers ethnic elements, one or another of several persistent and relatively stable types of body and of temperament rises into dominance at any given point. The situation, including the institutions in force at any given time, will favour the survival and dominance of one type of character in preference to another; and the type of man so selected to continue and to further elaborate the institutions handed down from the past will in some considerable measure shape these institutions in his own likeness. But apart from selection as between relatively stable types of character and habits of mind, there is no doubt simultaneously going on a process of selective adaptation of habits of thought within the general range of aptitudes which is characteristic of the dominant ethnic type or types. There may be a variation in the fundamental character of any population by selection between relatively stable types; but there is also a variation due to adaptation in detail within the range of the type, and to selection between specific habitual views regarding any given social relation or group of relations.

For the present purpose, however, the question as to the nature of the adaptive process—whether it is chiefly a selection between stable types of temperament and character, or chiefly an adaptation of men's habits of thought to changing circumstances—is of less importance than the fact that, by one method or another, institutions change and develop. Institutions must change with changing circumstances, since they are of the nature of an habitual method of responding to the stimuli which these changing circumstances afford. The development of these institutions is the development of society. The institutions are, in substance, prevalent habits of thought with respect to particular relations and particular functions of the individual and of the community; and the scheme of life, which is made up of the aggregate of institutions in force at a given time or at a given point in the development of any society, may, on the psychological side, be broadly characterised as a prevalent spiritual attitude or a prevalent theory of life. As regards its generic features, this spiritual attitude or theory of life is in the last analysis reducible to terms of a prevalent type of character.

The situation of to-day shapes the institutions of to-morrow through a selective, coercive process, by acting upon men's habitual view of things, and so altering or fortifying a point of view or a mental attitude handed down from the past. The institutions—that is to say the habits of thought—under the guidance of which men live are in this way received from an earlier time; more or less remotely earlier, but in any event they have been elaborated in and received from the past. Institutions are products of the past process, are adapted to past circumstances, and are therefore never in full accord with the requirements of the present. In the nature of the case, this process of selective adaptation can never catch up with the progressively changing situation in which the community finds itself at any given time; for the environment, the situation, the exigencies of life which enforce the adaptation and exercise the selection, change from day to day; and each successive situation of the community in its turn tends to obsolescence as soon as it has been established. When a step in the development has been taken, this step itself constitutes a change of situation which requires a new adaptation; it becomes the point of departure for a new step in the adjustment, and so on interminably.

It is to be noted then, although it may be a tedious truism, that the institutions of to-day—the present accepted scheme of life—do not entirely fit the situation of to-day. At the same time, men's present habits of thought tend to persist indefinitely, except as circumstances enforce a change. These institutions which have so been handed down, these habits of thought, points of view, mental attitudes and aptitudes, or what not, are therefore themselves a conservative factor. This is the factor of social inertia, psychological inertia, conservatism.

Social structure changes, develops, adapts itself to an altered situation, only through a change in the habits of thought of the several classes of the community; or in the last analysis, through a change in the habits of thought of the individuals which make up the community. The evolution of society is substantially a process of mental adaptation on the part of individuals under the stress of circumstances which will no longer tolerate habits of thought formed under and conforming to a different set of circumstances in the past. For the immediate purpose it need not be a question of serious importance whether this adaptive process is a process of selection and survival of persistent ethnic types or a process of individual adaptation and an inheritance of acquired traits.

Social advance, especially as seen from the point of view of economic theory, consists in a continued progressive approach to an approximately exact "adjustment of inner relations to outer relations"; but this adjustment is never definitely established, since the "outer relations" are subject to constant change as a consequence of the progressive changes going on in the "inner relations." But the degree of approximation may be greater or less, depending on the facility with which an adjustment is made. A readjustment of men's habits of thought to conform with the exigencies of an altered situation is in any case made only tardily and reluctantly, and only under the coercion exercised by a situation which has made the accredited views untenable. The readjustment of institutions and habitual views to an altered environment is made in response to pressure from without; it is of the nature of a response to stimulus. Freedom and facility of readjustment, that is to say capacity for growth in social structure, therefore depends in great measure on the degree of freedom with which the situation at any given time acts on the individual members of the community—the degree of exposure of the individual members to the constraining forces of the environment. If any portion or class of society is sheltered from the action of the environment in any essential respect, that portion of the community, or that class, will adapt its views and its scheme of life more tardily to the altered general situation; it will in so far tend to retard the process of social transformation. The wealthy leisure class is in such a sheltered position with respect to the economic forces that make for change and readjustment. And it may be said that the forces which make for a readjustment of institutions, especially in the case of a modern industrial community, are, in the last analysis, almost entirely of an economic nature.

Any community may be viewed as an industrial or economic mechanism, the structure of which is made up of what is called its economic institutions. These institutions are habitual methods of carrying on the life process of the community in contact with the material environment in which it lives. When given methods of unfolding human activity in this given environment have been elaborated in this way, the life of the community will express itself with some facility in these habitual directions. The community will make use of the forces of the environment for the purposes of its life according to methods learned in the past and embodied in these institutions. But as population increases, and as men's knowledge and skill in directing the forces of nature widen, the habitual methods of relation between the members of the group, and the habitual method of carrying on the life process of the group as a whole, no longer give the same result as before; nor are the resulting conditions of life distributed and apportioned in the same manner or with the same effect among the various members as before. If the scheme according to which the life process of the group was carried on under the earlier conditions gave approximately the highest attainable result—under the circumstances—in the way of efficiency or facility of the life process of the group; then the same scheme of life unaltered will not yield the highest result attainable in this respect under the altered conditions. Under the altered conditions of population, skill, and knowledge, the facility of life as carried on according to the traditional scheme may not be lower than under the earlier conditions; but the chances are always that it is less than might be if the scheme were altered to suit the altered conditions.

The group is made up of individuals, and the group's life is the life of individuals carried on in at least ostensible severalty. The group's accepted scheme of life is the consensus of views held by the body of these individuals as to what is right, good, expedient, and beautiful in the way of human life. In the redistribution of the conditions of life that comes of the altered method of dealing with the environment, the outcome is not an equable change in the facility of life throughout the group. The altered conditions may increase the facility of life for the group as a whole, but the redistribution will usually result in a decrease of facility or fulness of life for some members of the group. An advance in technical methods, in population, or in industrial organisation will require at least some of the members of the community to change their habits of life, if they are to enter with facility and effect into the altered industrial methods; and in doing so they will be unable to live up to the received notions as to what are the right and beautiful habits of life.

Any one who is required to change his habits of life and his habitual relations to his fellow-men will feel the discrepancy between the method of life required of him by the newly arisen exigencies, and the traditional scheme of life to which he is accustomed. It is the individuals placed in this position who have the liveliest incentive to reconstruct the received scheme of life and are most readily persuaded to accept new standards; and it is through the need of the means of livelihood that men are placed in such a position. The pressure exerted by the environment upon the group, and making for a readjustment of the group's scheme of life, impinges upon the members of the group in the form of pecuniary exigencies; and it is owing to this fact—that external forces are in great part translated into the form of pecuniary or economic exigencies—it is owing to this fact that we can say that the forces which count toward a readjustment of institutions in any modern industrial community are chiefly economic forces; or more specifically, these forces take the form of pecuniary pressure. Such a readjustment as is here contemplated is substantially a change in men's views as to what is good and right, and the means through which a change is wrought in men's apprehension of what is good and right is in large part the pressure of pecuniary exigencies.

Any change in men's views as to what is good and right in human life makes its way but tardily at the best. Especially is this true of any change in the direction of what is called progress; that is to say, in the direction of divergence from the archaic position—from the position which may be accounted the point of departure at any step in the social evolution of the community. Retrogression, reapproach to a standpoint to which the race has been long habituated in the past, is easier. This is especially true in case the development away from this past standpoint has not been due chiefly to a substitution of an ethnic type whose temperament is alien to the earlier standpoint.

The cultural stage which lies immediately back of the present in the life history of Western civilisation is what has here been called the quasi-peaceable stage. At this quasi-peaceable stage the law of status is the dominant feature in the scheme of life. There is no need of pointing out how prone the men of to-day are to revert to the spiritual attitude of mastery and of personal subservience which characterises that stage. It may rather be said to be held in an uncertain abeyance by the economic exigencies of to-day, than to have been definitively supplanted by a habit of mind that is in full accord with these later-developed exigencies. The predatory and quasi-peaceable stages of economic evolution seem to have been of long duration in the life history of all the chief ethnic elements which go to make up the populations of the Western culture. The temperament and the propensities proper to those cultural stages have, therefore, attained such a persistence as to make a speedy reversion to the broad features of the corresponding psychological constitution inevitable in the case of any class or community which is removed from the action of those forces that make for a maintenance of the later-developed habits of thought.

It is a matter of common notoriety that when individuals, or even considerable groups of men, are segregated from a higher industrial culture and exposed to a lower cultural environment, or to an economic situation of a more primitive character, they quickly show evidence of reversion toward the spiritual features which characterise the predatory type; and it seems probable that the dolicho-blond type of European man is possessed of a greater facility for such reversion to barbarism than the other ethnic elements with which that type is associated in the Western culture. Examples of such a reversion on a small scale abound in the later history of migration and colonisation. Except for the fear of offending that chauvinistic patriotism which is so characteristic a feature of the predatory culture, and the presence of which is frequently the most striking mark of reversion in modern communities, the case of the American colonies might be cited as an example of such a reversion on an unusually large scale, though it was not a reversion of very large scope.

—

The leisure class is in great measure sheltered from the stress of those economic exigencies which prevail in any modern, highly organised industrial community. The exigencies of the struggle for the means of life are less exacting for this class than for any other; and as a consequence of this privileged position we should expect to find it one of the least responsive of the classes of society to the demands which the situation makes for a further growth of institutions and a readjustment to an altered industrial situation. The leisure class is the conservative class. The exigencies of the general economic situation of the community do not freely or directly impinge upon the members of this class. They are not required under penalty of forfeiture to change their habits of life and their theoretical views of the external world to suit the demands of an altered industrial technique, since they are not in the full sense an organic part of the industrial community. Therefore these exigencies do not readily produce, in the members of this class, that degree of uneasiness with the existing order which alone can lead any body of men to give up views and methods of life that have become habitual to them. The office of the leisure class in social evolution is to retard the movement and to conserve what is obsolescent. This proposition is by no means novel; it has long been one of the commonplaces of popular opinion.

The prevalent conviction that the wealthy class is by nature conservative has been popularly accepted without much aid from any theoretical view as to the place and relation of that class in the cultural development. When an explanation of this class conservatism is offered, it is commonly the invidious one that the wealthy class opposes innovation because it has a vested interest, of an unworthy sort, in maintaining the present conditions. The explanation here put forward imputes no unworthy motive. The opposition of the class to changes in the cultural scheme is instinctive, and does not rest primarily on an interested calculation of material advantages; it is an instinctive revulsion at any departure from the accepted way of doing and of looking at things—a revulsion common to all men and only to be overcome by stress of circumstances. All change in habits of life and of thought is irksome. The difference in this respect between the wealthy and the common run of mankind lies not so much in the motive which prompts to conservatism as in the degree of exposure to the economic forces that urge a change. The members of the wealthy class do not yield to the demand for innovation as readily as other men because they are not constrained to do so.

This conservatism of the wealthy class is so obvious a feature that it has even come to be recognised as a mark of respectability. Since conservatism is a characteristic of the wealthier and therefore more reputable portion of the community, it has acquired a certain honorific or decorative value. It has become prescriptive to such an extent that an adherence to conservative views is comprised as a matter of course in our notions of respectability; and it is imperatively incumbent on all who would lead a blameless life in point of social repute. Conservatism, being an upper-class characteristic, is decorous; and conversely, innovation, being a lower-class phenomenon, is vulgar. The first and most unreflected element in that instinctive revulsion and reprobation with which we turn from all social innovators is this sense of the essential vulgarity of the thing. So that even in cases where one recognises the substantial merits of the case for which the innovator is spokesman—as may easily happen if the evils which he seeks to remedy are sufficiently remote in point of time or space or personal contact—still one cannot but be sensible of the fact that the innovator is a person with whom it is at least distasteful to be associated, and from whose social contact one must shrink. Innovation is bad form.

The fact that the usages, actions, and views of the well-to-do leisure class acquire the character of a prescriptive canon of conduct for the rest of society, gives added weight and reach to the conservative influence of that class. It makes it incumbent upon all reputable people to follow their lead. So that, by virtue of its high position as the avatar of good form, the wealthier class comes to exert a retarding influence upon social development far in excess of that which the simple numerical strength of the class would assign it. Its prescriptive example acts to greatly stiffen the resistance of all other classes against any innovation, and to fix men's affections upon the good institutions handed down from an earlier generation.

There is a second way in which the influence of the leisure class acts in the same direction, so far as concerns hindrance to the adoption of a conventional scheme of life more in accord with the exigencies of the time. This second method of upper-class guidance is not in strict consistency to be brought under the same category as the instinctive conservatism and aversion to new modes of thought just spoken of; but it may as well be dealt with here, since it has at least this much in common with the conservative habit of mind that it acts to retard innovation and the growth of social structure. The code of proprieties, conventionalities, and usages in vogue at any given time and among any given people has more or less of the character of an organic whole; so that any appreciable change in one point of the scheme involves something of a change or readjustment at other points also, if not a reorganisation all along the line. When a change is made which immediately touches only a minor point in the scheme, the consequent derangement of the structure of conventionalities may be inconspicuous; but even in such a case it is safe to say that some derangement of the general scheme, more or less far-reaching, will follow. On the other hand, when an attempted reform involves the suppression or thoroughgoing remodelling of an institution of first-rate importance in the conventional scheme, it is immediately felt that a serious derangement of the entire scheme would result; it is felt that a readjustment of the structure to the new form taken on by one of its chief elements would be a painful and tedious, if not a doubtful process.

In order to realise the difficulty which such a radical change in any one feature of the conventional scheme of life would involve, it is only necessary to suggest the suppression of the monogamic family, or of the agnatic system of consanguinity, or of private property, or of the theistic faith, in any country of the Western civilisation; or suppose the suppression of ancestor worship in China, or of the caste system in India, or of slavery in Africa, or the establishment of equality of the sexes in Mohammedan countries. It needs no argument to show that the derangement of the general structure of conventionalities in any of these cases would be very considerable. In order to effect such an innovation a very far-reaching alteration of men's habits of thought would be involved also at other points of the scheme than the one immediately in question. The aversion to any such innovation amounts to a shrinking from an essentially alien scheme of life.

The revulsion felt by good people at any proposed departure from the accepted methods of life is a familiar fact of everyday experience. It is not unusual to hear those persons who dispense salutary advice and admonition to the community express themselves forcibly upon the far-reaching pernicious effects which the community would suffer from such relatively slight changes as the disestablishment of the Anglican Church, an increased facility of divorce, adoption of female suffrage, prohibition of the manufacture and sale of intoxicating beverages, abolition or restriction of inheritance, etc. Any one of these innovations would, we are told, "shake the social structure to its base," "reduce society to chaos," "subvert the foundations of morality," "make life intolerable," "confound the order of nature," etc. These various locutions are, no doubt, of the nature of hyperbole; but, at the same time, like all overstatement, they are evidence of a lively sense of the gravity of the consequences which they are intended to describe. The effect of these and like innovations in deranging the accepted scheme of

life is felt to be of much graver consequence than the simple alteration of an isolated item in a series of contrivances for the convenience of men in society. What is true in so obvious a degree of
innovations of first-rate importance is true in a less degree of
changes of a smaller immediate importance. The aversion to
change is in large part an aversion to the bother of making the
readjustment which any given change will necessitate; and this solidarity of the system of institutions of any given culture or of any
given people strengthens the instinctive resistance offered to any
change in men's habits of thought, even in matters which, taken by
themselves, are of minor importance.

A consequence of this increased reluctance, due to the solidarity of human institutions, is that any innovation calls for a greater
expenditure of nervous energy in making the necessary readjustment than would otherwise be the case. It is not only that a change
in established habits of thought is distasteful. The process of readjustment of the accepted theory of life involves a degree of mental
effort—a more or less protracted and laborious effort to find and to
keep one's bearings under the altered circumstances. This process
requires a certain expenditure of energy, and so presumes, for its
successful accomplishment, some surplus of energy beyond that
absorbed in the daily struggle for subsistence. Consequently it follows that progress is hindered by underfeeding and excessive physical hardship, no less effectually than by such a luxurious life as will
shut out discontent by cutting off the occasion for it. The abjectly
poor, and all those persons whose energies are entirely absorbed by
the struggle for daily sustenance, are conservative because they
cannot afford the effort of taking thought for the day after to-
morrow; just as the highly prosperous are conservative because
they have small occasion to be discontented with the situation as it
stands to-day.

From this proposition it follows that the institution of a leisure
class acts to make the lower classes conservative by withdrawing
from them as much as it may of the means of sustenance, and so re-
ducing their consumption, and consequently their available energy,
to such a point as to make them incapable of the effort required for

the learning and adoption of new habits of thought. The accumulation of wealth at the upper end of the pecuniary scale implies privation at the lower end of the scale. It is a commonplace that, wherever it occurs, a considerable degree of privation among the body of the people is a serious obstacle to any innovation.

This direct inhibitory effect of the unequal distribution of wealth is seconded by an indirect effect tending to the same result. As has already been seen, the imperative example set by the upper class in fixing the canons of reputability fosters the practice of conspicuous consumption. The prevalence of conspicuous consumption as one of the main elements in the standard of decency among all classes is of course not traceable wholly to the example of the wealthy leisure class, but the practice and the insistence on it are no doubt strengthened by the example of the leisure class. The requirements of decency in this matter are very considerable and very imperative; so that even among classes whose pecuniary position is sufficiently strong to admit a consumption of goods considerably in excess of the subsistence minimum, the disposable surplus left over after the more imperative physical needs are satisfied is not infrequently diverted to the purpose of a conspicuous decency, rather than to added physical comfort and fulness of life. Moreover, such surplus energy as is available is also likely to be expended in the acquisition of goods for conspicuous consumption or conspicuous hoarding. The result is that the requirements of pecuniary reputability tend (1) to leave but a scanty subsistence minimum available for other than conspicuous consumption, and (2) to absorb any surplus energy which may be available after the bare physical necessities of life have been provided for. The outcome of the whole is a strengthening of the general conservative attitude of the community. The institution of a leisure class hinders cultural development immediately (1) by the inertia proper to the class itself, (2) through its prescriptive example of conspicuous waste and of conservatism, and (3) indirectly through that system of unequal distribution of wealth and sustenance on which the institution itself rests.

To this is to be added that the leisure class has also a material interest in leaving things as they are. Under the circumstances prevailing at any given time this class is in a privileged position, and any departure from the existing order may be expected to work to the detriment of the class rather than the reverse. The attitude of the class, simply as influenced by its class interest, should therefore be to let well-enough alone. This interested motive comes in to supplement the strong instinctive bias of the class, and so to render it even more consistently conservative than it otherwise would be.

All this, of course, has nothing to say in the way of eulogy or deprecation of the office of the leisure class as an exponent and vehicle of conservatism or reversion in social structure. The inhibition which it exercises may be salutary or the reverse. Whether it is the one or the other in any given case is a question of casuistry rather than of general theory. There may be truth in the view (as a question of policy) so often expressed by the spokesmen of the conservative element, that without some such substantial and consistent resistance to innovation as is offered by the conservative well-to-do classes, social innovation and experiment would hurry the community into untenable and intolerable situations; the only possible result of which would be discontent and disastrous reaction. All this, however, is beside the present argument.

But apart from all deprecation, and aside from all question as to the indispensability of some such check on headlong innovation, the leisure class, in the nature of things, consistently acts to retard that adjustment to the environment which is called social advance or development. The characteristic attitude of the class may be summed up in the maxim: "Whatever is, is right"; whereas the law of natural selection, as applied to human institutions, gives the axiom: "Whatever is, is wrong." Not that the institutions of to-day are wholly wrong for the purposes of the life of to-day, but they are, always and in the nature of things, wrong to some extent. They are the result of a more or less inadequate adjustment of the methods of living to a situation which prevailed at some point in the past development; and they are therefore wrong by something more than the interval which separates the present situation from that of the past. "Right" and "wrong" are of course here used without conveying any reflection as to what ought or ought not to be. They are applied simply from the (morally colourless) evolutionary stand-point, and are intended to designate compatibility or incompatibility with the effective evolutionary process. The institution of a leisure class, by force of class interest and instinct, and by precept and prescriptive example, makes for the perpetuation of the existing maladjustment of institutions, and even favours a reversion to a somewhat more archaic scheme of life; a scheme which would be still farther out of adjustment with the exigencies of life under the existing situation even than the accredited, obsolescent scheme that has come down from the immediate past.

But after all has been said on the head of conservation of the good old ways, it remains true that institutions change and develop. There is a cumulative growth of customs and habits of thought; a selective adaptation of conventions and methods of life. Something is to be said of the office of the leisure class in guiding this growth as well as in retarding it; but little can be said here of its relation to institutional growth except as it touches the institutions that are primarily and immediately of an economic character. These institutions—the economic structure—may be roughly distinguished into two classes or categories, according as they serve one or the other of two divergent purposes of economic life.

To adapt the classical terminology, they are institutions of acquisition or of production; or to revert to terms already employed in a different connection in earlier chapters, they are pecuniary or industrial institutions; or in still other terms, they are institutions serving either the invidious or the non-invidious economic interest. The former category have to do with "business," the latter with industry, taking the latter word in the mechanical sense. The latter class are not often recognised as institutions, in great part because they do not immediately concern the ruling class, and are, therefore, seldom the subject of legislation or of deliberate convention. When they do receive attention they are commonly approached from the pecuniary or business side; that being the side or phase of economic life that chiefly occupies men's deliberations in our time, especially the deliberations of the upper classes. These classes have little else than a business interest in things economic, and on them at the same time it is chiefly incumbent to deliberate upon the community's affairs.

The relation of the leisure (that is, propertied non-industrial) class to the economic process is a pecuniary relation—a relation of acquisition, not of production; of exploitation, not of serviceability. Indirectly their economic office may, of course, be of the utmost importance to the economic life process; and it is by no means here intended to depreciate the economic function of the propertied class or of the captains of industry. The purpose is simply to point out what is the nature of the relation of these classes to the industrial process and to economic institutions. Their office is of a parasitic character, and their interest is to divert what substance they may to their own use, and to retain whatever is under their hand. The conventions of the business world have grown up under the selective surveillance of this principle of predation or parasitism. They are conventions of ownership; derivatives, more or less remote, of the ancient predatory culture. But these pecuniary institutions do not entirely fit the situation of to-day, for they have grown up under a past situation differing somewhat from the present. Even for effectiveness in the pecuniary way, therefore, they are not as apt as might be. The changed industrial life requires changed methods of acquisition; and the pecuniary classes have some interest in so adapting the pecuniary institutions as to give them the best effect for acquisition of private gain that is compatible with the continuance of the industrial process out of which this gain arises. Hence there is a more or less consistent trend in the leisure-class guidance of institutional growth, answering to the pecuniary ends which shape leisure-class economic life.

The effect of the pecuniary interest and the pecuniary habit of mind upon the growth of institutions is seen in those enactments and conventions that make for security of property, enforcement of contracts, facility of pecuniary transactions, vested interests. Of such bearing are changes affecting bankruptcy and receiverships, limited liability, banking and currency, coalitions of labourers or employers, trusts and pools. The community's institutional furniture of this kind is of immediate consequence only to the propertied classes, and in proportion as they are propertied; that is to say, in proportion as they are to be ranked with the leisure class. But indirectly these conventions of business life are of the gravest consequence for the industrial process and for the life of the community. And in guiding the institutional growth in this respect, the pecuniary classes, therefore, serve a purpose of the most serious importance to the community, not only in the conservation of the accepted social scheme, but also in shaping the industrial process proper.

The immediate end of this pecuniary institutional structure and of its amelioration is the greater facility of peaceable and orderly exploitation; but its remoter effects far outrun this immediate object. Not only does the more facile conduct of business permit industry and extra-industrial life to go on with less perturbation; but the resulting elimination of disturbances and complications calling for an exercise of astute discrimination in everyday affairs acts to make the pecuniary class itself superfluous. As fast as pecuniary transactions are reduced to routine, the captain of industry can be dispensed with. This consummation, it is needless to say, lies yet in the indefinite future. The ameliorations wrought in favour of the pecuniary interest in modern institutions tend, in another field, to substitute the "soulless" joint-stock corporation for the captain, and so they make also for the dispensability of the great leisure-class function of ownership. Indirectly, therefore, the bent given to the growth of economic institutions by the leisure-class influence is of very considerable industrial consequence.

CHAPTER IX

THE CONSERVATION OF ARCHAIC TRAITS

The institution of a leisure class has an effect not only upon social structure but also upon the individual character of the members of society. So soon as a given proclivity or a given point of view has won acceptance as an authoritative standard or norm of life it will react upon the character of the members of the society which has accepted it as a norm. It will to some extent shape their habits of thought and will exercise a selective surveillance over the development of men's aptitudes and inclinations. This effect is wrought partly by a coercive, educational adaptation of the habits of all individuals, partly by a selective elimination of the unfit individuals and lines of descent. Such human material as does not lend itself to the methods of life imposed by the accepted scheme suffers more or less elimination as well as repression. The principles of pecuniary emulation and of industrial exemption have in this way been erected into canons of life, and have become coercive factors of some importance in the situation to which men have to adapt themselves.

These two broad principles of conspicuous waste and industrial exemption affect the cultural development both by guiding men's habits of thought, and so controlling the growth of institutions, and by selectively conserving certain traits of human nature that conduce to facility of life under the leisure-class scheme, and so controlling the effective temper of the community. The proximate tendency of the institution of a leisure class in shaping human character runs in the direction of spiritual survival and reversion. Its effect upon the temper of a community is of the nature of an arrested spiritual development. In the later culture especially, the institution has, on the whole, a conservative trend. This proposition is familiar enough in substance, but it may to many have the appearance of novelty in its present application. Therefore a summary review of its logical grounds may not be uncalled for, even at the risk of some tedious repetition and formulation of commonplaces.

Social evolution is a process of selective adaptation of temperament and habits of thought under the stress of the circumstances of associated life. The adaptation of habits of thought is the growth of institutions. But along with the growth of institutions has gone a change of a more substantial character. Not only have the habits of men changed with the changing exigencies of the situation, but these changing exigencies have also brought about a correlative change in human nature. The human material of society itself varies with the changing conditions of life. This variation of human nature is held by the later ethnologists to be a process of selection between several relatively stable and persistent ethnic types or ethnic elements. Men tend to revert or to breed true, more or less closely, to one or another of certain types of human nature that have in their main features been fixed in approximate conformity to a situation in the past which differed from the situation of to-day. There are several of these relatively stable ethnic types of mankind comprised in the populations of the Western culture. These ethnic types survive in the race inheritance to-day, not as rigid and invariable moulds, each of a single precise and specific pattern, but in the form of a greater or smaller number of variants. Some variation of the ethnic types has resulted under the protracted selective process to which the several types and their hybrids have been subjected during the prehistoric and historic growth of culture.

This necessary variation of the types themselves, due to a selective process of considerable duration and of a consistent trend, has not been sufficiently noticed by the writers who have discussed ethnic survival. The argument is here concerned with two main divergent variants of human nature resulting from this, relatively late, selective adaptation of the ethnic types comprised in the Western culture; the point of interest being the probable effect of the situation of to-day in furthering variation along one or the other of these two divergent lines.

The ethnological position may be briefly summed up; and in order to avoid any but the most indispensable detail the schedule of types and variants and the scheme of reversion and survival in which they are concerned are here presented with a diagrammatic meagreness and simplicity which would not be admissible for any other purpose. The man of our industrial communities tends to breed true to one or the other of three main ethnic types: the dolichocephalic-blond, the brachycephalic-brunette, and the Mediterranean—disregarding minor and outlying elements of our culture. But within each of these main ethnic types the reversion tends to one or the other of at least two main directions of variation; the peaceable or ante-predatory variant and the predatory variant. The former of these two characteristic variants is nearer to the generic type in each case, being the reversional representative of its type as it stood at the earliest stage of associated life of which there is available evidence, either archæological or psychological. This variant is taken to represent the ancestors of existing civilised man at the peaceable, savage phase of life which preceded the predatory culture, the régime of status, and the growth of pecuniary emulation. The second or predatory variant of the types is taken to be a survival of a more recent modification of the main ethnic types and their hybrids,—of these types as they were modified, mainly by a selective adaptation, under the discipline of the predatory culture and the later emulative culture of the quasi-peaceable stage, or the pecuniary culture proper.

Under the recognised laws of heredity there may be a survival from a more or less remote past phase. In the ordinary, average, or normal case, if the type has varied, the traits of the type are transmitted approximately as they have stood in the recent past—which may be called the hereditary present. For the purpose in hand this hereditary present is represented by the later predatory and the quasi-peaceable culture.

It is to the variant of human nature which is characteristic of this recent—hereditarily still existing—predatory or quasi-predatory culture that the modern civilised man tends to breed true in the common run of cases. This proposition requires some qualification so far as concerns the descendants of the servile or repressed classes of barbarian times, but the qualification necessary is probably not so great as might at first thought appear. Taking the population as a whole, this predatory, emulative variant does not seem to have attained a high degree of consistency or stability. That is to say, the human nature inherited by modern Occidental man is not nearly uniform in respect of the range or the relative strength of the various aptitudes and propensities which go to make it up. The man of the hereditary present is slightly archaic as judged for the purposes of the latest exigencies of associated life. And the type to which the modern man chiefly tends to revert under the law of variation is a somewhat more archaic human nature. On the other hand, to judge by the reversional traits which show themselves in individuals that vary from the prevailing predatory style of temperament, the ante-predatory variant seems to have a greater stability and greater symmetry in the distribution or relative force of its temperamental elements.

This divergence of inherited human nature, as between an earlier and a later variant of the ethnic type to which the individual tends to breed true, is traversed and obscured by a similar divergence between the two or three main ethnic types that go to make up the Occidental populations. The individuals in these communities are conceived to be, in virtually every instance, hybrids of the prevailing ethnic elements combined in the most varied proportions; with the result that they tend to take back to one or the other of the component ethnic types. These ethnic types differ in temperament in a way somewhat similar to the difference between the predatory and the ante-predatory variants of the types; the dolicho-blond type showing more of the characteristics of the predatory temperament—or at least more of the violent disposition—than the brachycephalic-brunette type, and especially more than the Mediterranean. When the growth of institutions or of the effective sentiment of a given community shows a divergence from the predatory human nature, therefore, it is impossible to say with certainty that such a divergence indicates a reversion to the ante-predatory variant. It may be due to an increasing dominance of the one or the other of the "lower" ethnic elements in the population. Still, although the evidence is not as conclusive as might be desired, there are indications that the variations in the effective temperament of modern communities is not altogether due to a selection between stable ethnic types. It seems to be to some appreciable extent a selection between the predatory and the peaceable variants of the several types.

This conception of contemporary human evolution is not indispensable to the discussion. The general conclusions reached by the use of these concepts of selective adaptation would remain substantially true if the earlier, Darwinian and Spencerian, terms and concepts were substituted. Under the circumstances, some latitude may be admissible in the use of terms. The word "type" is used loosely, to denote variations of temperament which the ethnologists would perhaps recognise only as trivial variants of the type rather than as distinct ethnic types. Wherever a closer discrimination seems essential to the argument, the effort to make such a closer discrimination will be evident from the context.

The ethnic types of to-day, then, are variants of the primitive racial types. They have suffered some alteration, and have attained some degree of fixity in their altered form, under the discipline of the barbarian culture. The man of the hereditary present is the barbarian variant, servile or aristocratic, of the ethnic elements that constitute him. But this barbarian variant has not attained the highest degree of homogeneity or of stability. The barbarian culture— the predatory and quasi-peaceable cultural stages—though of great absolute duration, has been neither protracted enough nor invariable enough in character to give an extreme fixity of type. Variations from the barbarian human nature occur with some frequency, and these cases of variation are becoming more noticeable to-day, because the conditions of modern life no longer act consistently to repress departures from the barbarian normal. The predatory temperament does not lend itself to all the purposes of modern life, and more especially not to modern industry.

Departures from the human nature of the hereditary present are most frequently of the nature of reversions to an earlier variant of the type. This earlier variant is represented by the temperament which characterises the primitive phase of peaceable savagery. The circumstances of life and the ends of effort that prevailed before the advent of the barbarian culture, shaped human nature and fixed it as regards certain fundamental traits. And it is to these ancient, generic features that modern men are prone to take back in case of variation from the human nature of the hereditary present. The conditions under which men lived in the most primitive stages of associated life that can properly be called human, seem to have been of a peaceful kind; and the character—the temperament and spiritual attitude—of men under these early conditions of environment and institutions seems to have been of a peaceful and un-aggressive, not to say an indolent, cast. For the immediate purpose this peaceable cultural stage may be taken to mark the initial phase of social development. So far as concerns the present argument, the dominant spiritual feature of this presumptive initial phase of culture seems to have been an unreflecting, unformulated sense of group solidarity, largely expressing itself in a complacent, but by no means strenuous, sympathy with all facility of human life, and an uneasy revulsion against apprehended inhibition or futility of life. Through its ubiquitous presence in the habits of thought of the ante-predatory savage man, this pervading but uneager sense of the generically useful seems to have exercised an appreciable constraining force upon his life and upon the manner of his habitual contact with other members of the group.

The traces of this initial, undifferentiated peaceable phase of culture seem faint and doubtful if we look merely to such categorical evidence of its existence as is afforded by usages and views in vogue within the historical present, whether in civilised or in rude communities; but less dubious evidence of its existence is to be found in psychological survivals, in the way of persistent and pervading traits of human character. These traits survive perhaps in an especial degree among those ethnic elements which were crowded into the background during the predatory culture. Traits that were suited to the earlier habits of life then became relatively useless in the individual struggle for existence. And those elements of the population, or those ethnic groups, which were by temperament less fitted to the predatory life were repressed and pushed into the background.

On the transition to the predatory culture the character of the struggle for existence changed in some degree from a struggle of the group against a non-human environment to a struggle against a human environment. This change was accompanied by an increasing antagonism and consciousness of antagonism between the individual members of the group. The conditions of success within the group, as well as the conditions of the survival of the group, changed in some measure; and the dominant spiritual attitude of the group gradually changed, and brought a different range of aptitudes and propensities into the position of legitimate dominance in the accepted scheme of life. Among these archaic traits that are to be regarded as survivals from the peaceable cultural phase, are that instinct of race solidarity which we call conscience, including the sense of truthfulness and equity, and the instinct of workmanship, in its naïve, non-invidious expression.

Under the guidance of the later biological and psychological science, human nature will have to be restated in terms of habit; and in the restatement, this, in outline, appears to be the only assignable place and ground of these traits. These habits of life are of too pervading a character to be ascribed to the influence of a late or brief discipline. The ease with which they are temporarily overborne by the special exigencies of recent and modern life argues that these habits are the surviving effects of a discipline of extremely ancient date, from the teachings of which men have frequently been constrained to depart in detail under the altered circumstances of a later time; and the almost ubiquitous fashion in which they assert themselves whenever the pressure of special exigencies is relieved, argues that the process by which the traits were fixed and incorporated into the spiritual make-up of the type must have lasted for a relatively very long time and without serious intermission. The point is not seriously affected by any question as to whether it was a process of habituation in the old-fashioned sense of the word or a process of selective adaptation of the race.

The character and exigencies of life, under that régime of status and of individual and class antithesis which covers the entire interval from the beginning of predatory culture to the present, argue that the traits of temperament here under discussion could scarcely have arisen and acquired fixity during that interval. It is entirely probable that these traits have come down from an earlier method of life, and have survived through the interval of predatory and quasi-peaceable culture in a condition of incipient, or at least imminent, desuetude, rather than that they have been brought out and fixed by this later culture. They appear to be hereditary characteristics of the race, and to have persisted in spite of the altered requirements of success under the predatory and the later pecuniary stages of culture. They seem to have persisted by force of the tenacity of transmission that belongs to an hereditary trait that is present in some degree in every member of the species, and which therefore rests on a broad basis of race continuity.

Such a generic feature is not readily eliminated, even under a process of selection so severe and protracted as that to which the traits here under discussion were subjected during the predatory and quasi-peaceable stages. These peaceable traits are in great part alien to the methods and the animus of barbarian life. The salient characteristic of the barbarian culture is an unremitting emulation and antagonism between classes and between individuals. This emulative discipline favours those individuals and lines of descent which possess the peaceable savage traits in a relatively slight degree. It therefore tends to eliminate these traits, and it has apparently weakened them, in an appreciable degree, in the populations that have been subject to it. Even where the extreme penalty for non-conformity to the barbarian type of temperament is not paid, there results at least a more or less consistent repression of the non-conforming individuals and lines of descent. Where life is largely a struggle between individuals within the group, the possession of the ancient peaceable traits in a marked degree would hamper an individual in the struggle for life.

Under any known phase of culture, other or later than the presumptive initial phase here spoken of, the gifts of good-nature, equity, and indiscriminate sympathy do not appreciably further the life of the individual. Their possession may serve to protect the individual from hard usage at the hands of a majority that insists on a modicum of these ingredients in their ideal of a normal man; but apart from their indirect and negative effect in this way, the individual fares better under the régime of competition in proportion as he has less of these gifts. Freedom from scruple, from sympathy, honesty and regard for life, may, within fairly wide limits, be said to further the success of the individual in the pecuniary culture. The highly successful men of all times have commonly been of this type; except those whose success has not been scored in terms of either wealth or power. It is only within narrow limits, and then only in a Pickwickian[1] sense, that honesty is the best policy.

As seen from the point of view of life under modern civilised conditions in an enlightened community of the Western culture, the primitive, ante-predatory savage, whose character it has been attempted to trace in outline above, was not a great success. Even for the purposes of that hypothetical culture to which his type of human nature owes what stability it has—even for the ends of the peaceable savage group—this primitive man has quite as many and as conspicuous economic failings as he has economic virtues,—as should be plain to any one whose sense of the case is not biassed by leniency born of a fellow-feeling. At his best he is "a clever, good-for-nothing fellow." The shortcomings of this presumptively primitive type of character are weakness, inefficiency, lack of initiative and ingenuity, and a yielding and indolent amiability, together with a lively but inconsequential animistic sense. Along with these traits go certain others which have some value for the collective life process, in the sense that they further the facility of life in the group. These traits are truthfulness, peaceableness, good-will, and a non-emulative, non-invidious interest in men and things.

With the advent of the predatory stage of life there comes a change in the requirements of the successful human character. Men's habits of life are required to adapt themselves to new exigencies under a new scheme of human relations. The same unfolding of energy, which had previously found expression in the traits of savage life recited above, is now required to find expression along a new line of action, in a new group of habitual responses to altered stimuli. The methods which, as counted in terms of facility of life, answered measurably under the earlier conditions, are no longer adequate under the new conditions. The earlier situation was characterised by a relative absence of antagonism or differentiation of interests, the later situation by an emulation constantly increasing in intensity and narrowing in scope. The traits which characterise the predatory and subsequent stages of culture, and which indicate the types of man best fitted to survive under the régime of status, are (in their primary expression) ferocity, self-seeking, clannishness, and disingenuousness—a free resort to force and fraud.

Under the severe and protracted discipline of the régime of competition, the selection of ethnic types has acted to give a somewhat pronounced dominance to these traits of character, by favouring the survival of those ethnic elements which are most richly endowed in these respects. At the same time the earlier-acquired, more generic habits of the race have never ceased to have some usefulness for the purposes of the life of the collectivity and have never fallen into definitive abeyance.

It may be worth while to point out that the dolicho-blond type of European man seems to owe much of its dominating influence and its masterful position in the recent culture to its possessing the characteristics of predatory man in an exceptional degree. These spiritual traits, together with a large endowment of physical energy,—itself probably a result of selection between groups and between lines of descent,—chiefly go to place any ethnic element in the position of a leisure or master class, especially during the earlier phases of the development of the institution of a leisure class. This need not mean that precisely the same complement of aptitudes in any individual would insure him an eminent personal success. Under the competitive régime, the conditions of success for the individual are not necessarily the same as those for a class. The success of a class or party presumes a strong element of clannishness, or loyalty to a chief, or adherence to a tenet; whereas the competitive individual can best achieve his ends if he combines the barbarian's energy, initiative, self-seeking and disingenuousness with the savage's lack of loyalty or clannishness. It may be remarked by the way, that the men who have scored a brilliant (Napoleonic) success on the basis of an impartial self-seeking and absence of scruple, have not uncommonly shown more of the physical characteristics of the brachycephalic-brunette than of the dolicho-blond. The greater proportion of moderately successful individuals, in a self-seeking way, however, seem, in physique, to belong to the last-named ethnic element.

The temperament induced by the predatory habit of life makes for the survival and fulness of life of the individual under a régime of emulation; at the same time it makes for the survival and success of the group if the group's life as a collectivity is also predominantly a life of hostile competition with other groups. But the evolution of economic life in the industrially more mature communities has now begun to take such a turn that the interest of the community no longer coincides with the emulative interests of the individual. In their corporate capacity, these advanced industrial communities are ceasing to be competitors for the means of life or for the right to live—except in so far as the predatory propensities of their ruling classes keep up the tradition of war and rapine. These communities are no longer hostile to one another by force of circumstances, other than the circumstances of tradition and temperament. Their material interests—apart, possibly, from the interests of the collective good fame—are not only no longer incompatible, but the success of any one of the communities unquestionably furthers the fulness of life of any other community in the group, for the present and for an incalculable time to come. No one of them any longer has any material interest in getting the better of any other. The same is not true in the same degree as regards individuals and their relations to one another.

The collective interests of any modern community centre in industrial efficiency. The individual is serviceable for the ends of the community somewhat in proportion to his efficiency in the productive employments, vulgarly so called. This collective interest is best served by honesty, diligence, peacefulness, good-will, an absence of self-seeking, and an habitual recognition and apprehension of causal sequence, without admixture of animistic belief and without a sense of dependence on any preternatural intervention in the course of events. Not much is to be said for the beauty, moral excellence, or general worthiness and reputability of such a prosy human nature as these traits imply; and there is little ground of enthusiasm for the manner of collective life that would result from the prevalence of these traits in unmitigated dominance. But that is beside the point. The successful working of a modern industrial community is best secured where these traits concur, and it is attained in the degree in which the human material is characterised by their possession. Their presence in some measure is required in order to a tolerable adjustment to the circumstances of the modern industrial situation. The complex, comprehensive, essentially peaceable, and highly organised mechanism of the modern industrial community works to the best advantage when these traits, or most of them, are present in the highest practicable degree. These traits are present in a markedly less degree in the man of the predatory type than is useful for the purposes of the modern collective life.

On the other hand, the immediate interest of the individual under the competitive régime is best served by shrewd trading and unscrupulous management. The characteristics named above as serving the interests of the community are disserviceable to the individual, rather than otherwise. The presence of these aptitudes in his make-up diverts his energies to other ends than those of pecuniary gain; and also in his pursuit of gain they lead him to seek gain by the indirect and ineffectual channels of industry, rather than by a free and unfaltering career of sharp practice. The industrial aptitudes are pretty consistently a hindrance to the individual. Under the régime of emulation the members of a modern industrial community are rivals, each of whom will best attain his individual and immediate advantage if, through an exceptional exemption from scruple, he is able serenely to overreach and injure his fellows when the chance offers.

It has already been noticed that modern economic institutions fall into two roughly distinct categories,—the pecuniary and the industrial. The like is true of employments. Under the former head are employments that have to do with ownership or acquisition; under the latter head, those that have to do with workmanship or production. As was found in speaking of the growth of institutions, so with regard to employments. The economic interests of the leisure class lie in the pecuniary employments; those of the working classes lie in both classes of employments, but chiefly in the industrial. Entrance to the leisure class lies through the pecuniary employments.

These two classes of employments differ materially in respect of the aptitudes required for each; and the training which they give similarly follows two divergent lines. The discipline of the pecuniary employments acts to conserve and to cultivate certain of the predatory aptitudes and the predatory animus. It does this both by educating those individuals and classes who are occupied with these employments and by selectively repressing and eliminating those individuals and lines of descent that are unfit in this respect. So far as men's habits of thought are shaped by the competitive process of acquisition and tenure; so far as their economic functions are comprised within the range of ownership of wealth as conceived in terms of exchange value, and its management and financiering through a permutation of values; so far their experience in economic life favours the survival and accentuation of the predatory temperament and habits of thought. Under the modern, peaceable system, it is of course the peaceable range of predatory habits and aptitudes that is chiefly fostered by a life of acquisition.

That is to say, the pecuniary employments give proficiency in the general line of practices comprised under fraud, rather than in those that belong under the more archaic method of forcible seizure.

These pecuniary employments, tending to conserve the predatory temperament, are the employments which have to do with ownership—the immediate function of the leisure class proper—and the subsidiary functions concerned with acquisition and accumulation. These cover that class of persons and that range of duties in the economic process which have to do with the ownership of enterprises engaged in competitive industry; especially those fundamental lines of economic management which are classed as financiering operations. To these may be added the greater part of mercantile occupations. In their best and clearest development these duties make up the economic office of the "captain of industry." The captain of industry is an astute man rather than an ingenious one, and his captaincy is a pecuniary rather than an industrial captaincy. Such administration of industry as he exercises is commonly of a permissive kind. The mechanically effective details of production and of industrial organisation are delegated to subordinates of a less "practical" turn of mind,—men who are possessed of a gift for workmanship rather than administrative ability. So far as regards their tendency in shaping human nature by education and selection, the common run of non-economic employments are to be classed with the pecuniary employments. Such are politics and ecclesiastical and military employments.

The pecuniary employments have also the sanction of reputability in a much higher degree than the industrial employments. In this way the leisure-class standards of good repute come in to sustain the prestige of those aptitudes that serve the invidious purpose; and the leisure-class scheme of decorous living, therefore, also furthers the survival and culture of the predatory traits. Employments fall into a hierarchical gradation of reputability. Those which have to do immediately with ownership on a large scale are the most reputable of economic employments proper. Next to these in good repute come those employments that are immediately subservient to ownership and financiering,—such as banking and the law. Banking employments also carry a suggestion of large ownership, and this fact is doubtless accountable for a share of the prestige that attaches to the business. The profession of the law does not imply large ownership; but since no taint of usefulness, for other than the competitive purpose, attaches to the lawyer's trade, it grades high in the conventional scheme. The lawyer is exclusively occupied with the details of predatory fraud, either in achieving or in checkmating chicane, and success in the profession is therefore accepted as marking a large endowment of that barbarian astuteness which has always commanded men's respect and fear. Mercantile pursuits are only half-way reputable, unless they involve a large element of ownership and a small element of usefulness. They grade high or low somewhat in proportion as they serve the higher or the lower needs; so that the business of retailing the vulgar necessaries of life descends to the level of the handicrafts and factory labour. Manual labour, or even the work of directing mechanical processes, is of course on a precarious footing as regards respectability.

A qualification is necessary as regards the discipline given by the pecuniary employments. As the scale of industrial enterprise grows larger, pecuniary management comes to bear less of the character of chicane and shrewd competition in detail. That is to say, for an ever-increasing proportion of the persons who come in contact with this phase of economic life, business reduces itself to a routine in which there is less immediate suggestion of overreaching or exploiting a competitor. The consequent exemption from predatory habits extends chiefly to subordinates employed in business. The duties of ownership and administration are virtually untouched by this qualification.

The case is different as regards those individuals or classes who are immediately occupied with the technique and manual operations of production. Their daily life is not in the same degree a course of habituation to the emulative and invidious motives and manoeuvres of the pecuniary side of industry. They are consistently held to the apprehension and coördination of mechanical facts and sequences, and to their appreciation and utilisation for the purposes of human life. So far as concerns this portion of the population, the educative and selective action of the industrial process with which they are immediately in contact acts to adapt their habits of thought to the non-invidious purposes of the collective life. For them, therefore, it hastens the obsolescence of the distinctively predatory aptitudes and propensities carried over by heredity and tradition from the barbarian past of the race.

The educative action of the economic life of the community, therefore, is not of a uniform kind throughout all its manifestations. That range of economic activities which is concerned immediately with pecuniary competition has a tendency to conserve certain predatory traits; while those industrial occupations which have to do immediately with the production of goods have in the main the contrary tendency. But with regard to the latter class of employments it is to be noticed in qualification that the persons engaged in them are nearly all to some extent also concerned with matters of pecuniary competition (as, for instance, in the competitive fixing of wages and salaries, in the purchase of goods for consumption, etc.). Therefore the distinction here made between classes of employments is by no means a hard and fast distinction between classes of persons.

The employments of the leisure classes in modern industry are such as to keep alive certain of the predatory habits and aptitudes. So far as the members of those classes take part in the industrial process, their training tends to conserve in them the barbarian temperament. But there is something to be said on the other side. Individuals so placed as to be exempt from strain may survive and transmit their characteristics even if they differ widely from the average of the species both in physique and in spiritual make-up. The chances for a survival and transmission of atavistic traits are greatest in those classes that are most sheltered from the stress of circumstances. The leisure class is in some degree sheltered from the stress of the industrial situation, and should, therefore, afford an exceptionally great proportion of reversions to the peaceable or savage temperament. It should be possible for such aberrant or atavistic individuals to unfold their life activity on ante-predatory lines without suffering as prompt a repression or elimination as in the lower walks of life.

Something of the sort seems to be true in fact. There is, for instance, an appreciable proportion of the upper classes whose inclinations lead them into philanthropic work, and there is a considerable body of sentiment in the class going to support efforts of reform and amelioration. And much of this philanthropic and reformatory effort, moreover, bears the marks of that amiable "cleverness" and incoherence that is characteristic of the primitive savage. But it may still be doubtful whether these facts are evidence of a larger proportion of reversions in the higher than in the lower strata. Even if the same inclinations were present in the impecunious classes, it would not as easily find expression there; since those classes lack the means and the time and energy to give effect to their inclinations in this respect. The *prima facie* evidence of the facts can scarcely go unquestioned.

In further qualification it is to be noted that the leisure class of to-day is recruited from those who have been successful in a pecuniary way, and who, therefore, are presumably endowed with more than an even complement of the predatory traits. Entrance into the leisure class lies through the pecuniary employments, and these employments, by selection and adaptation, act to admit to the upper levels only those lines of descent that are pecuniarily fit to survive under the predatory test. And so soon as a case of reversion to non-predatory human nature shows itself on these upper levels, it is commonly weeded out and thrown back to the lower pecuniary levels. In order to hold its place in the class, a stock must have the pecuniary temperament; otherwise its fortune would be dissipated and it would presently lose caste. Instances of this kind are sufficiently frequent.

The constituency of the leisure class is kept up by a continual selective process, whereby the individuals and lines of descent that are eminently fitted for an aggressive pecuniary competition are withdrawn from the lower classes. In order to reach the upper levels the aspirant must have, not only a fair average complement of the pecuniary aptitudes, but he must have these gifts in such an eminent degree as to overcome very material difficulties that stand in the way of his ascent. Barring accidents, the *nouveaux arrivés*[2] are a picked body.

This process of selective admission has, of course, always been going on; ever since the fashion of pecuniary emulation set in,—which is much the same as saying, ever since the institution of a leisure class was first installed. But the precise ground of selection has not always been the same, and the selective process has therefore not always given the same results. In the early barbarian, or predatory stage proper, the test of fitness was prowess, in the naïve sense of the word. To gain entrance to the class, the candidate must be gifted with clannishness, massiveness, ferocity, unscrupulousness, and tenacity of purpose. These were the qualities that counted toward the accumulation and continued tenure of wealth. The economic basis of the leisure class, then as later, was the possession of wealth; but the methods of accumulating wealth, and the gifts required for holding it, have changed in some degree since the early days of the predatory culture. In consequence of the selective process the dominant traits of the early barbarian leisure class were bold aggression, an alert sense of status, and a free resort to fraud. The members of the class held their place by tenure of prowess. In the later barbarian culture society attained settled methods of acquisition and possession under the quasi-peaceable régime of status. Simple aggression and unrestrained violence in great measure gave place to shrewd practice and chicanery, as the best approved method of accumulating wealth. A different range of aptitudes and propensities would then be conserved in the leisure class. Masterful aggression, and the correlative massiveness, together with a ruthlessly consistent sense of status, would still count among the most splendid traits of the class. These have remained in our traditions as the typical "aristocratic virtues." But with these were associated an increasing complement of the less obtrusive pecuniary virtues; such as providence, prudence, and chicane. As time has gone on, and the modern peaceable stage of pecuniary culture has been approached, the last-named range of aptitudes and habits has gained in relative effectiveness for pecuniary ends, and they have counted for relatively more in the selective process under which admission is gained and place is held in the leisure class.

The ground of selection has changed, until the aptitudes which now qualify for admission to the class are the pecuniary aptitudes only. What remains of the predatory barbarian traits is the tenacity of purpose or consistency of aim which distinguished the successful predatory barbarian from the peaceable savage whom he supplanted. But this trait can not be said characteristically to distinguish the pecuniarily successful upper-class man from the rank and file of the industrial classes. The training and the selection to which the latter are exposed in modern industrial life give a similarly decisive weight to this trait. Tenacity of purpose may rather be said to distinguish both these classes from two others: the shiftless ne'er-do-well and the lower-class delinquent. In point of natural endowment the pecuniary man compares with the delinquent in much the same way as the industrial man compares with the good-natured shiftless dependent. The ideal pecuniary man is like the ideal delinquent in his unscrupulous conversion of goods and persons to his own ends, and in a callous disregard of the feelings and wishes of others and of the remoter effects of his actions; but he is unlike him in possessing a keener sense of status, and in working more consistently and far-sightedly to a remoter end. The kinship of the two types of temperament is further shown in a proclivity to "sport" and gambling, and a relish of aimless emulation. The ideal pecuniary man also shows a curious kinship with the delinquent in one of the concomitant variations of the predatory human nature. The delinquent is very commonly of a superstitious habit of mind; he is a great believer in luck, spells, divination and destiny, and in omens and shamanistic ceremony. Where circumstances are favourable, this proclivity is apt to express itself in a certain servile devotional fervour and a punctilious attention to devout observances; it may perhaps be better characterised as devoutness than as religion. At this point the temperament of the delinquent has more in common with the pecuniary and leisure classes than with the industrial man or with the class of shiftless dependents.

Life in a modern industrial community, or in other words life under the pecuniary culture, acts by a process of selection to develop and conserve a certain range of aptitudes and propensities. The present tendency of this selective process is not simply a reversion to a given, immutable ethnic type. It tends rather to a modification of human nature differing in some respects from any of the types or variants transmitted out of the past. The objective point of the evolution is not a single one. The temperament which the evolution acts to establish as normal differs from any one of the archaic variants of human nature in its greater stability of aim— greater singleness of purpose and greater persistence in effort. So far as concerns economic theory, the objective point of the selective process is on the whole single to this extent; although there are minor tendencies of considerable importance diverging from this line of development. But apart from this general trend the line of development is not single. As concerns economic theory, the development in other respects runs on two divergent lines. So far as regards the selective conservation of capacities or aptitudes in individuals, these two lines may be called the pecuniary and the industrial. As regards the conservation of propensities, spiritual attitude, or animus, the two may be called the invidious or self-regarding and the non-invidious or economical. As regards the intellectual or cognitive bent of the two directions of growth, the former may be characterised as the personal standpoint, of conation, qualitative relation, status, or worth; the latter as the impersonal standpoint, of sequence, quantitative relation, mechanical efficiency, or use.

The pecuniary employments call into action chiefly the former of these two ranges of aptitudes and propensities, and act selectively to conserve them in the population. The industrial employments, on the other hand, chiefly exercise the latter range, and act to conserve them. An exhaustive psychological analysis will show that each of these two ranges of aptitudes and propensities is but the multiform expression of a given temperamental bent. By force of the unity or singleness of the individual, the aptitudes, animus, and interests comprised in the first-named range belong together as expressions of a given variant of human nature. The like is true of the latter range. The two may be conceived as alternative directions of human life, in such a way that a given individual inclines more or less consistently to the one or the other. The tendency of the pecuniary life is, in a general way, to conserve the barbarian temperament, but with the substitution of fraud and prudence, or administrative ability, in place of that predilection for physical damage that characterises the early barbarian. This substitution of chicane in place of devastation takes place only in an uncertain degree. Within the pecuniary employments the selective action runs pretty consistently in this direction, but the discipline of pecuniary life, outside the competition for gain, does not work consistently to the same effect. The discipline of modern life in the consumption of time and goods does not act unequivocally to eliminate the aristocratic virtues or to foster the bourgeois virtues. The conventional scheme of decent living calls for a considerable exercise of the earlier barbarian traits. Some details of this traditional scheme of life, bearing on this point, have been noticed in earlier chapters under the head of Leisure, and further details will be shown in later chapters.

From what has been said, it appears that the leisure-class life and the leisure-class scheme of life should further the conservation of the barbarian temperament; chiefly of the quasi-peaceable, or bourgeois, variant, but also in some measure of the predatory variant. In the absence of disturbing factors, therefore, it should be possible to trace a difference of temperament between the classes of society. The aristocratic and the bourgeois virtues—that is to say the destructive and pecuniary traits—should be found chiefly among the upper classes, and the industrial virtues—that is to say the peaceable traits—chiefly among the classes given to mechanical industry.

In a general and uncertain way this holds true, but the test is not so readily applied nor so conclusive as might be wished. There are several assignable reasons for its partial failure. All classes are in a measure engaged in the pecuniary struggle, and in all classes the possession of the pecuniary traits counts towards the success and survival of the individual. Wherever the pecuniary culture prevails, the selective process by which men's habits of thought are shaped, and by which the survival of rival lines of descent is decided, proceeds proximately on the basis of fitness for acquisition. Consequently, if it were not for the fact that pecuniary efficiency is on the whole incompatible with industrial efficiency, the selective action of all occupations would tend to the unmitigated dominance of the pecuniary temperament. The result would be the installation of what has been known as the "economic man," as the normal and definitive type of human nature. But the "economic man," whose only interest is the self-regarding one and whose only human trait is prudence, is useless for the purposes of modern industry.

The modern industry requires an impersonal, non-invidious interest in the work in hand. Without this the elaborate processes of industry would be impossible, and would, indeed, never have been conceived. This interest in work differentiates the workman from the criminal on the one hand, and from the captain of industry on the other. Since work must be done in order to the continued life of the community, there results a qualified selection favouring the spiritual aptitude for work, within a certain range of occupations. This much, however, is to be conceded, that even within the industrial occupations the selective elimination of the pecuniary traits is an uncertain process, and that there is consequently an appreciable survival of the barbarian temperament even within these occupations. On this account there is at present no broad distinction in this respect between the leisure-class character and the character of the common run of the population.

The whole question as to a class distinction in respect of spiritual make-up is also obscured by the presence, in all classes of society, of acquired habits of life that closely simulate inherited traits and at the same time act to develop in the entire body of the population the traits which they simulate. These acquired habits, or assumed traits of character, are most commonly of an aristocratic cast. The prescriptive position of the leisure class as the exemplar of reputability has imposed many features of the leisure-class theory of life upon the lower classes; with the result that there goes on, always and throughout society, a more or less persistent cultivation of these aristocratic traits. On this ground also these traits have a better chance of survival among the body of the people than would be the case if it were not for the precept and example of the leisure class. As one channel, and an important one, through which this transfusion of aristocratic views of life, and consequently more or less archaic traits of character, goes on, may be mentioned the class of domestic servants. These have their notions of what is good and beautiful shaped by contact with the master class and carry the preconceptions so acquired back among their low-born equals, and so disseminate the higher ideals abroad through the community without the loss of time which this dissemination might otherwise suffer. The saying, "Like master, like man," has a greater significance than is commonly appreciated for the rapid popular acceptance of many elements of upper-class culture.

There is also a further range of facts that go to lessen class differences as regards the survival of the pecuniary virtues. The pecuniary struggle produces an underfed class, of large proportions. This underfeeding consists in a deficiency of the necessaries of life or of the necessaries of a decent expenditure. In either case the result is a closely enforced struggle for the means with which to meet the daily needs; whether it be the physical or the higher needs. The strain of self-assertion against odds takes up the whole energy of the individual; he bends his efforts to compass his own invidious ends alone, and becomes continually more narrowly self-seeking. The industrial traits in this way tend to obsolescence through disuse. Indirectly, therefore, by imposing a scheme of pecuniary decency and by withdrawing as much as may be of the means of life from the lower classes, the institution of a leisure class acts to conserve the pecuniary traits in the body of the population. The result is an assimilation of the lower classes to the type of human nature that belongs primarily to the upper classes only.

It appears, therefore, that there is no wide difference in temperament between the upper and the lower classes; but it appears also that the absence of such a difference is in good part due to the prescriptive example of the leisure class and to the popular acceptance of those broad principles of conspicuous waste and pecuniary emulation on which the institution of a leisure class rests. The institution acts to lower the industrial efficiency of the community and retard the adaptation of human nature to the exigencies of modern industrial life. It affects the prevalent or effective human nature in a conservative direction, (1) by direct transmission of archaic traits, through inheritance within the class and wherever the leisure-class blood is transfused outside the class, and (2) by conserving and fortifying the traditions of the archaic régime, and so making the chances of survival of barbarian traits greater also outside the range of transfusion of leisure-class blood.

But little if anything has been done towards collecting or digesting data that are of special significance for the question of survival or elimination of traits in the modern populations. Little of a tangible character can therefore be offered in support of the view here taken, beyond a discursive review of such everyday facts as lie ready to hand. Such a recital can scarcely avoid being commonplace and tedious, but for all that it seems necessary to the completeness of the argument, even in the meagre outline in which it is here attempted. A degree of indulgence may therefore fairly be bespoken for the succeeding chapters, which offer a fragmentary recital of this kind.

CHAPTER X

MODERN SURVIVALS

OF PROWESS

The leisure class lives by the industrial community rather than in it. Its relations to industry are of a pecuniary rather than an industrial kind. Admission to the class is gained by exercise of the pecuniary aptitudes—aptitudes for acquisition rather than for serviceability. There is, therefore, a continued selective sifting of the human material that makes up the leisure class, and this selection proceeds on the ground of fitness for pecuniary pursuits. But the scheme of life of the class is in large part a heritage from the past, and embodies much of the habits and ideals of the earlier barbarian period. This archaic, barbarian scheme of life imposes itself also on the lower orders, with more or less mitigation. In its turn the scheme of life, of conventions, acts selectively and by education to shape the human material, and its action runs chiefly in the direction of conserving traits, habits, and ideals that belong to the early barbarian age,—the age of prowess and predatory life.

———

The most immediate and unequivocal expression of that archaic human nature which characterises man in the predatory stage is the fighting propensity proper. In cases where the predatory activity is a collective one, this propensity is frequently called the martial spirit, or, latterly, patriotism. It needs no insistence to find assent to the proposition that in the countries of civilised Europe the hereditary leisure class is endowed with this martial spirit in a higher degree than the middle classes. Indeed, the leisure class claims the distinction as a matter of pride, and no doubt with some grounds. War is honourable, and warlike prowess is eminently honorific in the eyes of the generality of men; and this admiration of warlike prowess is itself the best voucher of a predatory temperament in the admirer of war. The enthusiasm for war, and the predatory temper of which it is the index, prevail in the largest measure among the upper classes, especially among the hereditary leisure class. Moreover, the ostensible serious occupation of the upper class is that of government, which, in point of origin and developmental content, is also a predatory occupation.

The only class which could at all dispute with the hereditary leisure class the honour of an habitual bellicose frame of mind is that of the lower-class delinquents. In ordinary times, the large body of the industrial classes is relatively apathetic touching warlike interests. When unexcited, this body of the common people, which makes up the effective force of the industrial community, is rather averse to any other than a defensive fight; indeed, it responds a little tardily even to a provocation which makes for an attitude of defence. In the more civilised communities, or rather in the communities which have reached an advanced industrial development, the spirit of warlike aggression may be said to be obsolescent among the common people. This does not say that there is not an appreciable number of individuals among the industrial classes in whom the martial spirit asserts itself obtrusively. Nor does it say that the body of the people may not be fired with martial ardour for a time under the stimulus of some special provocation, such as is seen in operation to-day in more than one of the countries of Europe, and for the time in America. But except for such seasons of temporary exaltation, and except for those individuals who are endowed with an archaic temperament of the predatory type, together with the similarly endowed body of individuals among the higher and the lowest classes, the inertness of the mass of any modern civilised community in this respect is probably so great as would make war impracticable, except against actual invasion. The habits and aptitudes of the common run of men make for an unfolding of activity in other, less picturesque directions than that of war.

This class difference in temperament may be due in part to a difference in the inheritance of acquired traits in the several classes, but it seems also, in some measure, to correspond with a difference in ethnic derivation. The class difference is in this respect visibly less in those countries whose population is relatively homogeneous, ethnically, than in the countries where there is a broader divergence between the ethnic elements that make up the several classes of the community. In the same connection it may be noted that the later accessions to the leisure class in the latter countries, in a general way, show less of the martial spirit than contemporary representatives of the aristocracy of the ancient line. These *nouveaux arrivés* have recently emerged from the commonplace body of the population and owe their emergence into the leisure class to the exercise of traits and propensities which are not to be classed as prowess in the ancient sense.

Apart from warlike activity proper, the institution of the duel is also an expression of the same superior readiness for combat; and the duel is a leisure-class institution. The duel is in substance a more or less deliberate resort to a fight as a final settlement of a difference of opinion. In civilised communities it prevails as a normal phenomenon only where there is an hereditary leisure class, and almost exclusively among that class. The exceptions are (1) military and naval officers—who are ordinarily members of the leisure class, and who are at the same time specially trained to predatory habits of mind—and (2) the lower-class delinquents—who are by inheritance, or training, or both, of a similarly predatory disposition and habit. It is only the high-bred gentleman and the rowdy that normally resort to blows as the universal solvent of differences of opinion. The plain man will ordinarily fight only when excessive momentary irritation or alcoholic exaltation act to inhibit the more complex habits of response to the stimuli that make for provocation. He is then thrown back upon the simpler, less differentiated forms of the instinct of self-assertion; that is to say, he reverts temporarily and without reflection to an archaic habit of mind.

This institution of the duel as a mode of finally settling disputes and serious questions of precedence shades off into the obligatory, unprovoked private fight, as a social obligation due to one's good repute. As a leisure-class usage of this kind we have, particularly, that bizarre survival of bellicose chivalry, the German student duel.[1] In the lower or spurious leisure class of the delinquents there is in all countries a similar, though less formal, social obligation incumbent on the rowdy to assert his manhood in unprovoked combat with his fellows. And spreading through all grades of society, a similar usage prevails among the boys of the community. The boy usually knows to a nicety, from day to day, how he and his associates grade in respect of relative fighting capacity; and in the community of boys there is ordinarily no secure basis of reputability for any one who, by exception, will not or can not fight on invitation.

All this applies especially to boys above a certain somewhat vague limit of maturity. The child's temperament does not commonly answer to this description during infancy and the years of close tutelage, when the child still habitually seeks contact with its mother at every turn of its daily life. During this earlier period there is little aggression and little propensity for antagonism. The transition from this peaceable temper to the predaceous, and in extreme cases malignant, mischievousness of the boy is a gradual one, and it is accomplished with more completeness, covering a larger range of the individual's aptitudes, in some cases than in others. In the earlier stage of his growth, the child, whether boy or girl, shows less of initiative and aggressive self-assertion and less of an inclination to isolate himself and his interests from the domestic group in which he lives, and he shows more of sensitiveness to rebuke, bashfulness, timidity, and the need of friendly human contact. In the common run of cases this early temperament passes, by a gradual but somewhat rapid obsolescence of the infantile features, into the temperament of the boy proper; though there are also cases where the predaceous features of boy life do not emerge at all, or at the most emerge in but a slight and obscure degree.

In girls the transition to the predaceous stage is seldom accomplished with the same degree of completeness as in boys; and in a relatively large proportion of cases it is scarcely undergone at all. In such cases the transition from infancy to adolescence and maturity is a gradual and unbroken process of the shifting of interest from infantile purposes and aptitudes to the purposes, functions, and relations of adult life. In the girls there is a less general prevalence of a predaceous interval in the development; and in the cases where it occurs, the predaceous and isolating attitude during the interval is commonly less accentuated.

In the male child the predaceous interval is ordinarily fairly well marked and lasts for some time, but it is commonly terminated (if at all) with the attainment of maturity. This last statement may need very material qualification. The cases are by no means rare in which the transition from the boyish to the adult temperament is not made, or is made only partially—understanding by the "adult" temperament the average temperament of those adult individuals in modern industrial life who have some serviceability for the purposes of the collective life process, and who may therefore be said to make up the effective average of the industrial community.

The ethnic composition of the European populations varies. In some cases even the lower classes are in large measure made up of the peace-disturbing dolicho-blond; while in others this ethnic element is found chiefly among the hereditary leisure class. The fighting habit seems to prevail to a less extent among the working-class boys in the latter class of populations than among the boys of the upper classes or among those of the populations first named.

If this generalisation as to the temperament of the boy among the working classes should be found true on a fuller and closer scrutiny of the field, it would add force to the view that the bellicose temperament is in some appreciable degree a race characteristic; it appears to enter more largely into the make-up of the dominant, upper-class ethnic type—the dolicho-blond—of the European countries than into the subservient, lower-class types of man which are conceived to constitute the body of the population of the same communities.

The case of the boy may seem not to bear seriously on the question of the relative endowment of prowess with which the several classes of society are gifted; but it is at least of some value as going to show that this fighting impulse belongs to a more archaic temperament than that possessed by the average adult man of the industrious classes. In this, as in many other features of child life, the child reproduces, temporarily and in miniature, some of the earlier phases of the development of adult man. Under this interpretation, the boy's predilection for exploit and for isolation of his own interest is to be taken as a transient reversion to the human nature that is normal to the early barbarian culture—the predatory culture proper. In this respect, as in much else, the leisure-class and the delinquent-class character shows a persistence into adult life of traits that are normal to childhood and youth, and that are likewise normal or habitual to the earlier stages of culture. Unless the difference is traceable entirely to a fundamental difference between persistent ethnic types, the traits that distinguish the swaggering delinquent and the punctilious gentleman of leisure from the common crowd are, in some measure, marks of an arrested spiritual development. They mark an immature phase, as compared with the stage of development attained by the average of the adults in the modern industrial community. And it will appear presently that the puerile spiritual make-up of these representatives of the upper and the lowest social strata shows itself also in the presence of other archaic traits than this proclivity to ferocious exploit and isolation.

As if to leave no doubt about the essential immaturity of the fighting temperament, we have, bridging the interval between legitimate boyhood and adult manhood, the aimless and playful, but more or less systematic and elaborate, disturbances of the peace in vogue among schoolboys of a slightly higher age. In the common run of cases, these disturbances are confined to the period of adolescence. They recur with decreasing frequency and acuteness as youth merges into adult life, and so they reproduce, in a general way, in the life of the individual, the sequence by which the group has passed from the predatory to a more settled habit of life. In an appreciable number of cases the spiritual growth of the individual comes to a close before he emerges from this puerile phase; in these cases the fighting temper persists through life. Those individuals who in spiritual development eventually reach man's estate, therefore, ordinarily pass through a temporary archaic phase corresponding to the permanent spiritual level of the fighting and sporting men. Different individuals will, of course, achieve spiritual maturity and sobriety in this respect in different degrees; and those who fail of the average remain as an undissolved residue of crude humanity in the modern industrial community and as a foil for that selective process of adaptation which makes for a heightened industrial efficiency and the fulness of life of the collectivity.

This arrested spiritual development may express itself not only in a direct participation by adults in youthful exploits of ferocity, but also indirectly in aiding and abetting disturbances of this kind on the part of younger persons. It thereby furthers the formation of habits of ferocity which may persist in the later life of the growing generation, and so retard any movement in the direction of a more peaceable effective temperament on the part of the community. If a person so endowed with a proclivity for exploits is in a position to guide the development of habits in the adolescent members of the community, the influence which he exerts in the direction of conservation and reversion to prowess may be very considerable. This is the significance, for instance, of the fostering care latterly bestowed by many clergymen and other pillars of society upon "boys' brigades" and similar pseudo-military organisations. The same is true of the encouragement given to the growth of "college spirit," college athletics, and the like, in the higher institutions of learning.

These manifestations of the predatory temperament are all to be classed under the head of exploit. They are partly simple and unreflected expressions of an attitude of emulative ferocity, partly activities deliberately entered upon with a view to gaining repute for prowess. Sports of all kinds are of the same general character, including prize-fights, bull-fights, athletics, shooting, angling, yachting, and games of skill, even where the element of destructive physical efficiency is not an obtrusive feature. Sports shade off from the basis of hostile combat, through skill, to cunning and chicanery, without its being possible to draw a line at any point. The ground of an addiction to sports is an archaic spiritual constitution—the possession of the predatory emulative propensity in a relatively high potency. A strong proclivity to adventuresome exploit and to the infliction of damage is especially pronounced in those employments which are in colloquial usage specifically called sportsmanship.

It is perhaps truer, or at least more evident, as regards sports than as regards the other expressions of predatory emulation already spoken of, that the temperament which inclines men to them is essentially a boyish temperament. The addiction to sports, therefore, in a peculiar degree marks an arrested development of the man's moral nature. This peculiar boyishness of temperament in sporting men immediately becomes apparent when attention is directed to the large element of make-believe that is present in all sporting activity. Sports share this character of make-believe with the games and exploits to which children, especially boys, are habitually inclined. Make-believe does not enter in the same proportion into all sports, but it is present in a very appreciable degree in all. It is apparently present in a larger measure in sportsmanship proper and in athletic contests than in set games of skill of a more sedentary character; although this rule may not be found to apply with any great uniformity. It is noticeable, for instance, that even very mild-mannered and matter-of-fact men who go out shooting are apt to carry an excess of arms and accoutrements in order to impress upon their own imagination the seriousness of their undertaking. These huntsmen are also prone to a histrionic, prancing gait and to an elaborate exaggeration of the motions, whether of stealth or of onslaught, involved in their deeds of exploit. Similarly in athletic sports there is almost invariably present a good share of rant and swagger and ostensible mystification—features which mark the histrionic nature of these employments. In all this, of course, the reminder of boyish make-believe is plain enough. The slang of athletics, by the way, is in great part made up of extremely sanguinary locutions borrowed from the terminology of warfare. Except where it is adopted as a necessary means of secret communication, the use of a special slang in any employment is probably to be accepted as evidence that the occupation in question is substantially make-believe.

A further feature in which sports differ from the duel and similar disturbances of the peace is the peculiarity that they admit of other motives being assigned for them besides the impulses of exploit and ferocity. There is probably little if any other motive present in any given case, but the fact that other reasons for indulging in sports are frequently assigned goes to say that other grounds are sometimes present in a subsidiary way. Sportsmen—hunters and anglers—are more or less in the habit of assigning a love of nature, the need of recreation, and the like, as the incentives to their favourite pastime. These motives are no doubt frequently present and make up a part of the attractiveness of the sportsman's life; but these can not be the chief incentives. These ostensible needs could be more readily and fully satisfied without the accompaniment of a systematic effort to take the life of those creatures that make up an essential feature of that "nature" that is beloved by the sportsman. It is, indeed, the most noticeable effect of the sportsman's activity to keep nature in a state of chronic desolation by killing off all living things whose destruction he can compass.

Still, there is ground for the sportsman's claim that under the existing conventionalities his need of recreation and of contact with nature can best be satisfied by the course which he takes. Certain canons of good breeding have been imposed by the prescriptive example of a predatory leisure class in the past and have been somewhat painstakingly conserved by the usage of the latter-day representatives of that class; and these canons will not permit him, without blame, to seek contact with nature on other terms. From being an honourable employment handed down from the predatory culture as the highest form of everyday leisure, sports have come to be the only form of outdoor activity that has the full sanction of decorum. Among the proximate incentives to shooting and angling, then, may be the need of recreation and outdoor life. The remoter cause which imposes the necessity of seeking these objects under the cover of systematic slaughter is a prescription that can not be violated except at the risk of disrepute and consequent lesion to one's self-respect.

The case of other kinds of sport is somewhat similar. Of these, athletic games are the best example. Prescriptive usage with respect to what forms of activity, exercise, and recreation are permissible under the code of reputable living is of course present here also. Those who are addicted to athletic sports, or who admire them, set up the claim that these afford the best available means of recreation and of "physical culture." And prescriptive usage gives countenance to the claim. The canons of reputable living exclude from the scheme of life of the leisure class all activity that can not be classed as conspicuous leisure. And consequently they tend by prescription to exclude it also from the scheme of life of the community generally. At the same time purposeless physical exertion is tedious and distasteful beyond tolerance. As has been noticed in another connection, recourse is in such a case had to some form of activity which shall at least afford a colourable pretence of purpose, even if the object assigned be only a make-believe. Sports satisfy these requirements of substantial futility together with a colourable make-believe of purpose. In addition to this they afford scope for emulation, and are attractive also on that account. In order to be decorous, an employment must conform to the leisure-class canon of reputable waste; at the same time all activity, in order to be persisted in as an habitual, even if only partial, expression of life, must conform to the generically human canon of efficiency for some serviceable objective end. The leisure-class canon demands strict and comprehensive futility; the instinct of workmanship demands purposeful action. The leisure-class canon of decorum acts slowly and pervasively, by a selective elimination of all substantially useful or purposeful modes of action from the accredited scheme of life; the instinct of workmanship acts impulsively and may be satisfied, provisionally, with a proximate purpose. It is only as the apprehended ulterior futility of a given line of action enters the reflective complex of consciousness as an element essentially alien to the normally purposeful trend of the life process that its disquieting and deterrent effect on the consciousness of the agent is wrought.

The individual's habits of thought make an organic complex, the trend of which is necessarily in the direction of serviceability to the life process. When it is attempted to assimilate systematic waste or futility, as an end in life, into this organic complex, there presently supervenes a revulsion. But this revulsion of the organism may be avoided if the attention can be confined to the proximate, unreflected purpose of dexterous or emulative exertion. Sports—hunting, angling, athletic games, and the like—afford an exercise for dexterity and for the emulative ferocity and astuteness characteristic of predatory life. So long as the individual is but slightly gifted with reflection or with a sense of the ulterior trend of his actions,—so long as his life is substantially a life of naïve impulsive action,—so long the immediate and unreflected purposefulness of sports, in the way of an expression of dominance, will measurably satisfy his instinct of workmanship. This is especially true if his dominant impulses are the unreflecting emulative propensities of the predaceous temperament. At the same time the canons of decorum will commend sports to him as expressions of a pecuniarily blameless life. It is by meeting these two requirements, of ulterior wastefulness and proximate purposefulness, that any given employment holds its place as a traditional and habitual mode of decorous recreation. In the sense that other forms of recreation and exercise are morally impossible to persons of good breeding and delicate sensibilities, then, sports are the best available means of recreation under existing circumstances.

But those members of respectable society who advocate athletic games commonly justify their attitude on this head to themselves and to their neighbours on the ground that these games serve as an invaluable means of development. They not only improve the contestant's physique, but it is commonly added that they also foster a manly spirit, both in the participants and in the spectators. Football is the particular game which will probably first occur to any one in this community when the question of the serviceability of athletic games is raised, as this form of athletic contest is at present upper-most in the mind of those who plead for or against games as a means of physical or moral salvation. This typical athletic sport may, therefore, serve to illustrate the bearing of athletics upon the de-velopment of the contestant's character and physique. It has been said, not inaptly, that the relation of football to physical culture is much the same as that of the bull-fight to agriculture. Serviceabil-ity for these lusory institutions requires sedulous training or breed-ing. The material used, whether brute or human, is subjected to careful selection and discipline, in order to secure and accentuate certain aptitudes and propensities which are characteristic of the ferine state, and which tend to obsolescence under domestication. This does not mean that the result in either case is an all-around and consistent rehabilitation of the ferine or barbarian habit of mind and body. The result is rather a one-sided return to barbarism or to the *feræ naturæ*[2]—a rehabilitation and accentuation of those ferine traits which make for damage and desolation, without a corre-sponding development of the traits which would serve the individ-ual's self-preservation and fulness of life in a ferine environment. The culture bestowed in football gives a product of exotic ferocity and cunning. It is a rehabilitation of the early barbarian tempera-ment, together with a suppression of those details of temperament which, as seen from the standpoint of the social and economic exi-gencies, are the redeeming features of the savage character.

The physical vigour acquired in the training for athletic games—so far as the training may be said to have this effect—is of advantage both to the individual and to the collectivity, in that, other things being equal, it conduces to economic serviceability. The spiritual traits which go with athletic sports are likewise eco-nomically advantageous to the individual, as contradistinguished from the interests of the collectivity. This holds true in any com-munity where these traits are present in some degree in the population. Modern competition is in large part a process of self-assertion on the basis of these traits of predatory human nature. In the sophisticated form in which they enter into the modern, peace-able emulation, the possession of these traits in some measure is almost a necessary of life to the civilised man. But while they are indispensable to the competitive individual, they are not directly serviceable to the community. So far as regards the serviceability of the individual for the purposes of the collective life, emulative efficiency is of use only indirectly if at all. Ferocity and cunning are of no use to the community except in its hostile dealings with other communities; and they are useful to the individual only because there is so large a proportion of the same traits actively present in the human environment to which he is exposed. Any individual who enters the competitive struggle without the due endowment of these traits is at a disadvantage, somewhat as a hornless steer would find himself at a disadvantage in a drove of horned cattle.

The possession and the cultivation of the predatory traits of character may, of course, be desirable on other than economic grounds. There is a prevalent æsthetic or ethical predilection for the barbarian aptitudes, and the traits in question minister so effectively to this predilection that their serviceability in the æsthetic or ethical respect probably offsets any economic unserviceability which they may give. But for the present purpose that is beside the point. Therefore nothing is said here as to the desirability or advisability of sports on the whole, or as to their value on other than economic grounds.

In popular apprehension there is much that is admirable in the type of manhood which the life of sport fosters. There is self-reliance and good-fellowship, so termed in the somewhat loose colloquial use of the words. From a different point of view the qualities currently so characterised might be described as truculence and clannishness. The reason for the current approval and admiration of these manly qualities, as well as for their being called manly, is the same as the reason for their usefulness to the individual. The members of the community, and especially that class of the community which sets the pace in canons of taste, are endowed with this range of propensities in sufficient measure to make their absence in others felt as a shortcoming, and to make their possession in an exceptional degree appreciated as an attribute of superior merit. The traits of predatory man are by no means obsolete in the common run of modern populations. They are present and can be called out in bold relief at any time by any appeal to the sentiments in which they express themselves,—unless this appeal should clash with the specific activities that make up our habitual occupations and comprise the general range of our everyday interests. The common run of the population of any industrial community is emancipated from these, economically considered, untoward propensities only in the sense that, through partial and temporary disuse, they have lapsed into the background of sub-conscious motives. With varying degrees of potency in different individuals, they remain available for the aggressive shaping of men's actions and sentiments whenever a stimulus of more than everyday intensity comes in to call them forth. And they assert themselves forcibly in any case where no occupation alien to the predatory culture has usurped the individual's everyday range of interest and sentiment. This is the case among the leisure class and among certain portions of the population which are ancillary to that class. Hence the facility with which any new accessions to the leisure class take to sports; and hence the rapid growth of sports and of the sporting sentiment in any industrial community where wealth has accumulated sufficiently to exempt a considerable part of the population from work.

A homely and familiar fact may serve to show that the predaceous impulse does not prevail in the same degree in all classes. Taken simply as a feature of modern life, the habit of carrying a walking-stick may seem at best a trivial detail; but the usage has a significance for the point in question. The classes among whom the habit most prevails—the classes with whom the walking-stick is associated in popular apprehension—are the men of the leisure class proper, sporting men, and the lower-class delinquents. To these might perhaps be added the men engaged in the pecuniary employments. The same is not true of the common run of men engaged in industry; and it may be noted by the way that women do not carry a stick except in case of infirmity, where it has a use of a different kind. The practice is of course in great measure a matter of polite usage; but the basis of polite usage is, in turn, the proclivities of the class which sets the pace in polite usage. The walking-stick serves the purpose of an advertisement that the bearer's hands are employed otherwise than in useful effort, and it therefore has utility as an evidence of leisure. But it is also a weapon, and it meets a felt need of barbarian man on that ground. The handling of so tangible and primitive a means of offence is very comforting to any one who is gifted with even a moderate share of ferocity.

The exigencies of the language make it impossible to avoid an apparent implication of disapproval of the aptitudes, propensities, and expressions of life here under discussion. It is, however, not intended to imply anything in the way of deprecation or commendation of any one of these phases of human character or of the life process. The various elements of the prevalent human nature are taken up from the point of view of economic theory, and the traits discussed are gauged and graded with regard to their immediate economic bearing on the facility of the collective life process. That is to say, these phenomena are here apprehended from the economic point of view and are valued with respect to their direct action in furtherance or hindrance of a more perfect adjustment of the human collectivity to the environment and to the institutional structure required by the economic situation of the collectivity for the present and for the immediate future. For these purposes the traits handed down from the predatory culture are less serviceable than might be. Although even in this connection it is not to be overlooked that the energetic aggressiveness and pertinacity of predatory man is a heritage of no mean value. The economic value—with some regard also to the social value in the narrower sense—of these aptitudes and propensities is attempted to be passed upon without reflecting on their value as seen from another point of view. When contrasted with the prosy mediocrity of the latter-day industrial scheme of life, and judged by the accredited standards of morality, and more especially by the standards of æsthetics and of poetry, these survivals from a more primitive type of manhood may have a very different value from that here assigned them. But all this being foreign to the purpose in hand, no expression of opinion on this latter head would be in place here. All that is admissible is to enter the caution that these standards of excellence, which are alien to the present purpose, must not be allowed to influence our economic appreciation of these traits of human character or of the activities which foster their growth. This applies both as regards those persons who actively participate in sports and those whose sporting experience consists in contemplation only. What is here said of the sporting propensity is likewise pertinent to sundry reflections presently to be made in this connection on what would colloquially be known as the religious life.

The last paragraph incidentally touches upon the fact that everyday speech can scarcely be employed in discussing this class of aptitudes and activities without implying deprecation or apology. The fact is significant as showing the habitual attitude of the dispassionate common man toward the propensities which express themselves in sports and in exploit generally. And this is perhaps as convenient a place as any to discuss that undertone of deprecation which runs through all the voluminous discourse in defence or in laudation of athletic sports, as well as of other activities of a predominantly predatory character. The same apologetic frame of mind is at least beginning to be observable in the spokesmen of most other institutions handed down from the barbarian phase of life. Among these archaic institutions which are felt to need apology are comprised, with others, the entire existing system of the distribution of wealth, together with the resulting class distinctions of status; all or nearly all forms of consumption that come under the head of conspicuous waste; the status of women under the patriarchal system; and many features of the traditional creeds and devout observances, especially the exoteric expressions of the creed and the naïve apprehension of received observances. What is to be said in this connection of the apologetic attitude taken in commending sports and the sporting character will therefore apply, with a suitable change in phraseology, to the apologies offered in behalf of these other, related elements of our social heritage.

There is a feeling—usually vague and not commonly avowed in so many words by the apologist himself, but ordinarily perceptible in the manner of his discourse—that these sports, as well as the general range of predaceous impulses and habits of thought which underlie the sporting character, do not altogether commend themselves to common sense. "As to the majority of murderers, they are very incorrect characters." This aphorism offers a valuation of the predaceous temperament, and of the disciplinary effects of its overt expression and exercise, as seen from the moralist's point of view. As such it affords an indication of what is the deliverance of the sober sense of mature men as to the degree of availability of the predatory habit of mind for the purposes of the collective life. It is felt that the presumption is against any activity which involves habituation to the predatory attitude, and that the burden of proof lies with those who speak for the rehabilitation of the predaceous temper and for the practices which strengthen it. There is a strong body of popular sentiment in favour of diversions and enterprise of the kind in question; but there is at the same time present in the community a pervading sense that this ground of sentiment wants legitimation. The required legitimation is ordinarily sought by showing that although sports are substantially of a predatory, socially disintegrating effect; although their proximate effect runs in the direction of reversion to propensities that are industrially disserviceable; yet indirectly and remotely—by some not readily comprehensible process of polar induction, or counter-irritation perhaps—sports are conceived to foster a habit of mind that is serviceable for the social or industrial purpose. That is to say, although sports are essentially of the nature of invidious exploit, it is presumed that by some remote and obscure effect they result in the growth of a temperament conducive to non-invidious work. It is commonly attempted to show all this empirically; or it is rather assumed that this is the empirical generalisation which must be obvious to any one who cares to see it. In conducting the proof of this thesis the treacherous ground of inference from cause to effect is somewhat shrewdly avoided, except so far as to show that the "manly virtues" spoken of above are fostered by sports. But since it is these manly virtues that are (economically) in need of legitimation, the chain of proof breaks off where it should begin. In the most general economic terms, these apologies are an effort to show that, in spite of the logic of the thing, sports do in fact further what may broadly be called workmanship. So long as he has not succeeded in persuading himself or others that this is their effect the thoughtful apologist for sports will not rest content; and commonly, it is to be admitted, he does not rest content. His discontent with his own vindication of the practices in question is ordinarily shown by his truculent tone and by the eagerness with which he heaps up asseverations in support of his position.

But why are apologies needed? If there prevails a body of popular sentiment in favour of sports, why is not that fact a sufficient legitimation? The protracted discipline of prowess to which the race has been subjected under the predatory and quasi-peaceable culture has transmitted to the men of to-day a temperament that finds gratification in these expressions of ferocity and cunning. So, why not accept these sports as legitimate expressions of a normal and wholesome human nature? What other norm is there that is to be lived up to than that given in the aggregate range of propensities that express themselves in the sentiments of this generation, including the hereditary strain of prowess? The ulterior norm to which appeal is taken is the instinct of workmanship, which is an instinct more fundamental, of more ancient prescription, than the propensity to predatory emulation. The latter is but a special development of the instinct of workmanship, a variant, relatively late and ephemeral in spite of its great absolute antiquity. The emulative predatory impulse—or the instinct of sportsmanship, as it might well be called—is essentially unstable in comparison with the primordial instinct of workmanship out of which it has been developed and differentiated. Tested by this ulterior norm of life, predatory emulation, and therefore the life of sport, falls short.

The manner and the measure in which the institution of a leisure class conduces to the conservation of sports and invidious exploit can of course not be succinctly stated. From the evidence already recited it appears that, in sentiment and inclinations, the leisure class is more favourable to a warlike attitude and animus than the industrial classes. Something similar seems to be true as regards sports. But it is chiefly in its indirect effects, through the canons of decorous living, that the institution has its influence on the prevalent sentiment with respect to the sporting life. This indirect effect goes almost unequivocally in the direction of furthering a survival of the predatory temperament and habits; and this is true even with respect to those variants of the sporting life which the higher leisure-class code of proprieties proscribes; as, *e.g.,* prize-fighting, cock-fighting, and other like vulgar expressions of the sporting temper. Whatever the latest authenticated schedule of detail proprieties may say, the accredited canons of decency sanctioned by the institution say without equivocation that emulation and waste are good and their opposites are disreputable. In the crepuscular light of the social nether spaces the details of the code are not apprehended with all the facility that might be desired, and these broad underlying canons of decency are therefore applied somewhat unreflectingly, with little question as to the scope of their competence or the exceptions that have been sanctioned in detail.

Addiction to athletic sports, not only in the way of direct participation, but also in the way of sentiment and moral support, is, in a more or less pronounced degree, a characteristic of the leisure class; and it is a trait which that class shares with the lower-class delinquents, and with such atavistic elements throughout the body of the community as are endowed with a dominant predaceous trend. Few individuals among the populations of Western civilised countries are so far devoid of the predaceous instinct as to find no diversion in contemplating athletic sports and games, but with the common run of individuals among the industrial classes the inclination to sports does not assert itself to the extent of constituting what may fairly be called a sporting habit. With these classes sports are an occasional diversion rather than a serious feature of life. This common body of the people can therefore not be said to cultivate the sporting propensity. Although it is not obsolete in the average of them, or even in any appreciable number of individuals, yet the predilection for sports in the commonplace industrial classes is of the nature of a reminiscence, more or less diverting as an occasional interest, rather than a vital and permanent interest that counts as a dominant factor in shaping the organic complex of habits of thought into which it enters.

As it manifests itself in the sporting life of to-day, this propensity may not appear to be an economic factor of grave consequence. Taken simply by itself it does not count for a great deal in its direct effects on the industrial efficiency or the consumption of any given individual; but the prevalence and the growth of the type of human nature of which this propensity is a characteristic feature is a matter of some consequence. It affects the economic life of the collectivity both as regards the rate of economic development and as regards the character of the results attained by the development. For better or worse, the fact that the popular habits of thought are in any degree dominated by this type of character can not but greatly affect the scope, direction, standards, and ideals of the collective economic life, as well as the degree of adjustment of the collective life to the environment.

Something to a like effect is to be said of other traits that go to make up the barbarian character. For the purposes of economic theory, these further barbarian traits may be taken as concomitant variations of that predaceous temper of which prowess is an expression. In great measure they are not primarily of an economic character, nor do they have much direct economic bearing. They serve to indicate the stage of economic evolution to which the individual possessed of them is adapted. They are of importance, therefore, as extraneous tests of the degree of adaptation of the character in which they are comprised to the economic exigencies of to-day; but they are also to some extent important as being aptitudes which themselves go to increase or diminish the economic serviceability of the individual.

As it finds expression in the life of the barbarian, prowess manifests itself in two main directions,—force and fraud. In varying degrees these two forms of expression are similarly present in modern warfare, in the pecuniary occupations, and in sports and games. Both lines of aptitudes are cultivated and strengthened by the life of sport as well as by the more serious forms of emulative life. Strategy or cunning is an element invariably present in games, as also in warlike pursuits and in the chase. In all of these employments strategy tends to develop into finesse and chicane. Chicane, falsehood, brow-beating, hold a well-secured place in the method of procedure of any athletic contest and in games generally. The habitual employment of an umpire, and the minute technical regulations governing the limits and details of permissible fraud and strategic advantage, sufficiently attest the fact that fraudulent practices and attempts to overreach one's opponents are not adventitious features of the game. In the nature of the case habituation to sports should conduce to a fuller development of the aptitude for fraud; and the prevalence in the community of that predatory temperament which inclines men to sports connotes a prevalence of sharp practice and callous disregard of the interests of others, individually and collectively. Resort to fraud, in any guise and under any legitimation of law or custom, is an expression of a narrowly self-regarding habit of mind. It is needless to dwell at any length on the economic value of this feature of the sporting character.

In this connection it is to be noted that the most obvious characteristic of the physiognomy affected by athletic and other sporting men is that of an extreme astuteness. The gifts and exploits of Ulysses are scarcely second to those of Achilles, either in their substantial furtherance of the game or in the éclat which they give the astute sporting man among his associates. The pantomime of astuteness is commonly the first step in that assimilation to the professional sporting man which a youth undergoes after matriculation in any reputable school, of the secondary or the higher education, as the case may be. And the physiognomy of astuteness, as a decorative feature, never ceases to receive the thoughtful attention of men whose serious interest lies in athletic games, races, or other contests of a similar emulative nature. As a further indication of their spiritual kinship, it may be pointed out that the members of the lower delinquent class usually show this physiognomy of astuteness in a marked degree, and that they very commonly show the same histrionic exaggeration of it that is often seen in the young candidate for athletic honours. This, by the way, is the most legible mark of what is vulgarly called "toughness" in youthful aspirants for a bad name.

The astute man, it may be remarked, is of no economic value to the community—unless it be for the purpose of sharp practice in dealings with other communities. His functioning is not a furtherance of the generic life process. At its best, in its direct economic bearing, it is a conversion of the economic substance of the collectivity to a growth alien to the collective life process—very much after the analogy of what in medicine would be called a benign tumor, with some tendency to transgress the uncertain line that divides the benign from the malign growths.

The two barbarian traits, ferocity and astuteness, go to make up the predaceous temper or spiritual attitude. They are the expressions of a narrowly self-regarding habit of mind. Both are highly serviceable for individual expediency in a life looking to invidious success. Both also have a high æsthetic value. Both are fostered by the pecuniary culture. But both alike are of no use for the purposes of the collective life.

CHAPTER XI

THE BELIEF IN LUCK

The gambling propensity is another subsidiary trait of the barbarian temperament. It is a concomitant variation of character of almost universal prevalence among sporting men and among men given to warlike and emulative activities generally. This trait also has a direct economic value. It is recognised to be a hindrance to the highest industrial efficiency of the aggregate in any community where it prevails in an appreciable degree.

The gambling proclivity is doubtfully to be classed as a feature belonging exclusively to the predatory type of human nature. The chief factor in the gambling habit is the belief in luck; and this belief is apparently traceable, at least in its elements, to a stage in human evolution antedating the predatory culture. It may well have been under the predatory culture that the belief in luck was developed into the form in which it is present, as the chief element of the gambling proclivity, in the sporting temperament. It probably owes the specific form under which it occurs in the modern culture to the predatory discipline. But the belief in luck is in substance a habit of more ancient date than the predatory culture. It is one form of the animistic apprehension of things. The belief seems to be a trait carried over in substance from an earlier phase into the barbarian culture, and transmuted and transmitted through that culture to a later stage of human development under a specific form imposed by the predatory discipline. But in any case it is to be taken as an archaic trait, inherited from a more or less remote past, more or less incompatible with the requirements of the modern industrial process, and more or less of a hindrance to the fullest efficiency of the collective economic life of the present.

While the belief in luck is the basis of the gambling habit, it is not the only element that enters into the habit of betting. Betting on the issue of contests of strength and skill proceeds on a further motive, without which the belief in luck would scarcely come in as a prominent feature of sporting life. This further motive is the desire of the anticipated winner, or the partisan of the anticipated winning side, to heighten his side's ascendency at the cost of the loser. Not only does the stronger side score a more signal victory, and the losing side suffer a more painful and humiliating defeat, in proportion as the pecuniary gain and loss in the wager is large; although this alone is a consideration of material weight. But the wager is commonly laid also with a view, not avowed in words nor even recognised in set terms *in petto*,[1] to enhancing the chances of success for the contestant on which it is laid. It is felt that substance and solicitude expended to this end can not go for naught in the issue. There is here a special manifestation of the instinct of workmanship, backed by an even more manifest sense that the animistic congruity of things must decide for a victorious outcome for the side in whose behalf the propensity inherent in events has been propitiated and fortified by so much of conative and kinetic urging. This incentive to the wager expresses itself freely under the form of backing one's favourite in any contest, and it is unmistakably a predatory feature. It is as ancillary to the predaceous impulse proper that the belief in luck expresses itself in a wager. So that it may be set down that in so far as the belief in luck comes to expression in the form of laying a wager, it is to be accounted an integral element of the predatory type of character. The belief is, in its elements, an archaic habit which belongs substantially to early, undifferentiated human nature; but when this belief is helped out by the predatory emulative impulse, and so is differentiated into the specific form of the gambling habit, it is, in this higher-developed and specific form, to be classed as a trait of the barbarian character.

The belief in luck is a sense of fortuitous necessity in the sequence of phenomena. In its various mutations and expressions, it is of very serious importance for the economic efficiency of any community in which it prevails to an appreciable extent. So much so as to warrant a more detailed discussion of its origin and content and of the bearing of its various ramifications upon economic structure and function, as well as a discussion of the relation of the leisure class to its growth, differentiation, and persistence. In the developed, integrated form in which it is most readily observed in the barbarian of the predatory culture or in the sporting man of modern communities, the belief comprises at least two distinguishable elements,—which are to be taken as two different phases of the same fundamental habit of thought, or as the same psychological factor in two successive phases of its evolution. The fact that these two elements are successive phases of the same general line of growth of belief does not hinder their coexisting in the habits of thought of any given individual. The more primitive form (or the more archaic phase) is an incipient animistic belief, or an animistic sense of relations and things, that imputes a quasi-personal character to facts. To the archaic man all the obtrusive and obviously consequential objects and facts in his environment have a quasi-personal individuality. They are conceived to be possessed of volition, or rather of propensities, which enter into the complex of causes and affect events in an inscrutable manner. The sporting man's sense of luck and chance, or of fortuitous necessity, is an inarticulate or inchoate animism. It applies to objects and situations, often in a very vague way; but it is usually so far defined as to imply the possibility of propitiating, or of deceiving and cajoling, or otherwise disturbing the unfolding of propensities resident in the objects which constitute the apparatus and accessories of any game of skill or chance. There are few sporting men who are not in the habit of wearing charms or talismans to which more or less of efficacy is felt to belong. And the proportion is not much less of those who instinctively dread the "hoodooing" of the contestants or the apparatus engaged in any contest on which they lay a wager; or who feel that the fact of their backing a given contestant or side in the game does and ought to strengthen that side; or to whom the "mascot" which they cultivate means something more than a jest.

In its simple form the belief in luck is this instinctive sense of an inscrutable teleological propensity in objects or situations. Objects or events have a propensity to eventuate in a given end, whether this end or objective point of the sequence is conceived to be fortuitously given or deliberately sought. From this simple animism the belief shades off by insensible gradations into the second, derivative form or phase above referred to, which is a more or less articulate belief in an inscrutable preternatural agency. The preternatural agency works through the visible objects with which it is associated, but is not identified with these objects in point of individuality. The use of the term "preternatural agency" here carries no further implication as to the nature of the agency spoken of as preternatural. This is only a farther development of animistic belief. The preternatural agency is not necessarily conceived to be a personal agent in the full sense, but it is an agency which partakes of the attributes of personality to the extent of somewhat arbitrarily influencing the outcome of any enterprise, and especially of any contest. The pervading belief in the *hamingia* or *gipta* (*gæfa, auðna*)[2] which lends so much of colour to the Icelandic sagas specifically, and to early Germanic folk-legends generally, is an illustration of this sense of an extra-physical propensity in the course of events.

In this expression or form of the belief the propensity is scarcely personified, although to a varying extent an individuality is imputed to it; and this individuated propensity is sometimes conceived to yield to circumstances, commonly to circumstances of a spiritual or preternatural character. A well-known and striking exemplification of the belief—in a fairly advanced stage of differentiation and involving an anthropomorphic personification of the preternatural agent appealed to—is afforded by the wager of battle. Here the preternatural agent was conceived to act on request as umpire, and to shape the outcome of the contest in accordance with some stipulated ground of decision, such as the equity or legality of the respective contestants' claims. The like sense of an inscrutable but spiritually necessary tendency in events is still traceable as an obscure element in current popular belief, as shown, for instance, by the well-accredited maxim, "Thrice is he armed who knows his quarrel just,"—a maxim which retains much of its significance for the average unreflecting person even in the civilised communities of to-day. The modern reminiscence of the belief in the *hamingia,* or in the guidance of an unseen hand, which is traceable in the acceptance of this maxim is faint and perhaps uncertain; and it seems in any case to be blended with other psychological moments that are not clearly of an animistic character.

For the purpose in hand it is unnecessary to look more closely into the psychological process or the ethnological line of descent by which the later of these two animistic apprehensions of propensity is derived from the earlier. This question may be of the gravest importance to folk-psychology or to the theory of the evolution of creeds and cults. The same is true of the more fundamental question whether the two are related at all as successive phases in a sequence of development. Reference is here made to the existence of these questions only to remark that the interest of the present discussion does not lie in that direction. So far as concerns economic theory, these two elements or phases of the belief in luck, or in an extra-causal trend or propensity in things, are of substantially the same character. They have an economic significance as habits of thought which affect the individual's habitual view of the facts and sequences with which he comes in contact, and which thereby affect the individual's serviceability for the industrial purpose. Therefore, apart from all question of the beauty, worth, or beneficence of any animistic belief, there is place for a discussion of their economic bearing on the serviceability of the individual as an economic factor, and especially as an industrial agent.

It has already been noted in an earlier connection, that in order to the highest serviceability in the complex industrial processes of to-day, the individual must be endowed with the aptitude and the habit of readily apprehending and relating facts in terms of causal sequence. Both as a whole and in its details, the industrial process is a process of quantitative causation. The "intelligence" demanded of the workman, as well as of the director of an industrial process, is little else than a degree of facility in the apprehension of and adaptation to a quantitatively determined causal sequence. This facility of apprehension and adaptation is what is lacking in stupid workmen, and the growth of this facility is the end sought in their education—so far as their education aims to enhance their industrial efficiency.

In so far as the individual's inherited aptitudes or his training incline him to account for facts and sequences in other terms than those of causation or matter-of-fact, they lower his productive efficiency or industrial usefulness. This lowering of efficiency through a penchant for animistic methods of apprehending facts is especially apparent when taken in the mass—when a given population with an animistic turn is viewed as a whole. The economic drawbacks of animism are more patent and its consequences are more far-reaching under the modern system of large industry than under any other. In the modern industrial communities, industry is, to a constantly increasing extent, being organised in a comprehensive system of organs and functions mutually conditioning one another; and therefore freedom from all bias in the causal apprehension of phenomena grows constantly more requisite to efficiency on the part of the men concerned in industry. Under a system of handicraft an advantage in dexterity, diligence, muscular force, or endurance may, in a very large measure, offset such a bias in the habits of thought of the workmen.

Similarly in agricultural industry of the traditional kind, which closely resembles handicraft in the nature of the demands made upon the workman. In both, the workman is himself the prime mover chiefly depended upon, and the natural forces engaged are in large part apprehended as inscrutable and fortuitous agencies, whose working lies beyond the workman's control or discretion. In popular apprehension there is in these forms of industry relatively little of the industrial process left to the fateful swing of a comprehensive mechanical sequence which must be comprehended in terms of causation and to which the operations of industry and the movements of the workmen must be adapted. As industrial methods develop, the virtues of the handicraftsman count for less and less as an offset to scanty intelligence or a halting acceptance of the sequence of cause and effect. The industrial organisation assumes more and more of the character of a mechanism, in which it is man's office to discriminate and select what natural forces shall work out their effects in his service. The workman's part in industry changes from that of a prime mover to that of discrimination and valuation of quantitative sequences and mechanical facts. The faculty of a ready apprehension and unbiassed appreciation of causes in his environment grows in relative economic importance, and any element in the complex of his habits of thought which intrudes a bias at variance with this ready appreciation of matter-of-fact sequence gains proportionately in importance as a disturbing element acting to lower his industrial usefulness. Through its cumulative effect upon the habitual attitude of the population, even a slight or inconspicuous bias towards accounting for everyday facts by recourse to other ground than that of quantitative causation may work an appreciable lowering of the collective industrial efficiency of a community.

The animistic habit of mind may occur in the early, undifferentiated form of an inchoate animistic belief, or in the later and more highly integrated phase in which there is an anthropomorphic personification of the propensity imputed to facts. The industrial value of such a lively animistic sense, or of such recourse to a preternatural agency or the guidance of an unseen hand, is of course very much the same in either case. As affects the industrial serviceability of the individual, the effect is of the same kind in either case; but the extent to which this habit of thought dominates or shapes the complex of his habits of thought varies with the degree of immediacy, urgency, or exclusiveness with which the individual habitually applies the animistic or anthropomorphic formula in dealing with the facts of his environment. The animistic habit acts in all cases to blur the appreciation of causal sequence; but the earlier, less reflected, less defined animistic sense of propensity may be expected to affect the intellectual processes of the individual in a more pervasive way than the higher forms of anthropomorphism. Where the animistic habit is present in the naïve form, its scope and range of application are not defined or limited. It will therefore palpably affect his thinking at every turn of the person's life—wherever he has to do with the material means of life. In the later, maturer development of animism, after it has been defined through the process of anthropomorphic elaboration, when its application has been limited in a somewhat consistent fashion to the remote and the invisible, it comes about that an increasing range of everyday facts are provisionally accounted for without recourse to the preternatural agency in which a cultivated animism expresses itself. A highly integrated, personified preternatural agency is not a convenient means of handling the trivial occurrences of life, and a habit is therefore easily fallen into of accounting for many trivial or vulgar phenomena in terms of sequence. The provisional explanation so arrived at is by neglect allowed to stand as definitive, for trivial purposes, until special provocation or perplexity recalls the individual to his allegiance. But when special exigencies arise, that is to say, when there is peculiar need of a full and free recourse to the law of cause and effect, then the individual commonly has recourse to the preternatural agency as a universal solvent, if he is possessed of an anthropomorphic belief.

The extra-causal propensity or agent has a very high utility as a recourse in perplexity, but its utility is altogether of a non-economic kind. It is especially a refuge and a fund of comfort where it has attained the degree of consistency and specialisation that belongs to an anthropomorphic divinity. It has much to commend it even on other grounds than that of affording the perplexed individual a means of escape from the difficulty of accounting for phenomena in terms of causal sequence. It would scarcely be in place here to dwell on the obvious and well-accepted merits of an anthropomorphic divinity, as seen from the point of view of the æsthetic, moral, or spiritual interest, or even as seen from the less remote standpoint of political, military, or social policy. The question here concerns the less picturesque and less urgent economic value of the belief in such a preternatural agency, taken as a habit of thought which affects the industrial serviceability of the believer. And even within this narrow, economic range, the inquiry is perforce confined to the immediate bearing of this habit of thought upon the believer's workmanlike serviceability, rather than extended to include its remoter economic effects. These remoter effects are very difficult to trace. The inquiry into them is so encumbered with current preconceptions as to the degree in which life is enhanced by spiritual contact with such a divinity, that any attempt to inquire into their economic value must for the present be fruitless.

The immediate, direct effect of the animistic habit of thought upon the general frame of mind of the believer goes in the direction of lowering his effective intelligence in the respect in which intelligence is of especial consequence for modern industry. The effect follows, in varying degree, whether the preternatural agent or propensity believed in is of a higher or a lower cast. This holds true of the barbarian's and the sporting man's sense of luck and propensity, and likewise of the somewhat higher developed belief in an anthropomorphic divinity, such as is commonly possessed by the same class. It must be taken to hold true also—though with what relative degree of cogency is not easy to say—of the more adequately developed anthropomorphic cults, such as appeal to the devout civilised man. The industrial disability entailed by a popular adherence to one of the higher anthropomorphic cults may be relatively slight, but it is not to be overlooked. And even these high-class cults of the Western culture do not represent the last dissolving phase of this human sense of extra-causal propensity. Beyond these the same animistic sense shows itself also in such attenuations of anthropomorphism as the eighteenth-century appeal to an order of nature and natural rights, and in their modern representative, the ostensibly post-Darwinian concept of a meliorative trend in the process of evolution. This animistic explanation of phenomena is a form of the fallacy which the logicians knew by the name of *ignava ratio*.[3] For the purposes of industry or of science it counts as a blunder in the apprehension and valuation of facts.

Apart from its direct industrial consequences, the animistic habit has a certain significance for economic theory on other grounds. (1) It is a fairly reliable indication of the presence, and to some extent even of the degree of potency, of certain other archaic traits that accompany it and that are of substantial economic consequence; and (2) the material consequences of that code of devout proprieties to which the animistic habit gives rise in the development of an anthropomorphic cult are of importance both (*a*) as affecting the community's consumption of goods and the prevalent canons of taste, as already suggested in an earlier chapter, and (*b*) in inducing and conserving a certain habitual recognition of the relation to a superior, and so stiffening the current sense of status and allegiance.

As regards the point last named (*b*), that body of habits of thought which makes up the character of any individual is in some sense an organic whole. A marked variation in a given direction at any one point carries with it, as its correlative, a concomitant variation in the habitual expression of life in other directions or other groups of activities. These various habits of thought, or habitual expressions of life, are all phases of the single life sequence of the individual; therefore a habit formed in response to a given stimulus will necessarily affect the character of the response made to other stimuli. A modification of human nature at any one point is a modification of human nature as a whole. On this ground, and perhaps to a still greater extent on obscurer grounds that can not be discussed here, there are these concomitant variations as between the different traits of human nature. So, for instance, barbarian peoples with a well-developed predatory scheme of life are commonly also possessed of a strong prevailing animistic habit, a well-formed anthropomorphic cult, and a lively sense of status. On the other hand, anthropomorphism and the realising sense of an animistic propensity in material things are less obtrusively present in the life of the peoples at the cultural stages which precede and which follow the barbarian culture. The sense of status is also feebler, on the whole, in peaceable communities. It is to be remarked that a lively, but slightly specialised, animistic belief is to be found in most if not all peoples living in the ante-predatory, savage stage of culture. The primitive savage takes his animism less seriously than the barbarian or the degenerate savage. With him it eventuates in fantastic myth-making, rather than in coercive superstition. The barbarian culture shows sportsmanship, status, and anthropomorphism. There is commonly observable a like concomitance of variations in the same respects in the individual temperament of men in the civilised communities of to-day. Those modern representatives of the predaceous barbarian temper that make up the sporting element are commonly believers in luck; at least they have a strong sense of an animistic propensity in things, by force of which they are given to gambling. So also as regards anthropomorphism in this class. Such of them as give in their adhesion to some creed commonly attach themselves to one of the naïvely and consistently anthropomorphic creeds; there are relatively few sporting men who seek spiritual comfort in the less anthropomorphic cults, such as the Unitarian or the Universalist.

Closely bound up with this correlation of anthropomorphism and prowess is the fact that anthropomorphic cults act to conserve, if not to initiate, habits of mind favourable to a régime of status. As regards this point, it is quite impossible to say where the disciplinary effect of the cult ends and where the evidence of a concomitance of variations in inherited traits begins. In their finest development, the predatory temperament, the sense of status, and the anthropomorphic cult all together belong to the barbarian culture; and something of a mutual causal relation subsists between the three phenomena as they come into sight in communities on that cultural level. The way in which they recur in correlation in the habits and aptitudes of individuals and classes to-day goes far to imply a like causal or organic relation between the same psychological phenomena considered as traits or habits of the individual.

It has appeared at an earlier point in the discussion that the relation of status, as a feature of social structure, is a consequence of the predatory habit of life. As regards its line of derivation, it is substantially an elaborated expression of the predatory attitude. On the other hand, an anthropomorphic cult is a code of detailed relations of status superimposed upon the concept of a preternatural, inscrutable propensity in material things. So that, as regards the external facts of its derivation, the cult may be taken as an outgrowth of archaic man's pervading animistic sense, defined and in some degree transformed by the predatory habit of life, the result being a personified preternatural agency, which is by imputation endowed with a full complement of the habits of thought that characterise the man of the predatory culture.

The grosser psychological features in the case, which have an immediate bearing on economic theory and are consequently to be taken account of here, are therefore: (*a*) as has appeared in an earlier chapter, the predatory, emulative habit of mind here called prowess is but the barbarian variant of the generically human instinct of workmanship, which has fallen into this specific form under the guidance of a habit of invidious comparison of persons; (*b*) the relation of status is a formal expression of such an invidious comparison duly gauged and graded according to a sanctioned schedule; (*c*) an anthropomorphic cult, in the days of its early vigour at least, is an institution the characteristic element of which is a relation of status between the human subject as inferior and the personified preternatural agency as superior. With this in mind, there should be no difficulty in recognising the intimate relation which subsists between these three phenomena of human nature and of human life; the relation amounts to an identity in some of their substantial elements. On the one hand, the system of status and the predatory habit of life are an expression of the instinct of workmanship as it takes form under a custom of invidious comparison; on the other hand, the anthropomorphic cult and the habit of devout observances are an expression of men's animistic sense of a propensity in material things, elaborated under the guidance of substantially the same general habit of invidious comparison. The two categories—the emulative habit of life and the habit of devout observances—are therefore to be taken as complementary elements of the barbarian type of human nature and of its modern barbarian variants. They are expressions of much the same range of aptitudes, made in response to different sets of stimuli.

CHAPTER XII

DEVOUT OBSERVANCES

A discursive rehearsal of certain incidents of modern life will show the organic relation of the anthropomorphic cults to the barbarian culture and temperament. It will likewise serve to show how the survival and efficacy of the cults and the prevalence of their schedule of devout observances are related to the institution of a leisure class and to the springs of action underlying that institution. Without any intention to commend or to deprecate the practices to be spoken of under the head of devout observances, or the spiritual and intellectual traits of which these observances are the expression, the everyday phenomena of current anthropomorphic cults may be taken up from the point of view of the interest which they have for economic theory. What can properly be spoken of here are the tangible, external features of devout observances. The moral, as well as the devotional value of the life of faith lies outside of the scope of the present inquiry. Of course no question is here entertained as to the truth or beauty of the creeds on which the cults proceed. And even their remoter economic bearing can not be taken up here; the subject is too recondite and of too grave import to find a place in so slight a sketch.

Something has been said in an earlier chapter as to the influence which pecuniary standards of value exert upon the processes of valuation carried out on other bases, not related to the pecuniary interest. The relation is not altogether one-sided. The economic standards or canons of valuation are in their turn influenced by extra-economic standards of value. Our judgments of the economic bearing of facts are to some extent shaped by the dominant presence of these weightier interests. There is a point of view, indeed, from which the economic interest is of weight only as being ancillary to these higher, non-economic interests. For the present purpose, therefore, some thought must be taken to isolate the economic interest or the economic bearing of these phenomena of anthropomorphic cults. It takes some effort to divest oneself of the more serious point of view, and to reach an economic appreciation of these facts, with as little as may be of the bias due to higher interests extraneous to economic theory.

———

In the discussion of the sporting temperament, it has appeared that the sense of an animistic propensity in material things and events is what affords the spiritual basis of the sporting man's gambling habit. For the economic purpose, this sense of propensity is substantially the same psychological element as expresses itself, under a variety of forms, in animistic beliefs and anthropomorphic creeds. So far as concerns those tangible psychological features with which economic theory has to deal, the gambling spirit which pervades the sporting element shades off by insensible gradations into that frame of mind which finds gratification in devout observances. As seen from the point of view of economic theory, the sporting character shades off into the character of a religious devotee. Where the betting man's animistic sense is helped out by a somewhat consistent tradition, it has developed into a more or less articulate belief in a preternatural or hyperphysical agency, with something of an anthropomorphic content. And where this is the case, there is commonly a perceptible inclination to make terms with the preternatural agency by some approved method of approach and conciliation. This element of propitiation and cajoling has much in common with the crasser forms of worship—if not in historical derivation, at least in actual psychological content. It obviously shades off in unbroken continuity into what is recognised as superstitious practice and belief, and so asserts its claim to kinship with the grosser anthropomorphic cults.

The sporting or gambling temperament, then, comprises some of the substantial psychological elements that go to make a believer in creeds and an observer of devout forms, the chief point of coincidence being the belief in an inscrutable propensity or a preternatural interposition in the sequence of events. For the purpose of the gambling practice the belief in preternatural agency may be, and ordinarily is, less closely formulated, especially as regards the habits of thought and the scheme of life imputed to the preternatural agent; or, in other words, as regards his moral character and his purposes in interfering in events. With respect to the individuality or personality of the agency whose presence as luck, or chance, or hoodoo,[1] or mascot, etc., he feels and sometimes dreads and endeavours to evade, the sporting man's views are also less specific, less integrated and differentiated. The basis of his gambling activity is, in great measure, simply an instinctive sense of the presence of a pervasive extraphysical and arbitrary force or propensity in things or situations, which is scarcely recognised as a personal agent. The betting man is not infrequently both a believer in luck, in this naïve sense, and at the same time a pretty staunch adherent of some form of accepted creed. He is especially prone to accept so much of the creed as concerns the inscrutable power and the arbitrary habits of the divinity which has won his confidence. In such a case he is possessed of two, or sometimes more than two, distinguishable phases of animism. Indeed, the complete series of successive phases of animistic belief is to be found unbroken in the spiritual furniture of any sporting community. Such a chain of animistic conceptions will comprise the most elementary form of an instinctive sense of luck and chance and fortuitous necessity at one end of the series, together with the perfectly developed anthropomorphic divinity at the other end, with all intervening stages of integration. Coupled with these beliefs in preternatural agency goes an instinctive shaping of conduct to conform with the surmised requirements of the lucky chance on the one hand, and a more or less devout submission to the inscrutable decrees of the divinity on the other hand.

There is a relationship in this respect between the sporting temperament and the temperament of the delinquent classes; and the two are related to the temperament which inclines to an anthropomorphic cult. Both the delinquent and the sporting man are on an average more apt to be adherents of some accredited creed, and are also rather more inclined to devout observances, than the general average of the community. It is also noticeable that unbelieving members of these classes show more of a proclivity to become proselytes to some accredited faith than the average of unbelievers. This fact of observation is avowed by the spokesmen of sports, especially in apologising for the more naïvely predatory athletic sports. Indeed, it is somewhat insistently claimed as a meritorious feature of sporting life that the habitual participants in athletic games are in some degree peculiarly given to devout practices. And it is observable that the cult to which sporting men and the predaceous delinquent classes adhere, or to which proselytes from these classes commonly attach themselves, is ordinarily not one of the so-called higher faiths, but a cult which has to do with a thoroughly anthropomorphic divinity. Archaic, predatory human nature is not satisfied with abstruse conceptions of a dissolving personality that shades off into the concept of quantitative causal sequence, such as the speculative, esoteric creeds of Christendom impute to the First Cause, Universal Intelligence, World Soul, or Spiritual Aspect. As an instance of a cult of the character which the habits of mind of the athlete and the delinquent require, may be cited that branch of the church militant known as the Salvation Army. This is to some extent recruited from the lower-class delinquents, and it appears to comprise also, among its officers especially, a larger proportion of men with a sporting record than the proportion of such men in the aggregate population of the community.

College athletics afford a case in point. It is contended by exponents of the devout element in college life—and there seems to be no ground for disputing the claim—that the desirable athletic material afforded by any student body in this country is at the same time predominantly religious; or that it is at least given to devout observances to a greater degree than the average of those students whose interest in athletics and other college sports is less. This is what might be expected on theoretical grounds. It may be remarked, by the way, that from one point of view this is felt to reflect credit on the college sporting life, on athletic games, and on those persons who occupy themselves with these matters. It happens not infrequently that college sporting men devote themselves to the religious propaganda, either as a vocation or as a by-occupation; and it is observable that when this happens they are likely to become propagandists of some one of the more anthropomorphic cults. In their teaching they are apt to insist chiefly on the personal relation of status which subsists between an anthropomorphic divinity and the human subject.

This intimate relation between athletics and devout observance among college men is a fact of sufficient notoriety; but it has a special feature to which attention has not been called, although it is obvious enough. The religious zeal which pervades much of the college sporting element is especially prone to express itself in an unquestioning devoutness and a naïve and complacent submission to an inscrutable Providence. It therefore by preference seeks affiliation with some one of those lay religious organisations which occupy themselves with the spread of the exoteric forms of the faith,—as, *e.g.,* the Young Men's Christian Association or the Young People's Society for Christian Endeavour. These lay bodies are organised to further "practical" religion; and as if to enforce the argument and firmly establish the close relationship between the sporting temperament and the archaic devoutness, these lay religious bodies commonly devote some appreciable portion of their energies to the furtherance of athletic contests and similar games of chance and skill. It might even be said that sports of this kind are apprehended to have some efficacy as a means of grace. They are apparently useful as a means of proselyting, and as a means of sustaining the devout attitude in converts once made. That is to say, the games which give exercise to the animistic sense and to the emulative propensity help to form and to conserve that habit of mind to which the more exoteric cults are congenial. Hence, in the hands of the lay organisations, these sporting activities come to do duty as a novitiate or a means of induction into that fuller unfolding of the life of spiritual status which is the privilege of the full communicant alone.

That the exercise of the emulative and lower animistic proclivities are substantially useful for the devout purpose seems to be placed beyond question by the fact that the priesthood of many denominations is following the lead of the lay organisations in this respect. Those ecclesiastical organisations especially which stand nearest the lay organisations in their insistence on practical religion have gone some way towards adopting these or analogous practices in connection with the traditional devout observances. So there are "boys' brigades," and other organisations, under clerical sanction, acting to develop the emulative proclivity and the sense of status in the youthful members of the congregation. These pseudo-military organisations tend to elaborate and accentuate the proclivity to emulation and invidious comparison, and so strengthen the native facility for discerning and approving the relation of personal mastery and subservience. And a believer is eminently a person who knows how to obey and accept chastisement with good grace.

But the habits of thought which these practices foster and conserve make up but one-half of the substance of the anthropomorphic cults. The other, complementary element of devout life—the animistic habit of mind—is recruited and conserved by a second range of practices organised under clerical sanction. These are the class of gambling practices of which the church bazaar or raffle may be taken as the type. As indicating the degree of legitimacy of these practices in connection with devout observances proper, it is to be remarked that these raffles, and the like trivial opportunities for gambling, seem to appeal with more effect to the common run of the members of religious organisations than they do to persons of a less devout habit of mind.

All this seems to argue, on the one hand, that the same temperament inclines people to sports as inclines them to the anthropo-morphic cults, and on the other hand that the habituation to sports, perhaps especially to athletic sports, acts to develop the propensi-ties which find satisfaction in devout observances. Conversely; it also appears that habituation to these observances favours the growth of a proclivity for athletic sports and for all games that give play to the habit of invidious comparison and of the appeal to luck. Substantially the same range of propensities finds expression in both these directions of the spiritual life. That barbarian human nature in which the predatory instinct and the animistic standpoint predominate is normally prone to both. The predatory habit of mind involves an accentuated sense of personal dignity and of the relative standing of individuals. The social structure in which the predatory habit has been the dominant factor in the shaping of in-stitutions is a structure based on status. The pervading norm in the predatory community's scheme of life is the relation of superior and inferior, noble and base, dominant and subservient persons and classes, master and slave. The anthropomorphic cults have come down from that stage of industrial development and have been shaped by the same scheme of economic differentiation,—a differ-entiation into consumer and producer,—and they are pervaded by the same dominant principle of mastery and subservience. The cults impute to their divinity the habits of thought answering to the stage of economic differentiation at which the cults took shape. The anthropomorphic divinity is conceived to be punctilious in all questions of precedence and is prone to an assertion of mastery and an arbitrary exercise of power—an habitual resort to force as the final arbiter.

In the later and maturer formulations of the anthropomorphic creed this imputed habit of dominance on the part of a divinity of awful presence and inscrutable power is chastened into "the father-hood of God." The spiritual attitude and the aptitudes imputed to the preternatural agent are still such as belong under the régime of status, but they now assume the patriarchal cast characteristic of the quasi-peaceable stage of culture. Still it is to be noted that even in this advanced phase of the cult the observances in which devoutness finds expression consistently aim to propitiate the divinity by extolling his greatness and glory and by professing subservience and fealty. The act of propitiation or of worship is designed to appeal to a sense of status imputed to the inscrutable power that is thus approached. The propitiatory formulas most in vogue are still such as carry or imply an invidious comparison. A loyal attachment to the person of an anthropomorphic divinity endowed with such an archaic human nature implies the like archaic propensities in the devotee. For the purposes of economic theory, the relation of fealty, whether to a physical or to an extraphysical person, is to be taken as a variant of that personal subservience which makes up so large a share of the predatory and the quasi-peaceable scheme of life.

The barbarian conception of the divinity, as a warlike chieftain inclined to an overbearing manner of government, has been greatly softened through the milder manners and the soberer habits of life that characterise those cultural phases which lie between the early predatory stage and the present. But even after this chastening of the devout fancy, and the consequent mitigation of the harsher traits of conduct and character that are currently imputed to the divinity, there still remains in the popular apprehension of the divine nature and temperament a very substantial residue of the barbarian conception. So it comes about, for instance, that in characterising the divinity and his relations to the process of human life, speakers and writers are still able to make effective use of similes borrowed from the vocabulary of war and of the predatory manner of life, as well as of locutions which involve an invidious comparison. Figures of speech of this import are used with good effect even in addressing the less warlike modern audiences, made up of adherents of the blander variants of the creed. This effective use of barbarian epithets and terms of comparison by popular speakers argues that the modern generation has retained a lively appreciation of the dignity and merit of the barbarian virtues; and it argues also that there is a degree of congruity between the devout attitude and the predatory habit of mind. It is only on second thought, if at all, that the devout fancy of modern worshippers revolts at the imputation of ferocious and vengeful emotions and actions to the object of their adoration. It is a matter of common observation that sanguinary epithets applied to the divinity have a high æsthetic and honorific value in the popular apprehension. That is to say, suggestions which these epithets carry are very acceptable to our unreflecting apprehension.

Mine eyes have seen the glory of the coming of the Lord;
He is trampling out the vintage where the grapes of wrath are stored;
He hath loosed the fateful lightning of his terrible swift sword;
    His truth is marching on.

The guiding habits of thought of a devout person move on the plane of an archaic scheme of life which has outlived much of its usefulness for the economic exigencies of the collective life of to-day. In so far as the economic organisation fits the exigencies of the collective life of to-day, it has outlived the régime of status, and has no use and no place for a relation of personal subserviency. So far as concerns the economic efficiency of the community, the sentiment of personal fealty, and the general habit of mind of which that sentiment is an expression, are survivals which cumber the ground and hinder an adequate adjustment of human institutions to the existing situation. The habit of mind which best lends itself to the purposes of a peaceable, industrial community, is that matter-of-fact temper which recognises the value of material facts simply as opaque items in the mechanical sequence. It is that frame of mind which does not instinctively impute an animistic propensity to things, nor resort to preternatural intervention as an explanation of perplexing phenomena, nor depend on an unseen hand to shape the course of events to human use. To meet the requirements of the highest economic efficiency under modern conditions, the world process must habitually be apprehended in terms of quantitative, dispassionate force and sequence.

As seen from the point of view of the later economic exigencies, devoutness is, perhaps in all cases, to be looked upon as a survival from an earlier phase of associated life—a mark of arrested spiritual development. Of course it remains true that in a community where the economic structure is still substantially a system of status; where the attitude of the average of persons in the community is consequently shaped by and adapted to the relation of personal dominance and personal subservience; or where for any other reason—of tradition or of inherited aptitude—the population as a whole is strongly inclined to devout observances; there a devout habit of mind in any individual, not in excess of the average of the community, must be taken simply as a detail of the prevalent habit of life. In this light, a devout individual in a devout community can not be called a case of reversion, since he is abreast of the average of the community. But as seen from the point of view of the modern industrial situation, exceptional devoutness—devotional zeal that rises appreciably above the average pitch of devoutness in the community—may safely be set down as in all cases an atavistic trait.

It is, of course, equally legitimate to consider these phenomena from a different point of view. They may be appreciated for a different purpose, and the characterisation here offered may be turned about. In speaking from the point of view of the devotional interest, or the interest of devout taste, it may, with equal cogency be said that the spiritual attitude bred in men by the modern industrial life is unfavourable to a free development of the life of faith. It might fairly be objected to the later development of the industrial process that its discipline tends to "materialism," to the elimination of filial piety. From the æsthetic point of view, again, something to a similar purport might be said. But, however legitimate and valuable these and the like reflections may be for their purpose, they would not be in place in the present inquiry, which is exclusively concerned with the valuation of these phenomena from the economic point of view.

The grave economic significance of the anthropomorphic habit of mind and of the addiction to devout observances must serve as apology for speaking further on a topic which it can not but be distasteful to discuss at all as an economic phenomenon in a community so devout as ours. Devout observances are of economic importance as an index of a concomitant variation of temperament, accompanying the predatory habit of mind and so indicating the presence of industrially disserviceable traits. They indicate the presence of a mental attitude which has a certain economic value of its own by virtue of its influence upon the industrial serviceability of the individual. But they are also of importance more directly, in modifying the economic activities of the community, especially as regards the distribution and consumption of goods.

The most obvious economic bearing of these observances is seen in the devout consumption of goods and services. The consumption of ceremonial paraphernalia required by any cult, in the way of shrines, temples, churches, vestments, sacrifices, sacraments, holiday attire, etc., serves no immediate material end. All this material apparatus may, therefore, without implying depreciation, be broadly characterised as items of conspicuous waste. The like is true in a general way of the personal service consumed under this head; such as priestly education, priestly service, pilgrimages, fasts, holidays, household devotions, and the like. At the same time the observances in the execution of which this consumption takes place serve to extend and protract the vogue of those habits of thought on which an anthropomorphic cult rests. That is to say, they further the habits of thought characteristic of the régime of status. They are in so far an obstruction to the most effective organisation of industry under modern circumstances; and are, in the first instance, antagonistic to the development of economic institutions in the direction required by the situation of to-day. For the present purpose, the indirect as well as the direct effects of this consumption are of the nature of a curtailment of the community's economic efficiency. In economic theory, then, and considered in its proximate consequences, the consumption of goods and effort in the service of an anthropomorphic divinity means a lowering of the vitality of the community. What may be the remoter, indirect, moral effects of this class of consumption does not admit of a succinct answer, and it is a question which can not be taken up here.

It will be to the point, however, to note the general economic character of devout consumption, in comparison with consumption for other purposes. An indication of the range of motives and purposes from which devout consumption of goods proceeds will help toward an appreciation of the value both of this consumption itself and of the general habit of mind to which it is congenial. There is a striking parallelism, if not rather a substantial identity of motive, between the consumption which goes to the service of an anthropomorphic divinity and that which goes to the service of a gentleman of leisure—a chieftain or patriarch—in the upper class of society during the barbarian culture. Both in the case of the chieftain and in that of the divinity there are expensive edifices set apart for the behoof of the person served. These edifices, as well as the properties which supplement them in the service, must not be common in kind or grade; they always show a large element of conspicuous waste. It may also be noted that the devout edifices are invariably of an archaic cast in their structure and fittings. So also the servants, both of the chieftain and of the divinity, must appear in the presence clothed in garments of a special, ornate character. The characteristic economic feature of this apparel is a more than ordinarily accentuated conspicuous waste, together with the secondary feature—more accentuated in the case of the priestly servants than in that of the servants or courtiers of the barbarian potentate—that this court dress must always be in some degree of an archaic fashion. Also the garments worn by the lay members of the community when they come into the presence, should be of a more expensive kind than their everyday apparel. Here, again, the parallelism between the usage of the chieftain's audience hall and that of the sanctuary is fairly well marked. In this respect there is required a certain ceremonial "cleanness" of attire, the essential feature of which, in the economic respect, is that the garments worn on these occasions should carry as little suggestion as may be of any industrial occupation or of any habitual addiction to such employments as are of material use.

This requirement of conspicuous waste and of ceremonial cleanness from the traces of industry extends also to the apparel, and in a less degree to the food, which is consumed on sacred holidays; that is to say, on days set apart—tabu—for the divinity or for some member of the lower ranks of the preternatural leisure class. In economic theory, sacred holidays are obviously to be construed as a season of vicarious leisure performed for the divinity or saint in whose name the tabu is imposed and to whose good repute the abstention from useful effort on these days is conceived to inure. The characteristic feature of all such seasons of devout vicarious leisure is a more or less rigid tabu on all activity that is of human use. In the case of fast-days the conspicuous abstention from gainful occupations and from all pursuits that (materially) further human life is further accentuated by compulsory abstinence from such consumption as would conduce to the comfort or the fulness of life of the consumer.

It may be remarked, parenthetically, that secular holidays are of the same origin, by slightly remoter derivation. They shade off by degrees from the genuinely sacred days, through an intermediate class of semi-sacred birthdays of kings and great men who have been in some measure canonised, to the deliberately invented holiday set apart to further the good repute of some notable event or some striking fact, to which it is intended to do honour, or the good fame of which is felt to be in need of repair. This remoter refinement in the employment of vicarious leisure as a means of augmenting the good repute of a phenomenon or datum is seen at its best in its very latest application. A day of vicarious leisure has in some communities been set apart as Labour Day. This observance is designed to augment the prestige of the fact of labour, by the archaic, predatory method of a compulsory abstention from useful effort. To this datum of labour-in-general is imputed the good repute attributable to the pecuniary strength put in evidence by abstaining from labour.

Sacred holidays, and holidays generally, are of the nature of a tribute levied on the body of the people. The tribute is paid in vicarious leisure, and the honorific effect which emerges is imputed to the person or the fact for whose good repute the holiday has been instituted. Such a tithe of vicarious leisure is a perquisite of all members of the preternatural leisure class and is indispensable to their good fame. *Un saint qu'on ne chôme pas*[2] is indeed a saint fallen on evil days.

Besides this tithe of vicarious leisure levied on the laity, there are also special classes of persons—the various grades of priests and hierodules—whose time is wholly set apart for a similar service. It is not only incumbent on the priestly class to abstain from vulgar labour, especially so far as it is lucrative or is apprehended to contribute to the temporal well-being of mankind. The tabu in the case of the priestly class goes farther and adds a refinement in the form of an injunction against their seeking worldly gain even where it may be had without debasing application to industry. It is felt to be unworthy of the servant of the divinity, or rather unworthy the dignity of the divinity whose servant he is, that he should seek material gain or take thought for temporal matters. "Of all contemptible things a man who pretends to be a priest of God and is a priest to his own comforts and ambitions is the most contemptible."

There is a line of discrimination, which a cultivated taste in matters of devout observance finds little difficulty in drawing, between such actions and conduct as conduce to the fulness of human life and such as conduce to the good fame of the anthropomorphic divinity; and the activity of the priestly class, in the ideal barbarian scheme, falls wholly on the hither side of this line. What falls within the range of economics falls below the proper level of solicitude of the priesthood in its best estate. Such apparent exceptions to this rule as are afforded, for instance, by some of the mediæval orders of monks (the members of which actually laboured to some useful end), scarcely impugn the rule. These outlying orders of the priestly class are not a sacerdotal element in the full sense of the term. And it is noticeable also that these doubtfully sacerdotal orders, which countenanced their members in earning a living, fell into disrepute through offending the sense of propriety in the communities where they existed.

The priest should not put his hand to mechanically productive work; but he should consume in large measure. But even as regards his consumption it is to be noted that it should take such forms as do not obviously conduce to his own comfort or fulness of life; it should conform to the rules governing vicarious consumption, as explained under that head in an earlier chapter. It is not ordinarily in good form for the priestly class to appear well fed or in hilarious spirits. Indeed, in many of the more elaborate cults the injunction against other than vicarious consumption by this class frequently goes so far as to enjoin mortification of the flesh. And even in those modern denominations which have been organised under the latest formulations of the creed, in a modern industrial community, it is felt that all levity and avowed zest in the enjoyment of the good things of this world is alien to the true clerical decorum. Whatever suggests that these servants of an invisible master are living a life, not of devotion to their master's good fame, but of application to their own ends, jars harshly on our sensibilities as something fundamentally and eternally wrong. They are a servant class, although, being servants of a very exalted master, they rank high in the social scale by virtue of this borrowed light. Their consumption is vicarious consumption; and since, in the advanced cults, their master has no need of material gain, their occupation is vicarious leisure in the full sense. "Whether therefore ye eat, or drink, or whatsoever ye do, do all to the glory of God."[3]

It may be added that so far as the laity is assimilated to the priesthood in the respect that they are conceived to be servants of the divinity, so far this imputed vicarious character attaches also to the layman's life. The range of application of this corollary is somewhat wide. It applies especially to such movements for the reform or rehabilitation of the religious life as are of an austere, pietistic, ascetic cast,—where the human subject is conceived to hold his life by a direct servile tenure from his spiritual sovereign. That is to say, where the institution of the priesthood lapses, or where there is an exceptionally lively sense of the immediate and masterful presence of the divinity in the affairs of life, there the layman is conceived to stand in an immediate servile relation to the divinity, and his life is construed to be a performance of vicarious leisure directed to the enhancement of his master's repute. In such cases of reversion there is a return to the unmediated relation of subservience, as the dominant fact of the devout attitude. The emphasis is thereby thrown on an austere and discomforting vicarious leisure, to the neglect of conspicuous consumption as a means of grace.

A doubt will present itself as to the full legitimacy of this characterisation of the sacerdotal scheme of life, on the ground that a considerable proportion of the modern priesthood depart from the scheme in many details. The scheme does not hold good for the clergy of those denominations which have in some measure diverged from the old established schedule of beliefs or observances. These take thought, at least ostensibly or permissively, for the temporal welfare of the laity, as well as for their own. Their manner of life, not only in the privacy of their own household, but often even before the public, does not differ in an extreme degree from that of secular-minded persons, either in its ostensible austerity or in the archaism of its apparatus. This is truest for those denominations that have wandered the farthest. To this objection it is to be said that we have here to do not with a discrepancy in the theory of sacerdotal life, but with an imperfect conformity to the scheme on the part of this body of clergy. They are but a partial and imperfect representative of the priesthood, and must not be taken as exhibiting the sacerdotal scheme of life in an authentic and competent manner. The clergy of the sects and denominations might be characterised as a half-caste priesthood, or a priesthood in process of becoming or of reconstitution. Such a priesthood may be expected to show the characteristics of the sacerdotal office only as blended and obscured with alien motives and traditions, due to the disturbing presence of other factors than those of animism and status in the purposes of the organisations to which this non-conforming fraction of the priesthood belongs.

Appeal may be taken direct to the taste of any person with a discriminating and cultivated sense of the sacerdotal proprieties, or to the prevalent sense of what constitutes clerical decorum in any community at all accustomed to think or to pass criticism on what a clergyman may or may not do without blame. Even in the most extremely secularised denominations, there is some sense of a distinction that should be observed between the sacerdotal and the lay scheme of life. There is no person of sensibility but feels that where the members of this denominational or sectarian clergy depart from traditional usage, in the direction of a less austere or less archaic demeanour and apparel, they are departing from the ideal of priestly decorum. There is probably no community and no sect within the range of the Western culture in which the bounds of permissible indulgence are not drawn appreciably closer for the incumbent of the priestly office than for the common layman. If the priest's own sense of sacerdotal propriety does not effectually impose a limit, the prevalent sense of the proprieties on the part of the community will commonly assert itself so obtrusively as to lead to his conformity or his retirement from office.

Few if any members of any body of clergy, it may be added, would avowedly seek an increase of salary for gain's sake; and if such avowal were openly made by a clergyman, it would be found obnoxious to the sense of propriety among his congregation. It may also be noted in this connection that no one but the scoffers and the very obtuse are not instinctively grieved inwardly at a jest from the pulpit; and that there are none whose respect for their pastor does not suffer through any mark of levity on his part in any conjuncture of life, except it be levity of a palpably histrionic kind—a constrained unbending of dignity. The diction proper to the sanctuary and to the priestly office should also carry little if any suggestion of effective everyday life, and should not draw upon the vocabulary of modern trade or industry. Likewise, one's sense of the proprieties is readily offended by too detailed and intimate a handling of industrial and other purely human questions at the hands of the clergy. There is a certain level of generality below which a cultivated sense of the proprieties in homiletical discourse will not permit a well-bred clergyman to decline in his discussion of temporal interests. These matters that are of human and secular consequence simply, should properly be handled with such a degree of generality and aloofness as may imply that the speaker represents a master whose interest in secular affairs goes only so far as to permissively countenance them.

It is further to be noticed that the non-conforming sects and variants whose priesthood is here under discussion, vary among themselves in the degree of their conformity to the ideal scheme of sacerdotal life. In a general way it will be found that the divergence in this respect is widest in the case of the relatively young denominations, and especially in the case of such of the newer denominations as have chiefly a lower middle-class constituency. They commonly show a large admixture of humanitarian, philanthropic, or other motives which can not be classed as expressions of the devotional attitude; such as the desire of learning or of conviviality, which enter largely into the effective interest shown by members of these organisations. The non-conforming or sectarian movements have commonly proceeded from a mixture of motives, some of which are at variance with that sense of status on which the priestly office rests. Sometimes, indeed, the motive has been in good part a revulsion against a system of status. Where this is the case the institution of the priesthood has broken down in the transition, at least partially. The spokesman of such an organisation is at the outset a servant and representative of the organisation, rather than a member of a special priestly class and the spokesman of a divine master. And it is only by a process of gradual specialisation that, in succeeding generations, this spokesman regains the position of priest, with a full investiture of sacerdotal authority, and with its accompanying austere, archaic and vicarious manner of life. The like is true of the breakdown and redintegration of devout ritual after such a revulsion. The priestly office, the scheme of sacerdotal life, and the schedule of devout observances are rehabilitated only gradually, insensibly, and with more or less variation in details, as the persistent human sense of devout propriety reasserts its primacy in questions touching the interest in the preternatural,—and, it may be added, as the organisation increases in wealth, and so acquires more of the point of view and the habits of thought of a leisure class.

Beyond the priestly class, and ranged in an ascending hierarchy, ordinarily comes a superhuman vicarious leisure class of saints, angels, etc.,—or their equivalents in the ethnic cults. These rise in grade, one above another, according to an elaborate system of status. The principle of status runs through the entire hierarchical system, both visible and invisible. The good fame of these several orders of the supernatural hierarchy also commonly requires a certain tribute of vicarious consumption and vicarious leisure. In many cases they accordingly have devoted to their service suborders of attendants or dependents who perform a vicarious leisure for them, after much the same fashion as was found in an earlier chapter to be true of the dependent leisure class under the patriarchal system.

———

It may not appear without reflection how these devout observances and the peculiarity of temperament which they imply, or the consumption of goods and services which is comprised in the cult, stand related to the leisure class of a modern community, or to the economic motives of which that class is the exponent in the modern scheme of life. To this end a summary review of certain facts bearing on this relation will be useful.

It appears from an earlier passage in this discussion that for the purpose of the collective life of to-day, especially so far as concerns the industrial efficiency of the modern community, the characteristic traits of the devout temperament are a hindrance rather than a help. It should accordingly be found that the modern industrial life tends selectively to eliminate these traits of human nature from the spiritual constitution of the classes that are immediately engaged in the industrial process. It should hold true, approximately, that devoutness is declining or tending to obsolescence among the members of what may be called the effective industrial community. At the same time it should appear that this aptitude or habit survives in appreciably greater vigour among those classes which do not immediately or primarily enter into the community's life process as an industrial factor.

It has already been pointed out that these latter classes, which live by, rather than in, the industrial process, are roughly comprised under two categories: (1) the leisure class proper, which is shielded from the stress of the economic situation; and (2) the indigent classes, including the lower-class delinquents, which are unduly exposed to the stress. In the case of the former class an archaic habit of mind persists because no effectual economic pressure constrains this class to an adaptation of its habits of thought to the changing situation; while in the latter the reason for a failure to adjust their habits of thought to the altered requirements of industrial efficiency is innutrition, absence of such a surplus of energy as is needed in order to make the adjustment with facility, together with a lack of opportunity to acquire and become habituated to the modern point of view. The trend of the selective process runs in much the same direction in both cases.

From the point of view which the modern industrial life inculcates, phenomena are habitually subsumed under the quantitative relation of mechanical sequence. The indigent classes not only fall short of the modicum of leisure necessary in order to appropriate and assimilate the more recent generalisations of science which this point of view involves, but they also ordinarily stand in such a relation of personal dependence or subservience to their pecuniary superiors as materially to retard their emancipation from habits of thought proper to the régime of status. The result is that these classes in some measure retain that general habit of mind the chief expression of which is a strong sense of personal status, and of which devoutness is one feature.

In the older communities of the European culture, the hereditary leisure class, together with the mass of the indigent population, are given to devout observances in an appreciably higher degree than the average of the industrious middle class, wherever a considerable class of the latter character exists. But in some of these countries, the two categories of conservative humanity named above comprise virtually the whole population. Where these two classes greatly preponderate, their bent shapes popular sentiment to such an extent as to bear down any possible divergent tendency in the inconsiderable middle class, and imposes a devout attitude upon the whole community.

This must, of course, not be construed to say that such communities or such classes as are exceptionally prone to devout observances tend to conform in any exceptional degree to the specifications of any code of morals that we may be accustomed to associate with this or that confession of faith. A large measure of the devout habit of mind need not carry with it a strict observance of the injunctions of the Decalogue or of the common law. Indeed, it is becoming somewhat of a commonplace with observers of criminal life in European communities that the criminal and dissolute classes are, if anything, rather more devout, and more naïvely so, than the average of the population. It is among those who constitute the pecuniary middle class and the body of law-abiding citizens that a relative exemption from the devotional attitude is to be looked for. Those who best appreciate the merits of the higher creeds and observances would object to all this and say that the devoutness of the low-class delinquents is a spurious, or at the best a superstitious devoutness; and the point is no doubt well taken and goes directly and cogently to the purpose intended. But for the purpose of the present inquiry these extra-economic, extra-psychological distinctions must perforce be neglected, however valid and however decisive they may be for the purpose for which they are made.

What has actually taken place with regard to class emancipation from the habit of devout observance is shown by the latter-day complaint of the clergy,—that the churches are losing the sympathy of the artisan classes, and are losing their hold upon them. At the same time it is currently believed that the middle class, commonly so called, is also falling away in the cordiality of its support of the church, especially so far as regards the adult male portion of that class. These are currently recognised phenomena, and it might seem that a simple reference to these facts should sufficiently substantiate the general position outlined. Such an appeal to the general phenomena of popular church attendance and church membership may be sufficiently convincing for the proposition here advanced. But it will still be to the purpose to trace in some detail the course of events and the particular forces which have wrought this change in the spiritual attitude of the more advanced industrial communities of to-day. It will serve to illustrate the manner in which economic causes work towards a secularisation of men's habits of thought. In this respect the American community should afford an exceptionally convincing illustration, since this community has been the least trammelled by external circumstances of any equally important industrial aggregate.

After making due allowance for exceptions and sporadic departures from the normal, the situation here at the present time may be summarised quite briefly. As a general rule the classes that are low in economic efficiency, or in intelligence, or both, are peculiarly devout,—as, for instance, the negro population of the South, much of the lower-class foreign population, much of the rural population, especially in those sections which are backward in education, in the stage of development of their industry, or in respect of their industrial contact with the rest of the community. So also such fragments as we possess of a specialised or hereditary indigent class, or of a segregated criminal or dissolute class; although among these latter the devout habit of mind is apt to take the form of a naïve animistic belief in luck and in the efficacy of shamanistic practices perhaps more frequently than it takes the form of a formal adherence to any accredited creed. The artisan class, on the other hand, is notoriously falling away from the accredited anthropomorphic creeds and from all devout observances. This class is in an especial degree exposed to the characteristic intellectual and spiritual stress of modern organised industry, which requires a constant recognition of the undisguised phenomena of impersonal, matter-of-fact sequence and an unreserved conformity to the law of cause and effect. This class is at the same time not underfed nor overworked to such an extent as to leave no margin of energy for the work of adaptation.

The case of the lower or doubtful leisure class in America—the middle class commonly so called—is somewhat peculiar. It differs in respect of its devotional life from its European counterpart, but it differs in degree and method rather than in substance. The churches still have the pecuniary support of this class; although the creeds to which the class adheres with the greatest facility are relatively poor in anthropomorphic content. At the same time the effective middle-class congregation tends, in many cases, more or less remotely perhaps, to become a congregation of women and minors. There is an appreciable lack of devotional fervour among the adult males of the middle class, although to a considerable extent there survives among them a certain complacent, reputable assent to the outlines of the accredited creed under which they were born. Their everyday life is carried on in a more or less close contact with the industrial process.

This peculiar sexual differentiation, which tends to delegate devout observances to the women and their children, is due, at least in part, to the fact that the middle-class women are in great measure a (vicarious) leisure class. The same is true in a less degree of the women of the lower, artisan classes. They live under a régime of status handed down from an earlier stage of industrial development, and thereby they preserve a frame of mind and habits of thought which incline them to an archaic view of things generally. At the same time they stand in no such direct organic relation to the industrial process at large as would tend strongly to break down those habits of thought which, for the modern industrial purpose, are obsolete. That is to say, the peculiar devoutness of women is a particular expression of that conservatism which the women of civilised communities owe, in great measure, to their economic position. For the modern man the patriarchal relation of status is by no means the dominant feature of life; but for the women on the other hand, and for the upper middle-class women especially, confined as they are by prescription and by economic circumstances to their "domestic sphere," this relation is the most real and most formative factor of life. Hence a habit of mind favourable to devout observances and to the interpretation of the facts of life generally in terms of personal status. The logic, and the logical processes, of her everyday domestic life are carried over into the realm of the supernatural, and the woman finds herself at home and content in a range of ideas which to the man are in great measure alien and imbecile.

Still, the men of this class are also not devoid of piety, although it is commonly not piety of an aggressive or exuberant kind. The men of the upper middle class commonly take a more complacent attitude towards devout observances than the men of the artisan class. This may perhaps be explained in part by saying that what is true of the women of the class is true to a less extent also of the men. They are to an appreciable extent a sheltered class; and the patriarchal relation of status, which still persists in their conjugal life and in their habitual use of servants, may also act to conserve an archaic habit of mind and may exercise a retarding influence upon the process of secularisation which their habits of thought are undergoing. The relations of the American middle-class man to the economic community, however, are usually pretty close and exacting; although it may be remarked, by the way and in qualification, that their economic activity frequently also partakes in some degree of the patriarchal or quasi-predatory character. The occupations which are in good repute among this class, and which have most to do with shaping the class habits of thought, are the pecuniary occupations which have been spoken of in a similar connection in an earlier chapter. There is a good deal of the relation of arbitrary command and submission, and not a little of shrewd practice, remotely akin to predatory fraud. All this belongs on the plane of life of the predatory barbarian, to whom a devotional attitude is habitual. And in addition to this, the devout observances also commend themselves to this class on the ground of reputability. But this latter incentive to piety deserves treatment by itself and will be spoken of presently.

There is no hereditary leisure class of any consequence in the American community, except at the South. This Southern leisure class is somewhat given to devout observances; more so than any class of corresponding pecuniary standing in other parts of the country. It is also well known that the creeds of the South are of a more old-fashioned cast than their counterparts at the North. Corresponding to this more archaic devotional life of the South is the lower industrial development of that section. The industrial organisation of the South is at present, and especially it has been until quite recently, of a more primitive character than that of the American community taken as a whole. It approaches nearer to handicraft, in the paucity and rudeness of its mechanical appliances, and there is more of the element of mastery and subservience. It may also be noted that, owing to the peculiar economic circumstances of this section, the greater devoutness of the Southern population, both white and black, is correlated with a scheme of life which in many ways recalls the barbarian stages of industrial development. Among this population offences of an archaic character also are and have been relatively more prevalent and are less deprecated than they are elsewhere; as, for example, duels, brawls, feuds, drunkenness, horse-racing, cock-fighting, gambling, male sexual incontinence (evidenced by the considerable number of mulattoes). There is also a livelier sense of honour—an expression of sportsmanship and a derivative of predatory life.

As regards the wealthier class of the North, the American leisure class in the best sense of the term, it is, to begin with, scarcely possible to speak of an hereditary devotional attitude. This class is of too recent growth to be possessed of a well-formed transmitted habit in this respect, or even of a special homegrown tradition. Still, it may be noted in passing that there is a perceptible tendency among this class to give in at least a nominal, and apparently something of a real, adherence to some one of the accredited creeds. Also, weddings, funerals, and the like honorific events among this class are pretty uniformly solemnised with some especial degree of religious circumstance. It is impossible to say how far this adherence to a creed is a *bona fide* reversion to a devout habit of mind, and how far it is to be classed as a case of protective mimicry assumed for the purpose of an outward assimilation to canons of reputability borrowed from foreign ideals. Something of a substantial devotional propensity seems to be present, to judge especially by the somewhat peculiar degree of ritualistic observance which is in process of development in the upper-class cults. There is a tendency perceptible among the upper-class worshippers to affiliate themselves with those cults which lay relatively great stress on ceremonial and on the spectacular accessories of worship: and in the churches in which an upper-class membership predominates, there is at the same time a tendency to accentuate the ritualistic, at the cost of the intellectual features in the service and in the apparatus of the devout observances. This holds true even where the church in question belongs to a denomination with a relatively slight general development of ritual and paraphernalia. This peculiar development of the ritualistic element is no doubt due in part to a predilection for conspicuously wasteful spectacles, but it probably also in part indicates something of the devotional attitude of the worshippers. So far as the latter is true, it indicates a relatively archaic form of the devotional habit. The predominance of spectacular effects in devout observances is noticeable in all devout communities at a relatively primitive stage of culture and with a slight intellectual development. It is especially characteristic of the barbarian culture. Here there is pretty uniformly present in the devout observances a direct appeal to the emotions through all the avenues of sense. And a tendency to return to this naïve, sensational method of appeal is unmistakable in the upper-class churches of to-day. It is perceptible in a less degree in the cults which claim the allegiance of the lower leisure class and of the middle classes. There is a reversion to the use of coloured lights and brilliant spectacles, a freer use of symbols, orchestral music and incense, and one may even detect, in "processionals" and "recessionals" and in richly varied genuflexional evolutions, an incipient reversion to so antique an accessory of worship as the sacred dance.

This reversion to spectacular observances is not confined to the upper-class cults, although it finds its best exemplification and its highest accentuation in the higher pecuniary and social altitudes. The cults of the lower-class devout portion of the community, such as the Southern negroes and the backward foreign elements of the population, of course also show a strong inclination to ritual, symbolism, and spectacular effects; as might be expected from the antecedents and the cultural level of those classes. With these classes the prevalence of ritual and anthropomorphism are not so much a matter of reversion as of continued development out of the past. But the use of ritual and related features of devotion are also spreading in other directions. In the early days of the American community, the prevailing denominations started out with a ritual and paraphernalia of an austere simplicity; but it is a matter familiar to every one that in the course of time these denominations have, in a varying degree, adopted much of the spectacular elements which they once renounced. In a general way, this development has gone hand in hand with the growth of the wealth and the ease of life of the worshippers and has reached its fullest expression among those classes which grade highest in wealth and repute.

The causes to which this pecuniary stratification of devoutness is due have already been indicated in a general way in speaking of class differences in habits of thought. Class differences as regards devoutness are but a special expression of a generic fact. The lax allegiance of the lower middle class, or what may broadly be called the failure of filial piety among this class, is chiefly perceptible among the town populations engaged in the mechanical industries. In a general way, one does not, at the present time, look for a blameless filial piety among those classes whose employment approaches that of the engineer and the mechanician. These mechanical employments are in a degree a modern fact. The handicraftsmen of earlier times, who served an industrial end of a character similar to that now served by the mechanician, were not similarly refractory under the discipline of devoutness. The habitual activity of the men engaged in these branches of industry has greatly changed, as regards its intellectual discipline, since the modern industrial processes have come into vogue; and the discipline to which the mechanician is exposed in his daily employment affects the methods and standards of his thinking also on topics which lie outside his everyday work. Familiarity with the highly organised and highly impersonal industrial processes of the present acts to derange the animistic habits of thought. The workman's office is becoming more and more exclusively that of discretion and supervision in a process of mechanical, dispassionate sequences. So long as the individual is the chief and typical prime mover in the process; so long as the obtrusive feature of the industrial process is the dexterity and force of the individual handicraftsman; so long the habit of interpreting phenomena in terms of personal motive and propensity suffers no such considerable and consistent derangement through facts as to lead to its elimination. But under the later developed industrial processes, when the prime movers and the contrivances through which they work are of an impersonal, non-individual character, the grounds of generalisation habitually present in the workman's mind and the point of view from which he habitually apprehends phenomena is an enforced cognisance of matter-of-fact sequence. The result, so far as concerns the workman's life of faith, is a proclivity to undevout scepticism.

———

It appears, then, that the devout habit of mind attains its best development under a relatively archaic culture; the term "devout" being of course here used in its anthropological sense simply, and not as implying anything with respect to the spiritual attitude so characterised, beyond the fact of a proneness to devout observances. It appears also that this devout attitude marks a type of human nature which is more in consonance with the predatory mode of life than with the later-developed, more consistently and organically industrial life process of the community. It is in large measure an expression of the archaic habitual sense of personal status,—the relation of mastery and subservience,—and it therefore fits into the industrial scheme of the predatory and the quasi-peaceable culture, but does not fit into the industrial scheme of the present. It also appears that this habit persists with greatest tenacity among those classes in the modern communities whose everyday life is most remote from the mechanical processes of industry and which are the most conservative also in other respects; while for those classes that are habitually in immediate contact with modern industrial processes, and whose habits of thought are therefore exposed to the constraining force of technological necessities, that animistic interpretation of phenomena and that respect of persons on which devout observance proceeds are in process of obsolescence. And also—as bearing especially on the present discussion—it appears that the devout habit to some extent progressively gains in scope and elaboration among those classes in the modern communities to whom wealth and leisure accrue in the most pronounced degree. In this as in other relations, the institution of a leisure class acts to conserve, and even to rehabilitate, that archaic type of human nature and those elements of the archaic culture which the industrial evolution of society in its later stages acts to eliminate.

CHAPTER XIII

SURVIVALS OF THE
NON-INVIDIOUS INTEREST

In an increasing proportion as time goes on, the anthropomorphic cult, with its code of devout observances, suffers a progressive disintegration through the stress of economic exigencies and the decay of the system of status. As this disintegration proceeds, there come to be associated and blended with the devout attitude certain other motives and impulses that are not always of an anthropomorphic origin, nor traceable to the habit of personal subservience. Not all of these subsidiary impulses that blend with the habit of devoutness in the later devotional life are altogether congruous with the devout attitude or with the anthropomorphic apprehension of the sequence of phenomena. Their origin being not the same, their action upon the scheme of devout life is also not in the same direction. In many ways they traverse the underlying norm of subservience or vicarious life to which the code of devout observances and the ecclesiastical and sacerdotal institutions are to be traced as their substantial basis. Through the presence of these alien motives the social and industrial régime of status gradually disintegrates, and the canon of personal subservience loses the support derived from an unbroken tradition. Extraneous habits and proclivities encroach upon the field of action occupied by this

canon, and it presently comes about that the ecclesiastical and sacerdotal structures are partially converted to other uses, in some
measure alien to the purposes of the scheme of devout life as it
stood in the days of the most vigorous and characteristic development of the priesthood.

Among these alien motives which affect the devout scheme in its
later growth, may be mentioned the motives of charity and of social good-fellowship, or conviviality; or, in more general terms, the
various expressions of the sense of human solidarity and sympathy.
It may be added that these extraneous uses of the ecclesiastical
structure contribute materially to its survival in name and form
even among people who may be ready to give up the substance of
it. A still more characteristic and more pervasive alien element in
the motives which have gone to formally uphold the scheme of devout life is that non-reverent sense of æsthetic congruity with the
environment, which is left as a residue of the latter-day act of worship after elimination of its anthropomorphic content. This has
done good service for the maintenance of the sacerdotal institution
through blending with the motive of subservience. This sense or
impulse of æsthetic congruity is not primarily of an economic
character, but it has a considerable indirect effect in shaping the
habit of mind of the individual for economic purposes in the later
stages of industrial development; its most perceptible effect in this
regard goes in the direction of mitigating the somewhat pronounced self-regarding bias that has been transmitted by tradition
from the earlier, more competent phases of the régime of status.
The economic bearing of this impulse is therefore seen to traverse
that of the devout attitude; the former goes to qualify, if not to
eliminate, the self-regarding bias, through sublation of the antithesis or antagonism of self and not-self; while the latter, being an expression of the sense of personal subservience and mastery, goes to
accentuate this antithesis and to insist upon the divergence between the self-regarding interest and the interests of the generically human life process.

This non-invidious residue of the religious life,—the sense of
communion with the environment, or with the generic life

process,—as well as the impulse of charity or of sociability, act in a pervasive way to shape men's habits of thought for the economic purpose. But the action of all this class of proclivities is somewhat vague, and their effects are difficult to trace in detail. So much seems clear, however, as that the action of this entire class of motives or aptitudes tends in a direction contrary to the underlying principles of the institution of the leisure class as already formulated. The basis of that institution, as well as of the anthropomorphic cults associated with it in the cultural development, is the habit of invidious comparison; and this habit is incongruous with the exercise of the aptitudes now in question. The substantial canons of the leisure-class scheme of life are a conspicuous waste of time and substance and a withdrawal from the industrial process; while the particular aptitudes here in question assert themselves, on the economic side, in a deprecation of waste and of a futile manner of life, and in an impulse to participation in or identification with the life process, whether it be on the economic side or in any other of its phases or aspects.

It is plain that these aptitudes and the habits of life to which they give rise where circumstances favour their expression, or where they assert themselves in a dominant way, run counter to the leisure-class scheme of life; but it is not clear that life under the leisure-class scheme, as seen in the later stages of its development, tends consistently to the repression of these aptitudes or to exemption from the habits of thought in which they express themselves. The positive discipline of the leisure-class scheme of life goes pretty much all the other way. In its positive discipline, by prescription and by selective elimination, the leisure-class scheme favours the all-pervading and all-dominating primacy of the canons of waste and invidious comparison at every conjuncture of life. But in its negative effects the tendency of the leisure-class discipline is not so unequivocally true to the fundamental canons of the scheme. In its regulation of human activity for the purpose of pecuniary decency the leisure-class canon insists on withdrawal from the industrial process. That is to say, it inhibits activity in the directions in which the impecunious members of the community habitually put forth their efforts. Especially in the case of women, and more particularly as regards the upper-class and upper-middle-class women of advanced industrial communities, this inhibition goes so far as to insist on withdrawal even from the emulative process of accumulation by the quasi-predatory methods of the pecuniary occupations.

The pecuniary or the leisure-class culture, which set out as an emulative variant of the impulse of workmanship, is in its latest development beginning to neutralise its own ground, by eliminating the habit of invidious comparison in respect of efficiency, or even of pecuniary standing. On the other hand, the fact that members of the leisure class, both men and women, are to some extent exempt from the necessity of finding a livelihood in a competitive struggle with their fellows, makes it possible for members of this class not only to survive, but even, within bounds, to follow their bent in case they are not gifted with the aptitudes which make for success in the competitive struggle. That is to say, in the latest and fullest development of the institution, the livelihood of members of this class does not depend on the possession and the unremitting exercise of those aptitudes which characterise the successful predatory man. The chances of survival for individuals not gifted with those aptitudes are therefore greater in the higher grades of the leisure class than in the general average of a population living under the competitive system.

In an earlier chapter, in discussing the conditions of survival of archaic traits, it has appeared that the peculiar position of the leisure class affords exceptionally favourable chances for the survival of traits which characterise the types of human nature proper to an earlier and obsolete cultural stage. The class is sheltered from the stress of economic exigencies, and is in this sense withdrawn from the rude impact of forces which make for adaptation to the economic situation. The survival in the leisure class, and under the leisure-class scheme of life, of traits and types that are reminiscent of the predatory culture has already been discussed. These aptitudes and habits have an exceptionally favourable chance of survival under the leisure-class régime. Not only does the sheltered pecuniary position of the leisure class afford a situation favourable to the survival of such individuals as are not gifted with the complement of aptitudes required for serviceability in the modern industrial process; but the leisure-class canons of reputability at the same time enjoin the conspicuous exercise of certain predatory aptitudes. The employments in which the predatory aptitudes find exercise serve as an evidence of wealth, birth, and withdrawal from the industrial process. The survival of the predatory traits under the leisure-class culture is furthered both negatively, through the industrial exemption of the class, and positively, through the sanction of the leisure-class canons of decency.

With respect to the survival of traits characteristic of the ante-predatory savage culture the case is in some degree different. The sheltered position of the leisure class favours the survival also of these traits; but the exercise of the aptitudes for peace and good-will does not have the affirmative sanction of the code of proprieties. Individuals gifted with a temperament that is reminiscent of the ante-predatory culture are placed at something of an advantage within the leisure class, as compared with similarly gifted individuals outside the class, in that they are not under a pecuniary necessity to thwart these aptitudes that make for a non-competitive life; but such individuals are still exposed to something of a moral constraint which urges them to disregard these inclinations, in that the code of proprieties enjoins upon them habits of life based on the predatory aptitudes. So long as the system of status remains intact, and so long as the leisure class has other lines of nonindustrial activity to take to than obvious killing of time in aimless and wasteful fatigation, so long no considerable departure from the leisure-class scheme of reputable life is to be looked for. The occurrence of a non-predatory temperament within the class at that stage is to be looked upon as a case of sporadic reversion. But the reputable nonindustrial outlets for the human propensity to action presently fail, through the advance of economic development, the disappearance of large game, the decline of war, the obsolescence of proprietary government, and the decay of the priestly office. When this happens, the situation begins to change. Human life must seek expression in one direction if it may not in another; and if the predatory outlet fails, relief is sought elsewhere.

As indicated above, the exemption from pecuniary stress has been carried farther in the case of the leisure-class women of the advanced industrial communities than in that of any other considerable group of persons. The women may therefore be expected to show a more pronounced reversion to a non-invidious temperament than the men. But there is also among men of the leisure class a perceptible increase in the range and scope of activities that proceed from aptitudes which are not to be classed as self-regarding, and the end of which is not an invidious distinction. So, for instance, the greater number of men who have to do with industry in the way of pecuniarily managing an enterprise take some interest and some pride in seeing that the work is well done and is industrially effective, and this even apart from the profit which may result from any improvement of this kind. The efforts of commercial clubs and manufacturers' organisations in this direction of non-invidious advancement of industrial efficiency are also well known.

The tendency to some other than an invidious purpose in life has worked out in a multitude of organisations, the purpose of which is some work of charity or of social amelioration. These organisations are often of a quasi-religious or pseudo-religious character, and are participated in by both men and women. Examples will present themselves in abundance on reflection, but for the purpose of indicating the range of the propensities in question and of characterising them, some of the more obvious concrete cases may be cited. Such, for instance, are the agitation for temperance and similar social reforms, for prison reform, for the spread of education, for the suppression of vice, and for the avoidance of war by arbitration, disarmament, or other means; such are, in some measure, university settlements, neighbourhood guilds, the various organisations typified by the Young Men's Christian Association and the Young People's Society for Christian Endeavour, sewing-circles, social clubs, art clubs, and even commercial clubs; such are also, in some slight measure, the pecuniary foundations of semi-public establishments for charity, education, or amusement, whether they are endowed by wealthy individuals or by contributions collected from persons of smaller means—in so far as these establishments are not of a religious character.

It is of course not intended to say that these efforts proceed entirely from other motives than those of a self-regarding kind. What can be claimed is that other motives are present in the common run of cases, and that the perceptibly greater prevalence of effort of this kind under the circumstances of the modern industrial life than under the unbroken régime of the principle of status, indicates the presence in modern life of an effective scepticism with respect to the full legitimacy of an emulative scheme of life. It is a matter of sufficient notoriety to have become a commonplace jest that extraneous motives are commonly present among the incentives to this class of work—motives of a self-regarding kind, and especially the motive of an invidious distinction. To such an extent is this true, that many ostensible works of disinterested public spirit are no doubt initiated and carried on with a view primarily to the enhanced repute, or even to the pecuniary gain, of their promoters. In the case of some considerable groups of organisations or establishments of this kind the invidious motive is apparently the dominant motive both with the initiators of the work and with their supporters. This last remark would hold true especially with respect to such works as lend distinction to their doer through large and conspicuous expenditure; as, for example, the foundation of a university or of a public library or museum; but it is also, and perhaps equally, true of the more commonplace work of participation in such organisations and movements as are distinctively upper-class organisations. These serve to authenticate the pecuniary reputability of their members, as well as gratefully to keep them in mind of their superior status by pointing the contrast between themselves and the lower-lying humanity in whom the work of amelioration is to be wrought; as, for example, the university settlement, which now has some vogue. But after all allowances and deductions have been made, there is left some remainder of motives of a non-emulative kind. The fact itself that distinction or a decent good fame is sought by this method is evidence of a preva-

lent sense of the legitimacy, and of the presumptive effectual presence, of a non-emulative, non-invidious interest, as a constituent
factor in the habits of thought of modern communities.

In all this latter-day range of leisure-class activities that proceed
on the basis of a non-invidious and non-religious interest, it is to be
noted that the women participate more actively and more persistently than the men—except, of course, in the case of such works
as require a large expenditure of means. The dependent pecuniary
position of the women disables them for work requiring large expenditure. As regards the general range of ameliorative work, the
members of the priesthood or clergy of the less naïvely devout
sects, or the secularised denominations, are associated with the
class of the women. This is as the theory would have it. In other
economic relations, also, this clergy stands in a somewhat equivocal
position between the class of women and that of the men engaged
in economic pursuits. By tradition and by the prevalent sense of the
proprieties, both the clergy and the women of the well-to-do
classes are placed in the position of a vicarious leisure class; with
both classes the characteristic relation which goes to form the
habits of thought of the class is a relation of subservience—that is
to say, an economic relation conceived in personal terms; in both
classes there is consequently perceptible a special proneness to
construe phenomena in terms of personal relation rather than of
causal sequence; both classes are so inhibited by the canons of decency from the ceremonially unclean processes of the lucrative or
productive occupations as to make participation in the industrial
life process of to-day a moral impossibility for them. The result of
this ceremonial exclusion from productive effort of the vulgar sort
is to draft a relatively large share of the energies of the modern
feminine and priestly classes into the service of other interests than
the self-regarding one. The code leaves no alternative direction in
which the impulse to purposeful action may find expression. The
effect of a consistent inhibition on industrially useful activity in the
case of the leisure-class women shows itself in a restless assertion
of the impulse to workmanship in other directions than that of
business activity.

As has been noticed already, the everyday life of the well-to-do women and the clergy contains a larger element of status than that of the average of the men, especially than that of the men engaged in the modern industrial occupations proper. Hence the devout attitude survives in a better state of preservation among these classes than among the common run of men in the modern communities. Hence an appreciable share of the energy which seeks expression in a non-lucrative employment among these members of the vicarious leisure classes may be expected to eventuate in devout observances and works of piety. Hence, in part, the excess of the devout proclivity in women, spoken of in the last chapter. But it is more to the present point to note the effect of this proclivity in shaping the action and colouring the purposes of the non-lucrative movements and organisations here under discussion. Where this devout colouring is present it lowers the immediate efficiency of the organisations for any economic end to which their efforts may be directed. Many organisations, charitable and ameliorative, divide their attention between the devotional and the secular well-being of the people whose interests they aim to further. It can scarcely be doubted that if they were to give an equally serious attention and effort undividedly to the secular interests of these people, the immediate economic value of their work should be appreciably higher than it is. It might of course similarly be said, if this were the place to say it, that the immediate efficiency of these works of amelioration for the devout end might be greater if it were not hampered with the secular motives and aims which are usually present.

Some deduction is to be made from the economic value of this class of non-invidious enterprise, on account of the intrusion of the devotional interest. But there are also deductions to be made on account of the presence of other alien motives which more or less broadly traverse the economic trend of this non-emulative expression of the instinct of workmanship. To such an extent is this seen to be true on a closer scrutiny, that, when all is told, it may even appear that this general class of enterprises is of an altogether dubious economic value—as measured in terms of the fulness or facility of life of the individuals or classes to whose amelioration the enterprise is directed. For instance, many of the efforts now in reputable vogue for the amelioration of the indigent population of large cities are of the nature, in great part, of a mission of culture. It is by this means sought to accelerate the rate of speed at which given elements of the upper-class culture find acceptance in the everyday scheme of life of the lower classes. The solicitude of "settlements," for example, is in part directed to enhance the industrial efficiency of the poor and to teach them the more adequate utilisation of the means at hand; but it is also no less consistently directed to the inculcation, by precept and example, of certain punctilios of upper-class propriety in manners and customs. The economic substance of these proprieties will commonly be found on scrutiny to be a conspicuous waste of time and goods. Those good people who go out to humanise the poor are commonly, and advisedly, extremely scrupulous and silently insistent in matters of decorum and the decencies of life. They are commonly persons of an exemplary life and gifted with a tenacious insistence on ceremonial cleanness in the various items of their daily consumption. The cultural or civilising efficacy of this inculcation of correct habits of thought with respect to the consumption of time and commodities is scarcely to be overrated; nor is its economic value to the individual who acquires these higher and more reputable ideals inconsiderable. Under the circumstances of the existing pecuniary culture, the reputability, and consequently the success, of the individual is in great measure dependent on his proficiency in demeanour and methods of consumption that argue habitual waste of time and goods. But as regards the ulterior economic bearing of this training in worthier methods of life, it is to be said that the effect wrought is in large part a substitution of costlier or less efficient methods of accomplishing the same material results, in relations where the material result is the fact of substantial economic value. The propaganda of culture is in great part an inculcation of new tastes, or rather of a new schedule of proprieties, which have been adapted to the upper-class scheme of life under the guidance of the leisure-class formulation of the principles of status and pecuniary decency. This new schedule of proprieties is intruded into the lower-class scheme of life from the code elaborated by an element of the population whose life lies outside the industrial process; and this intrusive schedule can scarcely be expected to fit the exigencies of life for these lower classes more adequately than the schedule already in vogue among them, and especially not more adequately than the schedule which they are themselves working out under the stress of modern industrial life.

All this of course does not question the fact that the proprieties of the substituted schedule are more decorous than those which they displace. The doubt which presents itself is simply a doubt as to the economic expediency of this work of regeneration—that is to say, the economic expediency in that immediate and material bearing in which the effects of the change can be ascertained with some degree of confidence, and as viewed from the standpoint not of the individual but of the facility of life of the collectivity. For an appreciation of the economic expediency of these enterprises of amelioration, therefore, their effective work is scarcely to be taken at its face value, even where the aim of the enterprise is primarily an economic one and where the interest on which it proceeds is in no sense self-regarding or invidious. The economic reform wrought is largely of the nature of a permutation in the methods of conspicuous waste.

But something further is to be said with respect to the character of the disinterested motives and canons of procedure in all work of this class that is affected by the habits of thought characteristic of the pecuniary culture; and this further consideration may lead to a further qualification of the conclusions already reached. As has been seen in an earlier chapter, the canons of reputability or decency under the pecuniary culture insist on habitual futility of effort as the mark of a pecuniarily blameless life. There results not only a habit of disesteem of useful occupations, but there results also what is of more decisive consequence in guiding the action of any organised body of people that lays claim to social good repute. There is a tradition which requires that one should not be vulgarly familiar with any of the processes or details that have to do with the material necessities of life. One may meritoriously show a quantitative interest in the well-being of the vulgar, through subscriptions or through work on managing committees and the like. One may, perhaps even more meritoriously, show solicitude in general and in detail for the cultural welfare of the vulgar, in the way of contrivances for elevating their tastes and affording them opportunities for spiritual amelioration. But one should not betray an intimate knowledge of the material circumstances of vulgar life, or of the habits of thought of the vulgar classes, such as would effectually direct the efforts of these organisations to a materially useful end. This reluctance to avow an unduly intimate knowledge of the lower-class conditions of life in detail of course prevails in very different degrees in different individuals; but there is commonly enough of it present collectively in any organisation of the kind in question profoundly to influence its course of action. By its cumulative action in shaping the usage and precedents of any such body, this shrinking from an imputation of unseemly familiarity with vulgar life tends gradually to set aside the initial motives of the enterprise, in favour of certain guiding principles of good repute, ultimately reducible to terms of pecuniary merit. So that in an organisation of long standing the initial motive of furthering the facility of life in these classes comes gradually to be an ostensible motive only, and the vulgarly effective work of the organisation tends to obsolescence.

What is true of the efficiency of organisations for non-invidious work in this respect is true also as regards the work of individuals proceeding on the same motives; though it perhaps holds true with more qualification for individuals than for organised enterprises. The habit of gauging merit by the leisure-class canons of wasteful expenditure and unfamiliarity with vulgar life, whether on the side of production or of consumption, is necessarily strong in the individuals who aspire to do some work of public utility. And if the individual should forget his station and turn his efforts to vulgar effectiveness, the common sense of the community—the sense of pecuniary decency—would presently reject his work and set him right. An example of this is seen in the administration of bequests made by public-spirited men for the single purpose (at least ostensibly) of furthering the facility of human life in some particular respect. The objects for which bequests of this class are most frequently made at present are schools, libraries, hospitals, and asylums for the infirm or unfortunate. The avowed purpose of the donor in these cases is the amelioration of human life in the particular respect which is named in the bequest; but it will be found an invariable rule that in the execution of the work not a little of other motives, frequently incompatible with the initial motive, is present and determines the particular disposition eventually made of a good share of the means which have been set apart by the bequest. Certain funds, for instance, may have been set apart as a foundation for a foundling asylum or a retreat for invalids. The diversion of expenditure to honorific waste in such cases is not uncommon enough to cause surprise or even to raise a smile. An appreciable share of the funds is spent in the construction of an edifice faced with some æsthetically objectionable but expensive stone, covered with grotesque and incongruous details, and designed, in its battlemented walls and turrets and its massive portals and strategic approaches, to suggest certain barbaric methods of warfare. The interior of the structure shows the same pervasive guidance of the canons of conspicuous waste and predatory exploit. The windows, for instance, to go no farther into detail, are placed with a view to impress their pecuniary excellence upon the chance beholder from the outside, rather than with a view to effectiveness for their ostensible end in the convenience or comfort of the beneficiaries within; and the detail of interior arrangement is required to conform itself as best it may to this alien but imperious requirement of pecuniary beauty.

In all this, of course, it is not to be presumed that the donor would have found fault, or that he would have done otherwise if he had taken control in person; it appears that in those cases where such a personal direction is exercised—where the enterprise is conducted by direct expenditure and superintendence instead of by bequest—the aims and methods of management are not different in this respect. Nor would the beneficiaries, or the outside observers whose ease or vanity are not immediately touched, be pleased with a different disposition of the funds. It would suit no one to have the enterprise conducted with a view directly to the most economical and effective use of the means at hand for the initial, material end of the foundation. All concerned, whether their interest is immediate and self-regarding, or contemplative only, agree that some considerable share of the expenditure should go to the higher or spiritual needs derived from the habit of an invidious comparison in predatory exploit and pecuniary waste. But this only goes to say that the canons of emulative and pecuniary reputability so far pervade the common sense of the community as to permit no escape or evasion, even in the case of an enterprise which ostensibly proceeds entirely on the basis of a non-invidious interest.

It may even be that the enterprise owes its honorific virtue, as a means of enhancing the donor's good repute, to the imputed presence of this non-invidious motive; but that does not hinder the invidious interest from guiding the expenditure. The effectual presence of motives of an emulative or invidious origin in non-emulative works of this kind might be shown at length and with detail, in any one of the classes of enterprise spoken of above. Where these honorific details occur, in such cases, they commonly masquerade under designations that belong in the field of the æsthetic, ethical, or economic interest. These special motives, derived from the standards and canons of the pecuniary culture, act surreptitiously to divert effort of a non-invidious kind from effective service, without disturbing the agent's sense of good intention or obtruding upon his consciousness the substantial futility of his work. Their effect might be traced through the entire range of that schedule of non-invidious, meliorative enterprise that is so considerable a feature, and especially so conspicuous a feature, in the overt scheme of life of the well-to-do. But the theoretical bearing is perhaps clear enough and may require no further illustration; especially as some detailed attention will be given to one of these lines of enterprise—the establishments for the higher learning—in another connection.

Under the circumstances of the sheltered situation in which the leisure class is placed there seems, therefore, to be something of a reversion to the range of non-invidious impulses that characterise the ante-predatory savage culture. The reversion comprises both the sense of workmanship and the proclivity to indolence and good-fellowship. But in the modern scheme of life canons of conduct based on pecuniary or invidious merit stand in the way of a free exercise of these impulses; and the dominant presence of these canons of conduct goes far to divert such efforts as are made on the basis of the non-invidious interest to the service of that invidious interest on which the pecuniary culture rests. The canons of pecuniary decency are reducible for the present purpose to the principles of waste, futility, and ferocity. The requirements of decency are imperiously present in meliorative enterprise as in other lines of conduct, and exercise a selective surveillance over the details of conduct and management in any enterprise. By guiding and adapting the method in detail, these canons of decency go far to make all non-invidious aspiration or effort nugatory. The pervasive, impersonal, uneager principle of futility is at hand from day to day and works obstructively to hinder the effectual expression of so much of the surviving ante-predatory aptitudes as is to be classed under the instinct of workmanship; but its presence does not preclude the transmission of those aptitudes or the continued recurrence of an impulse to find expression for them.

In the later and farther development of the pecuniary culture, the requirement of withdrawal from the industrial process in order to avoid social odium is carried so far as to comprise abstention from the emulative employments. At this advanced stage the pecuniary culture negatively favours the assertion of the non-invidious propensities by relaxing the stress laid on the merit of emulative, predatory, or pecuniary occupations, as compared with those of an industrial or productive kind. As was noticed above, the requirement of such withdrawal from all employment that is of human use applies more rigorously to the upper-class women than to any other class, unless the priesthood of certain cults might be cited as an exception, perhaps more apparent than real, to this rule. The reason for the more extreme insistence on a futile life for this class of women than for the men of the same pecuniary and social grade lies in their being not only an upper-grade leisure class but also at the same time a vicarious leisure class. There is in their case a double ground for a consistent withdrawal from useful effort.

It has been well and repeatedly said by popular writers and speakers who reflect the common sense of intelligent people on questions of social structure and function that the position of woman in any community is the most striking index of the level of culture attained by the community, and it might be added, by any given class in the community. This remark is perhaps truer as regards the stage of economic development than as regards development in any other respect. At the same time the position assigned to the woman in the accepted scheme of life, in any community or under any culture, is in a very great degree an expression of traditions which have been shaped by the circumstances of an earlier phase of development, and which have been but partially adapted to the existing economic circumstances, or to the existing exigencies of temperament and habits of mind by which the women living under this modern economic situation are actuated.

The fact has already been remarked upon incidentally in the course of the discussion of the growth of economic institutions generally, and in particular in speaking of vicarious leisure and of dress, that the position of women in the modern economic scheme is more widely and more consistently at variance with the promptings of the instinct of workmanship than is the position of the men of the same classes. It is also apparently true that the woman's temperament includes a larger share of this instinct that approves peace and disapproves futility. It is therefore not a fortuitous circumstance that the women of modern industrial communities show a livelier sense of the discrepancy between the accepted scheme of life and the exigencies of the economic situation.

The several phases of the "woman question" have brought out in intelligible form the extent to which the life of women in modern society, and in the polite circles especially, is regulated by a body of common sense formulated under the economic circumstances of an earlier phase of development. It is still felt that woman's life, in its civil, economic, and social bearing, is essentially and normally a vicarious life, the merit or demerit of which is, in the nature of things, to be imputed to some other individual who stands in some relation of ownership or tutelage to the woman. So, for instance, any action on the part of a woman which traverses an injunction of the accepted schedule of proprieties is felt to reflect immediately upon the honour of the man whose woman she is. There may of course be some sense of incongruity in the mind of any one passing an opinion of this kind on the woman's frailty or perversity; but the common-sense judgment of the community in such matters is, after all, delivered without much hesitation, and few men would question the legitimacy of their sense of an outraged tutelage in any case that might arise. On the other hand, relatively little discredit attaches to a woman through the evil deeds of the man with whom her life is associated.

The good and beautiful scheme of life, then—that is to say the scheme to which we are habituated—assigns to the woman a "sphere" ancillary to the activity of the man; and it is felt that any departure from the traditions of her assigned round of duties is unwomanly. If the question is as to civil rights or the suffrage, our common sense in the matter—that is to say the logical deliverance of our general scheme of life upon the point in question—says that the woman should be represented in the body politic and before the law, not immediately in her own person, but through the mediation of the head of the household to which she belongs. It is unfeminine in her to aspire to a self-directing, self-centred life; and our common sense tells us that her direct participation in the affairs of the community, civil or industrial, is a menace to that social order which expresses our habits of thought as they have been formed under the guidance of the traditions of the pecuniary culture. "All this fume and froth of 'emancipating woman from the slavery of man' and so on, is, to use the chaste and expressive language of Elizabeth Cady Stanton[1] inversely, 'utter rot.' The social relations of the sexes are fixed by nature. Our entire civilisation— that is whatever is good in it—is based on the home." The "home" is the household with a male head. This view, but commonly expressed even more chastely, is the prevailing view of the woman's

260 · *Thorstein Veblen*

status, not only among the common run of the men of civilised communities, but among the women as well. Women have a very alert sense of what the scheme of proprieties requires, and while it is true that many of them are ill at ease under the details which the code imposes, there are few who do not recognise that the existing moral order, of necessity and by the divine right of prescription, places the woman in a position ancillary to the man. In the last analysis, according to her own sense of what is good and beautiful, the woman's life is, and in theory must be, an expression of the man's life at the second remove.

But in spite of this pervading sense of what is the good and natural place for the woman, there is also perceptible an incipient development of sentiment to the effect that this whole arrangement of tutelage and vicarious life and imputation of merit and demerit is somehow a mistake. Or, at least, that even if it may be a natural growth and a good arrangement in its time and place, and in spite of its patent æsthetic value, still it does not adequately serve the more everyday ends of life in a modern industrial community. Even that large and substantial body of well-bred, upper and middle-class women to whose dispassionate, matronly sense of the traditional proprieties this relation of status commends itself as fundamentally and eternally right—even these, whose attitude is conservative, commonly find some slight discrepancy in detail between things as they are and as they should be in this respect. But that less manageable body of modern women who, by force of youth, education, or temperament, are in some degree out of touch with the traditions of status received from the barbarian culture, and in whom there is, perhaps, an undue reversion to the impulse of self-expression and workmanship,—these are touched with a sense of grievance too vivid to leave them at rest.

In this "New-Woman" movement,—as these blind and incoherent efforts to rehabilitate the woman's pre-glacial standing have been named,—there are at least two elements discernible, both of which are of an economic character. These two elements or motives are expressed by the double watchword, "Emancipation" and "Work." Each of these words is recognised to stand for something in the way of a wide-spread sense of grievance. The prevalence of the sentiment is recognised even by people who do not see that there is any real ground for a grievance in the situation as it stands to-day. It is among the women of the well-to-do classes, in the communities which are farthest advanced in industrial development, that this sense of a grievance to be redressed is most alive and finds most frequent expression. That is to say, in other words, there is a demand, more or less serious, for emancipation from all relation of status, tutelage, or vicarious life; and the revulsion asserts itself especially among the class of women upon whom the scheme of life handed down from the régime of status imposes with least mitigation a vicarious life, and in those communities whose economic development has departed farthest from the circumstances to which this traditional scheme is adapted. The demand comes from that portion of womankind which is excluded by the canons of good repute from all effectual work, and which is closely reserved for a life of leisure and conspicuous consumption.

More than one critic of this new-woman movement has misapprehended its motive. The case of the American "new woman" has lately been summed up with some warmth by a popular observer of social phenomena: "She is petted by her husband, the most devoted and hard-working of husbands in the world. . . . She is the superior of her husband in education, and in almost every respect. She is surrounded by the most numerous and delicate attentions. Yet she is not satisfied. . . . The Anglo-Saxon 'new woman' is the most ridiculous production of modern times, and destined to be the most ghastly failure of the century." Apart from the deprecation—perhaps well placed—which is contained in this presentment, it adds nothing but obscurity to the woman question. The grievance of the new woman is made up of those things which this typical characterisation of the movement urges as reasons why she should be content. She is petted, and is permitted, or even required, to consume largely and conspicuously—vicariously for her husband or other natural guardian. She is exempted, or debarred, from vulgarly useful employment—in order to perform leisure vicariously for the good repute of her natural (pecuniary) guardian. These offices are the conventional marks of the un-free, at the same time that they are incompatible with the human impulse to purposeful activity. But the woman is endowed with her share—which there is reason to believe is more than an even share—of the instinct of workmanship, to which futility of life or of expenditure is obnoxious. She must unfold her life activity in response to the direct, unmediated stimuli of the economic environment with which she is in contact. The impulse is perhaps stronger upon the woman than upon the man to live her own life in her own way and to enter the industrial process of the community at something nearer than the second remove.

So long as the woman's place is consistently that of a drudge, she is, in the average of cases, fairly contented with her lot. She not only has something tangible and purposeful to do, but she has also no time or thought to spare for a rebellious assertion of such human propensity to self-direction as she has inherited. And after the stage of universal female drudgery is passed, and a vicarious leisure without strenuous application becomes the accredited employment of the women of the well-to-do classes, the prescriptive force of the canon of pecuniary decency, which requires the observance of ceremonial futility on their part, will long preserve high-minded women from any sentimental leaning to self-direction and a "sphere of usefulness." This is especially true during the earlier phases of the pecuniary culture, while the leisure of the leisure class is still in great measure a predatory activity, an active assertion of mastery in which there is enough of tangible purpose of an invidious kind to admit of its being taken seriously as an employment to which one may without shame put one's hand. This condition of things has obviously lasted well down into the present in some communities. It continues to hold to a different extent for different individuals, varying with the vividness of the sense of status and with the feebleness of the impulse to workmanship with which the individual is endowed. But where the economic structure of the community has so far outgrown the scheme of life based on status that the relation of personal subservience is no longer felt to be the sole "natural" human relation; there the ancient habit of purposeful activity will begin to assert itself in the less conformable indi-viduals, against the more recent, relatively superficial, relatively ephemeral habits and views which the predatory and the pecuniary culture have contributed to our scheme of life. These habits and views begin to lose their coercive force for the community or the class in question so soon as the habit of mind and the views of life due to the predatory and the quasi-peaceable discipline cease to be in fairly close accord with the later-developed economic situation. This is evident in the case of the industrious classes of modern communities; for them the leisure-class scheme of life has lost much of its binding force, especially as regards the element of sta-tus. But it is also visibly being verified in the case of the upper classes, though not in the same manner.

The habits derived from the predatory and quasi-peaceable cul-ture are relatively ephemeral variants of certain underlying propensities and mental characteristics of the race; which it owes to the protracted discipline of the earlier, proto-anthropoid cultural stage of peaceable, relatively undifferentiated economic life car-ried on in contact with relatively simple and invariable material environment. When the habits superinduced by the emulative method of life have ceased to enjoy the sanction of existing eco-nomic exigencies, a process of disintegration sets in whereby the habits of thought of more recent growth and of a less generic char-acter to some extent yield the ground before the more ancient and more pervading spiritual characteristics of the race.

In a sense, then, the new-woman movement marks a reversion to a more generic type of human character, or to a less differentiated expression of human nature. It is a type of human nature which is to be characterised as proto-anthropoid, and, as regards the sub-stance if not the form of its dominant traits, it belongs to a cultural stage that may be classed as possibly sub-human. The particular movement or evolutional feature in question of course shares this characterisation with the rest of the later social development, in so far as this social development shows evidence of a reversion to the spiritual attitude that characterises the earlier, undifferentiated stage of economic evolution. Such evidence of a general tendency to reversion from the dominance of the invidious interest is not entirely wanting, although it is neither plentiful nor unquestionably convincing. The general decay of the sense of status in modern industrial communities goes some way as evidence in this direction; and the perceptible return to a disapproval of futility in human life, and a disapproval of such activities as serve only the individual gain at the cost of the collectivity or at the cost of other social groups, is evidence to a like effect. There is a perceptible tendency to deprecate the infliction of pain, as well as to discredit all marauding enterprises, even where these expressions of the invidious interest do not tangibly work to the material detriment of the community or of the individual who passes an opinion on them. It may even be said that in the modern industrial communities the average, dispassionate sense of men says that the ideal human character is a character which makes for peace, good-will, and economic efficiency, rather than for a life of self-seeking, force, fraud, and mastery.

The influence of the leisure class is not consistently for or against the rehabilitation of this proto-anthropoid human nature. So far as concerns the chance of survival of individuals endowed with an exceptionally large share of the primitive traits, the sheltered position of the class favours its members directly by withdrawing them from the pecuniary struggle; but indirectly, through the leisure-class canons of conspicuous waste of goods and effort, the institution of a leisure class lessens the chance of survival of such individuals in the entire body of the population. The decent requirements of waste absorb the surplus energy of the population in an invidious struggle and leave no margin for the non-invidious expression of life. The remoter, less tangible, spiritual effects of the discipline of decency go in the same direction and work perhaps more effectually to the same end. The canons of decent life are an elaboration of the principle of invidious comparison, and they accordingly act consistently to inhibit all non-invidious effort and to inculcate the self-regarding attitude.

CHAPTER XIV

The Higher Learning as an Expression of the Pecuniary Culture

To the end that suitable habits of thought on certain heads may be conserved in the incoming generation, a scholastic discipline is sanctioned by the common sense of the community and incorporated into the accredited scheme of life. The habits of thought which are so formed under the guidance of teachers and scholastic traditions have an economic value—a value as affecting the serviceability of the individual—no less real than the similar economic value of the habits of thought formed without such guidance under the discipline of everyday life. Whatever characteristics of the accredited scholastic scheme and discipline are traceable to the predilections of the leisure class or to the guidance of the canons of pecuniary merit are to be set down to the account of that institution, and whatever economic value these features of the educational scheme possess are the expression in detail of the value of that institution. It will be in place, therefore, to point out any peculiar features of the educational system which are traceable to the leisure-class scheme of life, whether as regards the aim and method of the discipline, or as regards the compass and character of the body of knowledge inculcated. It is in learning proper, and more particularly in the higher learning, that the influence of leisure-class ideals is most patent; and since the purpose here is not to make an exhaustive collation of data showing the effect of the pecuniary culture upon education, but rather to illustrate the method and trend of leisure-class influence in education, a survey of certain salient features of the higher learning, such as may serve this purpose, is all that will be attempted.

In point of derivation and early development, learning is somewhat closely related to the devotional function of the community, particularly to the body of observances in which the service rendered the supernatural leisure class expresses itself. The service by which it is sought to conciliate supernatural agencies in the primitive cults is not an industrially profitable employment of the community's time and effort. It is, therefore, in great part, to be classed as a vicarious leisure performed for the supernatural powers with whom negotiations are carried on and whose good-will the service and the professions of subservience are conceived to procure. In great part, the early learning consisted in an acquisition of knowledge and facility in the service of a supernatural agent. It was therefore closely analogous in character to the training required for the domestic service of a temporal master. To a great extent, the knowledge acquired under the priestly teachers of the primitive community was a knowledge of ritual and ceremonial; that is to say, a knowledge of the most proper, most effective, or most acceptable manner of approaching and of serving the preternatural agents. What was learned was how to make oneself indispensable to these powers, and so to put oneself in a position to ask, or even to require, their intercession in the course of events or their abstention from interference in any given enterprise. Propitiation was the end, and this end was sought, in great part, by acquiring facility in subservience. It appears to have been only gradually that other elements than those of efficient service of the master found their way into the stock of priestly or shamanistic instruction.

The priestly servitor of the inscrutable powers that move in the external world came to stand in the position of a mediator between these powers and the common run of uninstructed humanity; for he was possessed of a knowledge of the supernatural etiquette which would admit him into the presence. And as commonly happens with mediators between the vulgar and their masters, whether the masters be natural or preternatural, he found it expedient to have the means at hand tangibly to impress upon the vulgar the fact that these inscrutable powers would do what he might ask of them. Hence, presently, a knowledge of certain natural processes which could be turned to account for spectacular effect, together with some sleight of hand, came to be an integral part of priestly lore. Knowledge of this kind passes for knowledge of the "unknowable," and it owes its serviceability for the sacerdotal purpose to its recondite character. It appears to have been from this source that learning, as an institution, arose, and its differentiation from this its parent stock of magic ritual and shamanistic fraud has been slow and tedious, and is scarcely yet complete even in the most advanced of the higher seminaries of learning.

The recondite element in learning is still, as it has been in all ages, a very attractive and effective element for the purpose of impressing, or even imposing upon, the unlearned; and the standing of the savant in the mind of the altogether unlettered is in great measure rated in terms of intimacy with the occult forces. So, for instance, as a typical case, even so late as the middle of this century, the Norwegian peasants have instinctively formulated their sense of the superior erudition of such doctors of divinity as Luther, Melanchthon, Peder Dass, and even so late a scholar in divinity as Grundtvig,[1] in terms of the Black Art. These, together with a very comprehensive list of minor celebrities, both living and dead, have been reputed masters in all magical arts; and a high position in the ecclesiastical personnel has carried with it, in the apprehension of these good people, an implication of profound familiarity with magical practice and the occult sciences. There is a parallel fact nearer home, similarly going to show the close relationship, in popular apprehension, between erudition and the unknowable; and it will at the same time serve to illustrate, in somewhat coarse outline, the bent which leisure-class life gives to the cognitive interest. While the belief is by no means confined to the leisure class, that class to-day comprises a disproportionately large number of believers in occult sciences of all kinds and shades. By those whose habits of thought are not shaped by contact with modern industry, the knowledge of the unknowable is still felt to be the ultimate if not the only true knowledge.

Learning, then, set out with being in some sense a by-product of the priestly vicarious leisure class; and, at least until a recent date, the higher learning has since remained in some sense a by-product or by-occupation of the priestly classes. As the body of systematised knowledge increased, there presently arose a distinction, traceable very far back in the history of education, between esoteric and exoteric knowledge; the former—so far as there is a substantial difference between the two—comprising such knowledge as is primarily of no economic or industrial effect, and the latter comprising chiefly knowledge of industrial processes and of natural phenomena which were habitually turned to account for the material purposes of life. This line of demarcation has in time become, at least in popular apprehension, the normal line between the higher learning and the lower.

It is significant, not only as an evidence of their close affiliation with the priestly craft, but also as indicating that their activity to a good extent falls under that category of conspicuous leisure known as manners and breeding, that the learned class in all primitive communities are great sticklers for form, precedent, gradations of rank, ritual, ceremonial vestments, and learned paraphernalia generally. This is of course to be expected, and it goes to say that the higher learning, in its incipient phase, is a leisure-class occupation—more specifically an occupation of the vicarious leisure class employed in the service of the supernatural leisure class. But this predilection for the paraphernalia of learning goes also to indicate a further point of contact or of continuity between the priestly office and the office of the savant. In point of derivation, learning, as well as the priestly office, is largely an outgrowth of sympathetic magic; and this magical apparatus of form and ritual therefore finds its place with the learned class of the primitive community as a matter of course. The ritual and paraphernalia have an occult efficacy for the magical purpose; so that their presence as an integral factor in the earlier phases of the development of magic and science is a matter of expediency, quite as much as of affectionate regard for symbolism simply.

This sense of the efficacy of symbolic ritual, and of sympathetic effect to be wrought through dexterous rehearsal of the traditional accessories of the act or end to be compassed, is of course present more obviously and in larger measure in magical practice than in the discipline of the sciences, even of the occult sciences. But there are, I apprehend, few persons with a cultivated sense of scholastic merit to whom the ritualistic accessories of science are altogether an idle matter. The very great tenacity with which these ritualistic paraphernalia persist through the later course of the development is evident to any one who will reflect on what has been the history of learning in our civilisation. Even to-day there are such things in the usage of the learned community as the cap and gown, matriculation, initiation, and graduation ceremonies, and the conferring of scholastic degrees, dignities, and prerogatives in a way which suggests some sort of a scholarly apostolic succession. The usage of the priestly orders is no doubt the proximate source of all these features of learned ritual, vestments, sacramental initiation, the transmission of peculiar dignities and virtues by the imposition of hands, and the like; but their derivation is traceable back of this point, to the source from which the specialised priestly class proper received them in the course of differentiation by which the priest came to be distinguished from the sorcerer on the one hand and from the menial servant of a temporal master on the other hand. So far as regards both their derivation and their psychological content, these usages and the conceptions on which they rest belong to a stage in cultural development no later than that of the angekok and the rain-maker. Their place in the later phases of devout observance, as well as in the higher educational system, is that of a survival from a very early animistic phase of the development of human nature.

These ritualistic features of the educational system of the present and of the recent past, it is quite safe to say, have their place primarily in the higher, liberal, and classic institutions and grades of learning, rather than in the lower, technological, or practical grades and branches of the system. So far as they possess them, the lower and less reputable branches of the educational scheme have evidently borrowed these things from the higher grades; and their continued persistence among the practical schools, without the sanction of the continued example of the higher and classic grades, would be highly improbable, to say the least. With the lower and practical schools and scholars, the adoption and cultivation of these usages is a case of mimicry—due to a desire to conform as far as may be to the standards of scholastic reputability maintained by the upper grades and classes, who have come by these accessory features legitimately, by the right of lineal devolution.

The analysis may even be safely carried a step farther. Ritualistic survivals and reversions come out in fullest vigour and with the freest air of spontaneity among those seminaries of learning which have to do primarily with the education of the priestly and leisure classes. Accordingly it should appear, and it does pretty plainly appear, on a survey of recent developments in college and university life, that wherever schools founded for the instruction of the lower classes in the immediately useful branches of knowledge grow into institutions of the higher learning, the growth of ritualistic ceremonial and paraphernalia and of elaborate scholastic "functions" goes hand in hand with the transition of the schools in question from the field of homely practicality into the higher, classical sphere. The initial purpose of these schools, and the work with which they have chiefly had to do at the earlier of these two stages of their evolution, has been that of fitting the young of the industrious classes for work. On the higher, classical plane of learning to which they commonly tend, their dominant aim becomes the preparation of the youth of the priestly and the leisure classes—or of an incipient leisure class—for the consumption of goods, material and immaterial, according to a conventionally accepted, reputable scope and method. This happy issue has commonly been the fate of schools founded by "friends of the people" for the aid of struggling young men, and where this transition is made in good form there is commonly, if not invariably, a coincident change to a more ritualistic life in the schools.

In the school life of to-day, learned ritual is in a general way best at home in schools whose chief end is the cultivation of the "humanities." This correlation is shown, perhaps more neatly than anywhere else, in the life-history of the American colleges and universities of recent growth. There may be many exceptions from the rule, especially among those schools which have been founded by the typically reputable and ritualistic churches, and which, therefore, started on the conservative and classical plane or reached the classical position by a shortcut; but the general rule as regards the colleges founded in the newer American communities during the present century has been that so long as the community has remained poor, and so long as the constituency from which the colleges have drawn their pupils has been dominated by habits of industry and thrift, so long the reminiscences of the medicine-man have found but a scant and precarious acceptance in the scheme of college life. But so soon as wealth begins appreciably to accumulate in the community, and so soon as a given school begins to lean on a leisure-class constituency, there comes also a perceptibly increased insistence on scholastic ritual and on conformity to the ancient forms as regards vestments and social and scholastic solemnities. So, for instance, there has been an approximate coincidence between the growth of wealth among the constituency which supports any given college of the Middle West and the date of acceptance—first into tolerance and then into imperative vogue— of evening dress for men and of the décolleté for women, as the scholarly vestments proper to occasions of learned solemnity or to the seasons of social amenity within the college circle. Apart from the mechanical difficulty of so large a task, it would scarcely be a difficult matter to trace this correlation. The like is true of the vogue of the cap and gown.

Cap and gown have been adopted as learned insignia by many colleges of this section within the last few years; and it is safe to say that this could scarcely have occurred at a much earlier date, or until there had grown up a leisure-class sentiment of sufficient volume in the community to support a strong movement of reversion towards an archaic view as to the legitimate end of education. This particular item of learned ritual, it may be noted, would not only commend itself to the leisure-class sense of the fitness of things, as appealing to the archaic propensity for spectacular effect and the predilection for antique symbolism; but it at the same time fits into the leisure-class scheme of life as involving a notable element of conspicuous waste. The precise date at which the reversion to cap and gown took place, as well as the fact that it affected so large a number of schools at about the same time, seems to have been due in some measure to a wave of atavistic sense of conformity and reputability that passed over the community at that period.

It may not be entirely beside the point to note that in point of time this curious reversion seems to coincide with the culmination of a certain vogue of atavistic sentiment and tradition in other directions also. The wave of reversion seems to have received its initial impulse in the psychologically disintegrating effects of the Civil War. Habituation to war entails a body of predatory habits of thought, whereby clannishness in some measure replaces the sense of solidarity, and a sense of invidious distinction supplants the impulse to equitable, everyday serviceability. As an outcome of the cumulative action of these factors, the generation which follows a season of war is apt to witness a rehabilitation of the element of status, both in its social life and in its scheme of devout observances and other symbolic or ceremonial forms. Throughout the eighties, and less plainly traceable through the seventies also, there was perceptible a gradually advancing wave of sentiment favouring quasi-predatory business habits, insistence on status, anthropomorphism, and conservatism generally. The more direct and unmediated of these expressions of the barbarian temperament, such as the recrudescence of outlawry and the spectacular quasi-predatory careers of fraud run by certain "captains of industry," came to a head earlier and were appreciably on the decline by the close of the seventies. The recrudescence of anthropomorphic sentiment also seems to have passed its most acute stage before the close of the eighties. But the learned ritual and paraphernalia here spoken of are a still remoter and more recondite expression of the barbarian animistic sense; and these, therefore, gained vogue and elaboration more slowly and reached their most effective development at a still later date. There is reason to believe that the culmination is now already past. Except for the new impetus given by a new war experience, and except for the support which the growth of a wealthy class affords to all ritual, and especially to whatever ceremonial is wasteful and pointedly suggests gradations of status, it is probable that the late improvements and augmentation of scholastic insignia and ceremonial would gradually decline. But while it may be true that the cap and gown, and the more strenuous observance of scholastic proprieties which came with them, were floated in on this post-bellum tidal wave of reversion to barbarism, it is also no doubt true that such a ritualistic reversion could not have been effected in the college scheme of life until the accumulation of wealth in the hands of a propertied class had gone far enough to afford the requisite pecuniary ground for a movement which should bring the colleges of the country up to the leisure-class requirements in the higher learning. The adoption of the cap and gown is one of the striking atavistic features of modern college life, and at the same time it marks the fact that these colleges have definitively become leisure-class establishments, either in actual achievement or in aspiration.

As further evidence of the close relation between the educational system and the cultural standards of the community, it may be remarked that there is some tendency latterly to substitute the captain of industry in place of the priest, as the head of seminaries of the higher learning. The substitution is by no means complete or unequivocal. Those heads of institutions are best accepted who combine the sacerdotal office with a high degree of pecuniary efficiency. There is a similar but less pronounced tendency to intrust the work of instruction in the higher learning to men of some pecuniary qualification. Administrative ability and skill in advertising the enterprise count for rather more than they once did, as qualifications for the work of teaching. This applies especially in those sciences that have most to do with the everyday facts of life, and it is particularly true of schools in the economically single-minded communities. This partial substitution of pecuniary for sacerdotal efficiency is a concomitant of the modern transition from conspicuous leisure to conspicuous consumption, as the chief means of reputability. The correlation of the two facts is probably clear without further elaboration.

The attitude of the schools and of the learned class towards the education of women serves to show in what manner and to what extent learning has departed from its ancient station of priestly and leisure-class prerogative, and it indicates also what approach has been made by the truly learned to the modern, economic or industrial, matter-of-fact standpoint. The higher schools and the learned professions were until recently tabu to the women. These establishments were from the outset, and have in great measure continued to be, devoted to the education of the priestly and leisure classes.

The women, as has been shown elsewhere, were the original subservient class, and to some extent, especially so far as regards their nominal or ceremonial position, they have remained in that relation down to the present. There has prevailed a strong sense that the admission of women to the privileges of the higher learning (as to the Eleusinian mysteries[2]) would be derogatory to the dignity of the learned craft. It is therefore only very recently, and almost solely in the industrially most advanced communities, that the higher grades of schools have been freely opened to women. And even under the urgent circumstances prevailing in the modern industrial communities, the highest and most reputable universities show an extreme reluctance in making the move. The sense of class worthiness, that is to say of status, of a honorific differentiation of the sexes according to a distinction between superior and inferior intellectual dignity, survives in a vigorous form in these corporations of the aristocracy of learning. It is felt that the women should, in all propriety, acquire only such knowledge as may be classed under one or the other of two heads: (1) such knowledge as conduces immediately to a better performance of domestic service—the domestic sphere; (2) such accomplishments and dexterity, quasi-scholarly and quasi-artistic, as plainly come in under the head of a performance of vicarious leisure. Knowledge is felt to be unfeminine if it is knowledge which expresses the unfolding of the learner's own life, the acquisition of which proceeds on the learner's own cognitive interest, without prompting from the canons of propriety, and without reference back to a master whose comfort or good repute is to be enhanced by the employment or the exhibition of it. So, also, all knowledge which is useful as evidence of leisure, other than vicarious leisure, is scarcely feminine.

For an appreciation of the relation which these higher seminaries of learning bear to the economic life of the community, the phenomena which have been reviewed are of importance rather as indications of a general attitude than as being in themselves facts of first-rate economic consequence. They go to show what is the instinctive attitude and animus of the learned class towards the life process of an industrial community. They serve as an exponent of the stage of development, for the industrial purpose, attained by the higher learning and by the learned class, and so they afford an indication as to what may fairly be looked for from this class at points where the learning and the life of the class bear more immediately upon the economic life and efficiency of the community, and upon the adjustment of its scheme of life to the requirements of the time. What these ritualistic survivals go to indicate is a prevalence of conservatism, if not of reactionary sentiment, especially among the higher schools where the conventional learning is cultivated.

To these indications of a conservative attitude is to be added another characteristic which goes in the same direction, but which is a symptom of graver consequence than this playful inclination to trivialities of form and ritual. By far the greater number of American colleges and universities, for instance, are affiliated to some religious denomination and are somewhat given to devout observances. Their putative familiarity with scientific methods and the scientific point of view should presumably exempt the faculties of these schools from animistic habits of thought; but there is still a considerable proportion of them who profess an attachment to the anthropomorphic beliefs and observances of an earlier culture. These professions of devotional zeal are, no doubt, to a good extent expedient and perfunctory, both on the part of the schools in their corporate capacity, and on the part of the individual members of the corps of instructors; but it can not be doubted that there is after all a very appreciable element of anthropomorphic sentiment present in the higher schools. So far as this is the case it must be set down as the expression of an archaic, animistic habit of mind. This habit of mind must necessarily assert itself to some extent in the instruction offered, and to this extent its influence in shaping the habits of thought of the student makes for conservatism and reversion; it acts to hinder his development in the direction of matter-of-fact knowledge, such as best serves the ends of industry.

The college sports, which have so great a vogue in the reputable seminaries of learning to-day, tend in a similar direction; and, indeed, sports have much in common with the devout attitude of the colleges, both as regards their psychological basis and as regards their disciplinary effect. But this expression of the barbarian temperament is to be credited primarily to the body of students, rather than to the temper of the schools as such; except in so far as the colleges or the college officials—as sometimes happens—actively countenance and foster the growth of sports. The like is true of college fraternities as of college sports, but with a difference. The latter are chiefly an expression of the predatory impulse simply; the former are more specifically an expression of that heritage of clannishness which is so large a feature in the temperament of the predatory barbarian. It is also noticeable that a close relation subsists between the fraternities and the sporting activity of the schools. After what has already been said in an earlier chapter on the sporting and gambling habit, it is scarcely necessary further to discuss the economic value of this training in sports and in factional organisation and activity.

But all these features of the scheme of life of the learned class, and of the establishments dedicated to the conservation of the higher learning, are in a great measure incidental only. They are scarcely to be accounted organic elements of the professed work of research and instruction for the ostensible pursuit of which the schools exist. But these symptomatic indications go to establish a presumption as to the character of the work performed—as seen from the economic point of view—and as to the bent which the serious work carried on under their auspices gives to the youth who resort to the schools. The presumption raised by the considerations already offered is that in their work also, as well as in their ceremonial, the higher schools may be expected to take a conservative position; but this presumption must be checked by a comparison of the economic character of the work actually performed, and by something of a survey of the learning whose conservation is intrusted to the higher schools. On this head, it is well known that the accredited seminaries of learning have, until a recent date, held a conservative position. They have taken an attitude of deprecation towards all innovations. As a general rule a new point of view or a new formulation of knowledge have been countenanced and taken up within the schools only after these new things have made their way outside of the schools. As exceptions from this rule are chiefly to be mentioned innovations of an inconspicuous kind and departures which do not bear in any tangible way upon the conventional point of view or upon the conventional scheme of life; as, for instance, details of fact in the mathematico physical sciences, and new readings and interpretations of the classics, especially such as have a philological or literary bearing only. Except within the domain of the "humanities," in the narrow sense, and except so far as the traditional point of view of the humanities has been left intact by the innovators, it has generally held true that the accredited learned class and the seminaries of the higher learning have looked askance at all innovation. New views, new departures in scientific theory, especially new departures which touch the theory of human relations at any point, have found a place in the scheme of the university tardily and by a reluctant tolerance, rather than by a cordial welcome; and the men who have occupied themselves with such efforts to widen the scope of human knowledge have not commonly been well received by their learned contemporaries. The higher schools have not commonly given their countenance to a serious advance in the methods or the content of knowledge until the innovations have outlived their youth and much of their usefulness—after they have become commonplaces of the intellectual furniture of a new generation which has grown up under, and has had its habits of thought shaped by, the new, extra-scholastic body of knowledge and the new standpoint. This is true of the recent past. How far it may be true of the immediate present it would be hazardous to say, for it is impossible to see present-day facts in such perspective as to get a fair conception of their relative proportions.

So far, nothing has been said of the Mæcenas[3] function of the well-to-do, which is habitually dwelt on at some length by writers and speakers who treat of the development of culture and of social structure. This leisure-class function is not without an important bearing on the higher learning and on the spread of knowledge and culture. The manner and the degree in which the class furthers learning through patronage of this kind is sufficiently familiar. It has been frequently presented in affectionate and effective terms by spokesmen whose familiarity with the topic fits them to bring home to their hearers the profound significance of this cultural factor. These spokesmen, however, have presented the matter from the point of view of the cultural interest, or of the interest of reputability, rather than from that of the economic interest. As apprehended from the economic point of view, and valued for the purpose of industrial serviceability, this function of the well-to-do, as well as the intellectual attitude of members of the well-to-do class, merits some attention and will bear illustration.

By way of characterisation of the Mæcenas relation, it is to be noted that, considered externally, as an economic or industrial relation simply, it is a relation of status. The scholar under patronage performs the duties of a learned life vicariously for his patron, to whom a certain repute inures after the manner of the good repute imputed to a master for whom any form of vicarious leisure is performed. It is also to be noted that, in point of historical fact, the furtherance of learning or the maintenance of scholarly activity through the Mæcenas relation has most commonly been a furtherance of proficiency in classical lore or in the humanities. This knowledge tends to lower rather than to heighten the industrial efficiency of the community.

Further, as regards the direct participation of the members of the leisure class in the furtherance of knowledge. The canons of reputable living act to throw such intellectual interest as seeks expression among the class on the side of classical and formal erudition, rather than on the side of the sciences that bear some relation to the community's industrial life. The most frequent excursions into other than classical fields of knowledge on the part of members of the leisure class are made into the discipline of law and of the political, and more especially the administrative, sciences. These so-called sciences are substantially bodies of maxims of expediency for guidance in the leisure-class office of government, as conducted on a proprietary basis. The interest with which this discipline is approached is therefore not commonly the intellectual or cognitive interest simply. It is largely the practical interest of the exigencies of that relation of mastery in which the members of the class are placed. In point of derivation, the office of government is a predatory function, pertaining integrally to the archaic leisure-class scheme of life. It is an exercise of control and coercion over the population from which the class draws its sustenance. This discipline, as well as the incidents of practice which give it its content, therefore has some attraction for the class apart from all questions of cognition. All this holds true wherever and so long as the governmental office continues, in form or in substance, to be a proprietary office; and it holds true beyond that limit, in so far as the tradition of the more archaic phase of governmental evolution has lasted on into the later life of those modern communities for whom proprietary government by a leisure class is now beginning to pass away.

For that field of learning within which the cognitive or intellectual interest is dominant—the sciences properly so called—the case is somewhat different, not only as regards the attitude of the leisure class, but as regards the whole drift of the pecuniary culture. Knowledge for its own sake, the exercise of the faculty of comprehension without ulterior purpose, should, it might be expected, be sought by men whom no urgent material interest diverts from such a quest. The sheltered industrial position of the leisure class should give free play to the cognitive interest in members of this class, and we should consequently have, as many writers confidently find that we do have, a very large proportion of scholars, scientists, savants derived from this class and deriving their incentive to scientific investigation and speculation from the discipline of a life of leisure. Some such result is to be looked for, but there are features of the leisure-class scheme of life, already sufficiently dwelt upon, which go to divert the intellectual interest of this class to other subjects than that causal sequence in phenomena which makes the content of the sciences. The habits of thought which characterise the life of the class run on the personal relation of dominance, and on the derivative, invidious concepts of honour, worth, merit, character, and the like. The causal sequence which makes up the subject matter of science is not visible from this point of view. Neither does good repute attach to knowledge of facts that are vulgarly useful. Hence it should appear probable that the interest of the invidious comparison with respect to pecuniary or other honorific merit should occupy the attention of the leisure class, to the neglect of the cognitive interest. Where this latter interest asserts itself it should commonly be diverted to fields of speculation or investigation which are reputable and futile, rather than to the quest of scientific knowledge. Such indeed has been the history of priestly and leisure-class learning so long as no considerable body of systematised knowledge had been intruded into the scholastic discipline from an extra-scholastic source. But since the relation of mastery and subservience is ceasing to be the dominant and formative factor in the community's life process, other features of the life process and other points of view are forcing themselves upon the scholars.

The true-bred gentleman of leisure should, and does, see the world from the point of view of the personal relation; and the cognitive interest, so far as it asserts itself in him, should seek to systematise phenomena on this basis. Such indeed is the case with the gentleman of the old school, in whom the leisure-class ideals have suffered no disintegration; and such is the attitude of his latter-day descendant, in so far as he has fallen heir to the full complement of upper-class virtues. But the ways of heredity are devious, and not every gentleman's son is to the manor born. Especially is the transmission of the habits of thought which characterise the predatory master somewhat precarious in the case of a line of descent in which but one or two of the latest steps have lain within the leisure-class discipline. The chances of occurrence of a strong congenital or acquired bent towards the exercise of the cognitive aptitudes are apparently best in those members of the leisure class who are of lower-class or middle-class antecedents,—that is to say, those who have inherited the complement of aptitudes proper to the industrious classes, and who owe their place in the leisure class to the possession of qualities which count for more to-day than they did in the times when the leisure-class scheme of life took shape. But even outside the range of these later accessions to the leisure class there are an appreciable number of individuals in whom the invidious interest is not sufficiently dominant to shape their theoretical views, and in whom the proclivity to theory is sufficiently strong to lead them into the scientific quest.

The higher learning owes the intrusion of the sciences in part to these aberrant scions of the leisure class, who have come under the dominant influence of the latter-day tradition of impersonal relation and who have inherited a complement of human aptitudes differing in certain salient features from the temperament which is characteristic of the régime of status. But it owes the presence of this alien body of scientific knowledge also in part, and in a higher degree, to members of the industrious classes who have been in sufficiently easy circumstances to turn their attention to other interests than that of finding daily sustenance, and whose inherited aptitudes run back of the régime of status in the respect that the invidious and anthropomorphic point of view does not dominate their intellectual processes. As between these two groups, which approximately comprise the effective force of scientific progress, it is the latter that has contributed the most. And with respect to both it seems to be true that they are not so much the source as the vehicle, or at the most they are the instrument of commutation, by which the habits of thought enforced upon the community, through contact with its environment under the exigencies of modern associated life and the mechanical industries, are turned to account for theoretical knowledge.

Science, in the sense of an articulate recognition of causal sequence in phenomena, whether physical or social, has been a feature of the Western culture only since the industrial process in the Western communities has come to be substantially a process of mechanical contrivances in which man's office is that of discrimination and valuation of material forces. Science has flourished somewhat in the same degree as the industrial life of the community has conformed to this pattern, and somewhat in the same degree as the industrial interest has dominated the community's life. And science, and scientific theory especially, has made headway in the several departments of human life and knowledge in proportion as each of these several departments has successively come into closer contact with the industrial process and the economic interest; or perhaps it is truer to say, in proportion as each of them has successively escaped from the dominance of the conceptions of personal relation or status, and of the derivative canons of anthropomorphic fitness and honorific worth.

It is only as the exigencies of modern industrial life have enforced the recognition of causal sequence in the practical contact of mankind with their environment, that men have come to systematise the phenomena of this environment, and the facts of their own contact with it, in terms of causal sequence. So that while the higher learning in its best development, as the perfect flower of scholasticism and classicism, was a by-product of the priestly office and the life of leisure, so modern science may be said to be a by-product of the industrial process. Through these groups of men, then—investigators, savants, scientists, inventors, speculators— most of whom have done their most telling work outside the shelter of the schools, the habits of thought enforced by the modern industrial life have found coherent expression and elaboration as a body of theoretical science having to do with the causal sequence of phenomena. And from this extra-scholastic field of scientific speculation, changes of method and purpose have from time to time been intruded into the scholastic discipline.

In this connection it is to be remarked that there is a very perceptible difference of substance and purpose between the instruction offered in the primary and secondary schools, on the one hand, and in the higher seminaries of learning, on the other hand. The difference in point of immediate practicality of the information imparted and of the proficiency acquired may be of some consequence and may merit the attention which it has from time to time received; but there is a more substantial difference in the mental and spiritual bent which is favoured by the one and the other discipline. This divergent trend in discipline between the higher and the lower learning is especially noticeable as regards the primary education in its latest development in the advanced industrial communities. Here the instruction is directed chiefly to proficiency or dexterity, intellectual and manual, in the apprehension and employment of impersonal facts, in their causal rather than in their honorific incidence. It is true, under the traditions of the earlier days, when the primary education was also predominantly a leisure-class commodity, a free use is still made of emulation as a spur to diligence in the common run of primary schools; but even this use of emulation as an expedient is visibly declining in the primary grades of instruction in communities where the lower education is not under the guidance of the ecclesiastical or military tradition. All this holds true in a peculiar degree, and more especially on the spiritual side, of such portions of the educational system as have been immediately affected by kindergarten methods and ideals.

The peculiarly non-invidious trend of the kindergarten discipline, and the similar character of the kindergarten influence in primary education beyond the limits of the kindergarten proper, should be taken in connection with what has already been said of the peculiar spiritual attitude of leisure-class womankind under the circumstances of the modern economic situation. The kindergarten discipline is at its best—or at its farthest remove from ancient patriarchal and pedagogical ideals—in the advanced industrial communities, where there is a considerable body of intelligent and idle women, and where the system of status has somewhat abated in rigour under the disintegrating influence of industrial life and in the absence of a consistent body of military and ecclesiastical traditions. It is from these women in easy circumstances that it gets its moral support. The aims and methods of the kindergarten commend themselves with especial effect to this class of women who are ill at ease under the pecuniary code of reputable life. The kindergarten, and whatever the kindergarten spirit counts for in modern education, therefore, is to be set down, along with the "new-woman movement," to the account of that revulsion against futility and invidious comparison which the leisure-class life under modern circumstances induces in the women most immediately exposed to its discipline. In this way it appears that, by indirection, the institution of a leisure class here again favours the growth of a non-invidious attitude, which may, in the long run, prove a menace to the stability of the institution itself, and even to the institution of individual ownership on which it rests.

———

During the recent past some tangible changes have taken place in the scope of college and university teaching. These changes have in the main consisted in a partial displacement of the humanities—those branches of learning which are conceived to make for the traditional "culture," character, tastes, and ideals—by those more matter-of-fact branches which make for civic and industrial efficiency. To put the same thing in other words, those branches of knowledge which make for efficiency (ultimately productive efficiency) have gradually been gaining ground against those branches which make for a heightened consumption or a lowered industrial efficiency and for a type of character suited to the régime of status. In this adaptation of the scheme of instruction the higher schools have commonly been found on the conservative side; each step which they have taken in advance has been to some extent of the nature of a concession. The sciences have been intruded into the

scholar's discipline from without, not to say from below. It is noticeable that the humanities which have so reluctantly yielded
ground to the sciences are pretty uniformly adapted to shape the
character of the student in accordance with a traditional self-
centred scheme of consumption; a scheme of contemplation and
enjoyment of the true, the beautiful, and the good, according to a
conventional standard of propriety and excellence, the salient feature of which is leisure—*otium cum dignitate.* In language veiled by
their own habituation to the archaic, decorous point of view, the
spokesmen of the humanities have insisted upon the ideal embodied in the maxim, *fruges consumere nati.*[4] This attitude should occasion no surprise in the case of schools which are shaped by and rest
upon a leisure-class culture.

The professed grounds on which it has been sought, as far as
might be, to maintain the received standards and methods of culture intact are likewise characteristic of the archaic temperament
and of the leisure-class theory of life. The enjoyment and the bent
derived from habitual contemplation of the life, ideals, speculations, and methods of consuming time and goods, in vogue among
the leisure class of classical antiquity, for instance, is felt to be
"higher," "nobler," "worthier," than what results in these respects
from a like familiarity with the everyday life and the knowledge
and aspirations of commonplace humanity in a modern community. That learning the content of which is an unmitigated knowledge of latter-day men and things is by comparison "lower," "base,"
"ignoble,"—one even hears the epithet "sub-human" applied to
this matter-of-fact knowledge of mankind and of everyday life.

This contention of the leisure-class spokesmen of the humanities seems to be substantially sound. In point of substantial fact, the
gratification and the culture, or the spiritual attitude or habit of
mind, resulting from an habitual contemplation of the anthropomorphism, clannishness, and leisurely self-complacency of the
gentleman of an early day, or from a familiarity with the animistic
superstitions and the exuberant truculence of the Homeric heroes,
for instance, is, æsthetically considered, more legitimate than the
corresponding results derived from a matter-of-fact knowledge of

things and a contemplation of latter-day civic or workmanlike efficiency. There can be but little question that the first-named habits have the advantage in respect of æsthetic or honorific value, and therefore in respect of the "worth" which is made the basis of award in the comparison. The content of the canons of taste, and more particularly of the canons of honour, is in the nature of things a resultant of the past life and circumstances of the race, transmitted to the later generation by inheritance or by tradition; and the fact that the protracted dominance of a predatory, leisure-class scheme of life has profoundly shaped the habit of mind and the point of view of the race in the past, is a sufficient basis for an æsthetically legitimate dominance of such a scheme of life in very much of what concerns matters of taste in the present. For the purpose in hand, canons of taste are race habits, acquired through a more or less protracted habituation to the approval or disapproval of the kind of things upon which a favourable or unfavourable judgment of taste is passed. Other things being equal, the longer and more unbroken the habituation, the more legitimate is the canon of taste in question. All this seems to be even truer of judgments regarding worth or honour than of judgments of taste generally.

But whatever may be the æsthetic legitimacy of the derogatory judgment passed on the newer learning by the spokesmen of the humanities, and however substantial may be the merits of the contention that the classic lore is worthier and results in a more truly human culture and character, it does not concern the question in hand. The question in hand is as to how far these branches of learning, and the point of view for which they stand in the educational system, help or hinder an efficient collective life under modern industrial circumstances,—how far they further a more facile adaptation to the economic situation of to-day. The question is an economic, not an æsthetic one; and the leisure-class standards of learning which find expression in the deprecatory attitude of the higher schools towards matter-of-fact knowledge are, for the present purpose, to be valued from this point of view only. For this purpose the use of such epithets as "noble," "base," "higher," "lower," etc., is significant only as showing the animus and the point of view of the disputants; whether they contend for the worthiness of the new or of the old. All these epithets are honorific or humilific terms; that is to say, they are terms of invidious comparison, which in the last analysis fall under the category of the reputable or the disreputable; that is, they belong within the range of ideas that characterises the scheme of life of the régime of status; that is, they are in substance an expression of sportsmanship—of the predatory and animistic habit of mind; that is, they indicate an archaic point of view and theory of life, which may fit the predatory stage of culture and of economic organisation from which they have sprung, but which are, from the point of view of economic efficiency in the broader sense, disserviceable anachronisms.

The classics, and their position of prerogative in the scheme of education to which the higher seminaries of learning cling with such a fond predilection, serve to shape the intellectual attitude and lower the economic efficiency of the new learned generation. They do this not only by holding up an archaic ideal of manhood, but also by the discrimination which they inculcate with respect to the reputable and the disreputable in knowledge. This result is accomplished in two ways: (1) by inspiring an habitual aversion to what is merely useful, as contrasted with what is merely honorific in learning, and so shaping the tastes of the novice that he comes in good faith to find gratification of his tastes solely, or almost solely, in such exercise of the intellect as normally results in no industrial or social gain; and (2) by consuming the learner's time and effort in acquiring knowledge which is of no use, except in so far as this learning has by convention become incorporated into the sum of learning required of the scholar, and has thereby affected the terminology and diction employed in the useful branches of knowledge. Except for this terminological difficulty—which is itself a consequence of the vogue of the classics in the past—a knowledge of the ancient languages, for instance, would have no practical bearing for any scientist or any scholar not engaged on work primarily of a linguistic character. Of course all this has nothing to say as to the cultural value of the classics, nor is there any intention to disparage the discipline of the classics or the bent which their study gives to the student. That bent seems to be of an economically disserviceable kind, but this fact—somewhat notorious indeed—need disturb no one who has the good fortune to find comfort and strength in the classical lore. The fact that classical learning acts to derange the learner's workmanlike aptitudes should fall lightly upon the apprehension of those who hold workmanship of small account in comparison with the cultivation of decorous ideals:

> Iam fides et pax et honos pudorque
> Priscus et neglecta redire virtus
> Audet.[5]

Owing to the circumstance that this knowledge has become part of the elementary requirements in our system of education, the ability to use and to understand certain of the dead languages of southern Europe is not only gratifying to the person who finds occasion to parade his accomplishments in this respect, but the evidence of such knowledge serves at the same time to recommend any savant to his audience, both lay and learned. It is currently expected that a certain number of years shall have been spent in acquiring this substantially useless information, and its absence creates a presumption of hasty and precarious learning, as well as of a vulgar practicality that is equally obnoxious to the conventional standards of sound scholarship and intellectual force.

The case is analogous to what happens in the purchase of any article of consumption by a purchaser who is not an expert judge of materials or of workmanship. He makes his estimate of the value of the article chiefly on the ground of the apparent expensiveness of the finish of those decorative parts and features which have no immediate relation to the intrinsic usefulness of the article; the presumption being that some sort of ill-defined proportion subsists between the substantial value of the article and the expense of adornment added in order to sell it. The presumption that there can ordinarily be no sound scholarship where a knowledge of the classics and humanities is wanting leads to a conspicuous waste of time and labour on the part of the general body of students in acquiring such knowledge. The conventional insistence on a modicum of conspicuous waste as an incident of all reputable scholarship has affected our canons of taste and of serviceability in matters of scholarship in much the same way as the same principle has influenced our judgment of the serviceability of manufactured goods.

It is true, since conspicuous consumption has gained more and more on conspicuous leisure as a means of repute, the acquisition of the dead languages is no longer so imperative a requirement as it once was, and its talismanic virtue as a voucher of scholarship has suffered a concomitant impairment. But while this is true, it is also true that the classics have scarcely lost in absolute value as a voucher of scholastic respectability, since for this purpose it is only necessary that the scholar should be able to put in evidence some learning which is conventionally recognised as evidence of wasted time; and the classics lend themselves with great facility to this use. Indeed, there can be little doubt that it is their utility as evidence of wasted time and effort, and hence of the pecuniary strength necessary in order to afford this waste, that has secured to the classics their position of prerogative in the scheme of the higher learning, and has led to their being esteemed the most honorific of all learning. They serve the decorative ends of leisure-class learning better than any other body of knowledge, and hence they are an effective means of reputability.

In this respect the classics have until lately had scarcely a rival. They still have no dangerous rival on the continent of Europe, but lately, since college athletics have won their way into a recognised standing as an accredited field of scholarly accomplishment, this latter branch of learning—if athletics may be freely classed as learning—has become a rival of the classics for the primacy in leisure-class education in American and English schools. Athletics have an obvious advantage over the classics for the purpose of leisure-class learning, since success as an athlete presumes, not only a waste of time, but also a waste of money, as well as the possession of certain highly unindustrial archaic traits of character and temperament. In the German universities the place of athletics and Greek-letter fraternities, as a leisure-class scholarly occupation, has in some measure been supplied by a skilled and graded inebriety and a perfunctory duelling.

The leisure class and its standards of virtue—archaism and waste—can scarcely have been concerned in the introduction of the classics into the scheme of the higher learning; but the tenacious retention of the classics by the higher schools, and the high degree of reputability which still attaches to them, are no doubt due to their conforming so closely to the requirements of archaism and waste.

"Classic" always carries this connotation of wasteful and archaic, whether it is used to denote the dead languages or the obsolete or obsolescent forms of thought and diction in the living language, or to denote other items of scholarly activity or apparatus to which it is applied with less aptness. So the archaic idiom of the English language is spoken of as "classic" English. Its use is imperative in all speaking and writing upon serious topics, and a facile use of it lends dignity to even the most commonplace and trivial string of talk. The newest form of English diction is of course never written; the sense of that leisure-class propriety which requires archaism in speech is present even in the most illiterate or sensational writers in sufficient force to prevent such a lapse. On the other hand, the highest and most conventionalised style of archaic diction is—quite characteristically—properly employed only in communications between an anthropomorphic divinity and his subjects. Midway between these extremes lies the everyday speech of leisure-class conversation and literature.

Elegant diction, whether in writing or speaking, is an effective means of reputability. It is of moment to know with some precision what is the degree of archaism conventionally required in speaking on any given topic. Usage differs appreciably from the pulpit to the market-place; the latter, as might be expected, admits the use of relatively new and effective words and turns of expression, even by fastidious persons. A discriminate avoidance of neologisms is honorific, not only because it argues that time has been wasted in acquiring the obsolescent habit of speech, but also as showing that the speaker has from infancy habitually associated with persons who have been familiar with the obsolescent idiom. It thereby goes to show his leisure-class antecedents. Great purity of speech is presumptive evidence of several successive lives spent in other than vulgarly useful occupations; although its evidence is by no means entirely conclusive to this point.

As felicitous an instance of futile classicism as can well be found, outside of the Far East, is the conventional spelling of the English language. A breach of the proprieties in spelling is extremely annoying and will discredit any writer in the eyes of all persons who are possessed of a developed sense of the true and beautiful. English orthography satisfies all the requirements of the canons of reputability under the law of conspicuous waste. It is archaic, cumbrous, and ineffective; its acquisition consumes much time and effort; failure to acquire it is easy of detection. Therefore it is the first and readiest test of reputability in learning, and conformity to its ritual is indispensable to a blameless scholastic life.

On this head of purity of speech, as at other points where a conventional usage rests on the canons of archaism and waste, the spokesmen for the usage instinctively take an apologetic attitude. It is contended, in substance, that a punctilious use of ancient and accredited locutions will serve to convey thought more adequately and more precisely than would the straightforward use of the latest form of spoken English; whereas it is notorious that the ideas of to-day are effectively expressed in the slang of to-day. Classic speech has the honorific virtue of dignity; it commands attention and respect as being the accredited method of communication under the leisure-class scheme of life, because it carries a pointed suggestion of the industrial exemption of the speaker. The advantage of the accredited locutions lies in their reputability; they are reputable because they are cumbrous and out of date, and therefore argue waste of time and exemption from the use and the need of direct and forcible speech.

NOTES

CHAPTER I: INTRODUCTORY

1. *Andamans:* An island chain in the Bay of Bengal to the east of the Indian mainland. The islands are noted here because, despite some colonization by Europeans, who used them as depots along Far East trade routes, the tribal system of the islanders remained largely intact until the modern era.
2. *Todas:* The Toda are a tribe living in the Nilgiri Hills of southern India. Like the inhabitants of the Andamans, they also maintained a tribal culture well into modern times.

CHAPTER III: CONSPICUOUS LEISURE

1. Nota notæ est nota rei ipsius: A Latin phrase derived from Aristotle and used in logic. It means "The mark of a mark is the mark of the thing itself"—in other words, a symbol that connotes another symbol that in turn represents a thing actually connotes the thing itself, and not just the symbol of the thing. Veblen is saying that markers of wealth, when wealth is a marker of virtue or supremacy, are themselves markers of supremacy.
2. *Summum crede . . . perdere causas:* From Juvenal, Satire VIII, lines 83–84: "Believe it to be the greatest evil to prefer life to shame (i.e., virtue) and for life to lose the reasons for living."

CHAPTER IV: CONSPICUOUS CONSUMPTION

1. *potlatch:* A traditional celebratory feast among the Native Americans of the Pacific Northwest in which expensive gifts are given to the guests as a display of wealth and power.

2. otium cum dignitate: More correctly, *cum dignitate otium,* "leisure with dignity." From Cicero's oration *Pro Sestio,* XLV.98.

CHAPTER V: THE PECUNIARY STANDARD OF LIVING

1. *hitherto . . . human being:* From book IV, chapter 6 of *Principles of Political Economy* (1848) by the English philosopher John Stuart Mill (1806–1873).

2. *Malthusian:* Thomas Robert Malthus (1766–1834) was an English economist whose major work, *An Essay on the Principle of Population* (1798), predicted a rise in population that would necessarily outstrip food production. Malthus's work served as the cornerstone for many later theories of population expansion and control.

CHAPTER VI: PECUNIARY CANONS OF TASTE

1. *dolicho:* Dolichocephalic (literally "long-headed"). Veblen is making reference to a system of describing races on the basis of measurable physical attributes, one of which is a ratio of head length to width. Here, Veblen is describing Nordic peoples; when he later refers to populations predominantly "brachycephalic-brunette," he is referring to Celts and Slavs.

2. *Columbian Exposition:* The exposition at the 1893 World's Fair in Chicago held to celebrate the four hundredth anniversary of Columbus's voyage to the New World. It showcased various technological and industrial inventions and had cultural and artistic exhibits.

3. *Diogenes:* A Greek philosopher who lived in Athens and died circa 320 B.C. He believed that the best life is the simplest life. Accordingly, he rid himself of even the smallest common comforts and chose to live a life of austerity.

4. *John Ruskin:* Although his personal life has come under great scrutiny since the time of his death, at the peak of his influence Ruskin (1819–1900) was Britain's preeminent art critic.

5. *William Morris:* An influential Victorian designer, Morris (1834–1896) was also a painter, poet, and social critic. Veblen later mentions one of his last undertakings, the creation of Kelmscott Press, which saw the reintroduction of traditional methods of book production; the volumes produced by the press are considered to be among the most beautiful ever produced.

CHAPTER IX: THE CONSERVATION OF ARCHAIC TRAITS

1. *Pickwickian:* In the kind and idiosyncratic manner of Samuel Pickwick, the main character in Charles Dickens's *The Pickwick Papers* (1837).
2. nouveaux arrivés: "Newcomers" in French.

CHAPTER X: MODERN SURVIVALS OF PROWESS

1. *student duel:* Well after the practice of dueling with swords had been abandoned in Europe, certain fraternal orders, especially within German universities, kept the custom alive in a modified form as a rite of passage for membership and good standing.
2. feræ natura: "Nature of wild animals" in Latin.

CHAPTER XI: THE BELIEF IN LUCK

1. in petto: Held back, secret, unexpressed. (The phrase is Italian and literally means "in the breast.")
2. hamingia (... auđna): Norse words for spirits or forces granting luck, especially in battle or heroic exploits.
3. ignava ratio: "Inactive (faculty of) reasoning" in Latin.

CHAPTER XII: DEVOUT OBSERVANCES

1. *hoodoo:* Variant of "voodoo." In this case, a practitioner of voodoo or an element in voodoo that can invoke powers of good or bad luck.
2. Un saint qu'on ne chôme pas: "A saint whom we do not celebrate" in French.
3. *Whether therefore ... glory of God:* 1 Corinthians 10:31.

CHAPTER XIII: SURVIVALS OF THE NON-INVIDIOUS INTEREST

1. *Elizabeth Cady Stanton:* An early leader of the women's-rights movement in America, Stanton (1815–1902) was a tireless speaker and writer who worked for women's suffrage and the abolition of slavery.

CHAPTER XIV: THE HIGHER LEARNING AS AN EXPRESSION OF THE PECUNIARY CULTURE

1. *Luther . . . Grundtvig:* Martin Luther (1483–1546), a German priest, wrote ninety-five theses that questioned some established Catholic practices and beliefs and proclaimed the doctrine of salvation by faith alone; his actions helped spark the Protestant Reformation. Philipp Melanchthon (1497–1560), a Lutheran humanist writer and theologian, wrote the *Confession of Augsburg*, the fundamental statement of Lutheran doctrine. Petter Dass (1647–1707) was a Norwegian poet who wrote both secular and sacred lyrics. Nikolai Frederik Severin Grundtvig (1783–1872), a Danish writer and bishop, started a movement to reform and revitalize the Danish church.

2. *Eleusinian mysteries:* Secret religious rites in ancient Greece that were associated with the goddess of fertility, Demeter. Initiates to the Eleusinian cult would take part in a procession from Athens to Eleusis and perform these rites, which promised spiritual benefit in the under-world. The nature of these rites is still unclear.

3. *Mæcenas:* A Roman diplomat and statesman and close friend of Augus-tus, Maecenas (c. 70 B.C.–8 B.C.) is chiefly remembered as a patron of the arts. Among the poets he supported and promoted were Virgil and Horace.

4. fruges consumere nati: From Horace, Epistles, I.2: "born to consume the fruits (of the earth)."

5. *Iam fides . . . Audet:* From Horace, lines 57–59 of the *Carmen Saeculare:* "Al-ready loyalty and peace and honor and traditional morality and ne-glected virtue are ready to return."

READING GROUP GUIDE

1. Describe the process by which property and ownership gain an important status in the early stages of a civilization's development. What relationship does Veblen see between the accumulation of wealth, the establishment and maintenance of a leisure class, and the display of virtue and prowess in early cultures? What are the distinctions between those members of an early community who display virtue and those who, because of position or capacity, cannot?

2. "Conspicuous consumption" is Veblen's most famous coinage. What is the role of the conspicuous consumer in the leisure class? How is conspicuous consumption related to conspicuous leisure? Give examples of people in or associated with the leisure class who devote their lives to conspicuous displays of consumption or leisure and describe how doing so enhances their position in their society. Similarly, describe the function of vicarious consumption and vicarious leisure.

3. A standard criticism of *The Theory of the Leisure Class* is that, although Veblen's analysis of the development of a leisure class does describe social pressure to maintain or acquire certain social distinctions, he focuses too closely on the economic aspects of class and does not give the proper due to purely social processes. Do you believe, as Veblen can be said to, that the upper or leisure class is primarily an economic entity, or are there characteristics of this class that are as important as money,

or perhaps more important? If so, what are they and how do they relate to the purely economic aspects of the leisure class and its development?

4. One of the most striking recurring elements of Veblen's description of the leisure class is his depiction of the role of women and servants. Describe and account for the change in the role of women in the upper class as they cease to be servants and property of men and become conspicuous consumers. How do servants fulfill roles similar to those of women in each step of the development of the leisure class? Although the first chapter clearly explains how the status of the head of a household is enhanced by his ability to treat women and servants as property, the effect of conspicuous consumption by women and servants on the status of the head of a household is less clear. Describe the process by which consumption by women and servants enhances the position of a household, especially in the middle class, where, according to Veblen, the wife is "the ceremonial consumer of goods."

5. Describe the ways that dress, religious observances, gambling, and education have come to serve as markers of social position. To what extent is Veblen's description of them accurate? To what extent are these still effective markers of class?

6. In the last paragraph of chapter II, Veblen claims that, with regard to his use of the word "invidious," "there is no intention to extol or depreciate, or to commend or deplore any of the phenomena which the word is used to characterise," that "the term is used in a technical sense." Is this a legitimate claim on his part? Does his use of terms such as "invidious pecuniary comparison" and "waste" and "chattel" really lack a pejorative connotation, as he claims, or is he making moral judgments? Do you believe that Veblen provides an objective account of the leisure class, or is there an implied moral content in his writing?

A Note on the Type

The principal text of this Modern Library edition was set in a digitized version of Janson, a typeface that dates from about 1690 and was cut by Nicholas Kis, a Hungarian working in Amsterdam. The original matrices have survived and are held by the Stempel foundry in Germany. Hermann Zapf redesigned some of the weights and sizes for Stempel, basing his revisions on the original design.